The Apocalypse Explained

THE
APOCALYPSE
EXPLAINED

Originally titled *The Apocalypse of St. John*

H. M. Féret, O.P.

Translated by
Elizabethe Corathiel

Roman Catholic Books

A Division of Catholic Media Apostolate
Distribution Center: Post Office Box 2286, Fort Collins, CO 80522

Nihil obstat: Hubertus Richards, S.T.L., L.S.S.
Censor deputatus

Imprimatur: E. Morrogh Bernard
Vic. Gen.

Westmonasterii, die 15a Martii, 1958

ISBN 0-912141-69-7

CONTENTS

FOREWORD

Invited in 1941 to give a series of lectures at the Cours St Jacques of Paris, the author took the Apocalypse as his theme. For about a year this inspired book had been the subject of his daily meditations as a theologian and historian. It appeared to him to contain a message particularly applicable to that troublesome time and well calculated to raise the spirits of those who consulted it.

As a result of many requests he agreed to publish the substance of these lectures although he would personally have preferred to let the material ripen. He is well aware of this volume's shortcomings compared to the Apocalypse itself. All the same, he hopes that it may perhaps induce the lay reader to acquire a taste for the text which at first must appear somewhat forbidding, and his object has been to provide the major clues that will enable such a reader to follow the unfolding of the profound lessons which are conveyed by this inspired work, the greatest that Christianity has ever produced.

The very nature of the work has made it necessary to include as many critical and historical comments as possible on this difficult book, taken as a whole and in detail. Specialists who read these pages will have no trouble in discerning the reasons for the options and interpretations which are suggested. One hopes that they will not be considered too arbitrary.

As for non-specialists, the foregoing should suffice, if need be, to warn them of what they must not expect from this volume. The very nature of the Apocalypse has laid it open to all kinds of fantastic commentaries. In periods of unrest the most far-fetched treatises have been written about it, and even in our day it is not uncommon to be asked quite seriously whether prophecies in this mysterious book do not apply to living personalities or current events. Such little diversions are quite futile, and the true believer may regard them as somewhat disrespectful to the word of God. These pages aim to show what the book holds for the religious soul.

Bibliographical references have been reduced to a minimum. It is no longer possible at this stage to tell at which points the book owes acknowledgement for its contents to the Rev. Father E. B. Allo's 'Apocalypse of St John' (Paris, Gabalda, 'Etudes Bibliques,' 1921; the quotations here all taken from the third edition, 1933). It was frequent re-reading of this great book, with all its critical information in the true Catholic tradition, that led the author to embark on his personal meditations of St John's prophecies, and he is now unable to tell which particular details of the present volume are borrowed and which are his own. If at a few points he has parted company with his guide (for instance, in the matter of the 144,000 of chapter 14, or the reign of the saints on earth, or the millennium of chapter 20, etc.) he remains none the less indebted for the very light which has led him to this independent opinion. He trusts that Father Allo will accept this expression of his profound gratitude.

In publishing this volume he has had no other ambition than to help fellow Christians, in their turn, to explore, in the faith and under the direction of the holy Church, the boundless riches and illumination of the word of God in the New Testament and to draw from it incessantly, as did the Evangelist, *nova et vetera*.

Le Saulchoir, March-June, 1942.

CHAPTER I

HISTORIC CONTEXT AND LITERARY STYLE

Eusebius writes in his Ecclesiastical History (Book III, Caps. 17 and 18) Cap. 17: 'After having behaved with great cruelty towards many of his subjects, condemning several nobles and other persons of distinction to death without fair trial, and banishing others beyond the frontiers of the Empire, with confiscation of all their possessions, Domitian (who reigned from A.D. 81 to 96) proved himself a worthy successor to Nero in his hatred of Christians and hostility towards God. Hence he let loose upon us all the horrors of a second persecution, even though his father, Vespasian, had never shown us any mark of disfavour.'

Cap. 18: 'About this time the apostle John was still living, and he was exiled to the Island of Patmos, because he preached the word of God. We have this on the authority of Irenaeus and many others. Dealing with the subject of Antichrist in the Apocalypse attributed to St John, he writes this of the Evangelist in the fifth book on Heresies: "If his name (that of Antichrist) could have been mentioned openly, he who saw the Apocalypse would not have made a mystery of it. For it was not long since he had had the vision, which was almost in our own generation, towards the end of the reign of Domitian".'

We need not enter into all the controversies that have been waged round statements by the father of ecclesiastical history. In all essentials the issue is not affected by them.

Let us take it as proved that John, the exile on Patmos, was the inspired prophet whose work we are about to study, and that he was identical with John the apostle and Evangelist. Not a single author prior to Denys of Alexandria (bishop of that town in A.D. 248-264) casts any doubt on that identity in quoting the Apocalypse. And such authors

1

are relatively numerous. Denys himself only appears to question it because of a misunderstanding. If he is the first to introduce some misgiving, he does so solely because he refuses to attribute responsibility to an apostle of Our Lord for the message from Patmos, the meaning of which he has misunderstood. Actually, anyone who, allowing for the difference in literary styles, has perceived the unmistakable relationship that exists between the doctrine and the inspiration of the Apocalypse and the other writings of St John will have no difficulty in accepting the tradition of the Church, that the son of Zebedee was the author of all of them.

Eusebius's statement based on Irenaeus (which is particularly valuable because this saint, being practically a contemporary, must have personally witnessed the things he writes about) actually gives us the date of the book, as having been written towards the close of Domitian's reign. And we know from the same author's Chronicles that many Christians suffered for their faith in the year 2120 of Abraham, that is to say, when Domitian had been on the throne for fifteen years. Hence A.D. 56-7 is the most probable year in which St John's prophecies were written. The date agrees with the evidence of the book itself. Literary detection justifies us in identifying Domitian with the sixth king in 16, 10, Nero with the 'head wounded unto death' in 13, 3, and the reign of Vespasian with the healing of the mysterious wound.

Geography also comes to our aid in accepting the authority of Eusebius. Patmos is the island of which St John writes. It is a tiny islet in a group situated practically mid-way between Naxos and the Anatolian coast. He addresses his message to the seven Christian communities nearest to that coast. No choice could have been more appropriate for the particular purpose he has in view.

I, John . . .
Was on the isle that is called Patmos for the word of God and the testimony of Jesus Christ. I was in the spirit on the Lord's Day, and heard behind me a great voice . . . which said :
What thou seest write in a book and send it unto the seven churches . . . unto Ephesus, and unto Smyrna, and unto Pergamos, and unto Thyatira, and unto Sardis, and unto Philadelphia, and unto Laodicea . . . (1, 9-11).

It is also clear that in view of the symbolism of the number 7 throughout the book, the churches mentioned were not to have the exclusive benefit of the revelation. They represented the whole Christian population of Asia Minor, which was then the kernel of the Christian Church, and they were expected to pass the message on. Apostolic writings were always rapidly circulated in this way. And even if these Churches were chosen in preference to all others, there was nothing haphazard about it. Doubtless it was determined by their location in the most densely populated districts, districts throbbing with life, the richest, the most effervescent and the most civilised urban areas in the whole Empire at that time. It had long been the custom to launch major missions there (witness the apostolic campaigns which St Paul had conducted for half a century). There can also be no doubt that these cities were most directly affected by Domitian's persecutions. They were acutely conscious of the problems the Apocalypse was designed to counter. As we shall presently see, the central theme of the message itself explains why these particular cities were chosen.

So, having established the authorship of the book, its date, and its place of origin, let us take a look at the spiritual and religious environment in which it was launched. Naturally, its teachings and the manner in which they were conveyed were strongly coloured by this. We shall first have to examine the external husk of the work, leaving the process whereby its inner theme insinuated itself into the evolution of early Christian thought to a later chapter.

Asia Minor at that time is of particular interest to the historian of religions because of the various currents of ideas known as the Greco-Oriental religious Syncretism that met and mingled there. Almost at once the temptation arises to deal with the Apocalypse as if it were fundamentally a reflection of this background, and to read and interpret it accordingly. Countless commentators have fallen into this trap. The most ingenious and varied ideas have been advanced to clarify the book in its entirety and in its smallest details by the light of the themes and the imagery inherent in the pagan philosophies that constituted this great religious movement. Father Allo lists and discusses these theses with inexhaustible patience. We shall be coming back later to his commentary.

We shall also see later on how this has led to delusions. We cannot, of course, arbitrarily dismiss the possible influence of contemporary thought on some passages of the book, so let us take a look at the great religious phenomena of Domitian's day, and try to determine how far they may have influenced the seer of Patmos in his warnings and messages of encouragement to the Christian communities.

For a very long time, religion had been so tied up with politics in the ancient systems of government that the popular mind could not distinguish one from the other. The Lares of the hearth and of the cities joined titular deities of streams, cross-roads and trade routes, celestial patrons of fields and harvests and every kind of activity until there were whole pantheons of divinities amalgamated in a national cult. They stood for everything held most holy, from religious sentiment and family solidarity to national loyalty, duty and patriotic fervour. Political reliability took its colour from the deference shown to the national gods. Their cause was the country's cause, and every wave of national sentiment produced a corresponding flood of religious enthusiasm. Changing one's religion was tantamount to treason. One proved one's confidence in the invincibility of the standards in exact proportion to the deference one paid to the gods. That was the law common to all society in ancient times.

Alexander's conquests, and the consequent complete disruption of temporal and spiritual values, the West impinging upon the East, and still more the East upon the West, broke up for the first time the close alliance between politics and religion. In that very area of Asia Minor with which we are at the moment concerned, the severance became even more marked as a result of the imperialist policy of the Roman Empire. It swept away national boundaries and unified the Mediterranean world. Whether they liked it or not, the subject races had to relinquish their national characteristics, not completely, perhaps, but sufficiently to permit a fluid intercourse. Separate religions, deprived of their own State frontiers, inevitably relaxed their exclusive rights, and the most varied cults found acceptance on soil which had formerly been foreign to them. The process was hastened by mythological analogies and kindred cultural practices. Ideas were borrowed, fusions occurred. People began to realise, mingling with one another on a new, non-militant basis, that their neighbours had gods and goddesses exactly like their own, and observed the same mystic cycles. Hence the term Greco-Oriental Syncretism, which has been forged to describe the phenomenon of this age in which all the ancient religions of Greece, Rome and the Orient met in Asia Minor and radiated outwards.

Widening horizons are always beneficial. They reveal the charm of the unknown, which is even more alluring when wrapt in mystery. The concerted aspiration which stimulates the soul-life of all whole communities at certain epochs was noticeable here, too, and made the period under discussion one of the greatest religious landmarks in human history. Swarms of sects, a plethora of initiation rites and Gnostic literary essays, appeared. New temples and places of worship were forever cropping up, and religious trends from the farthest Orient extended their influence to the limits of the western world and even into the heart of barbarian territories. They reflected the religious sensitivity which was characteristic of the age. And precisely at this time of emotional and religious excitement, Christianity appeared.

Superficially, Christianity would appear to be just another of the manifold religious developments which the period of Syncretism produced. It was born, and nurtured, as Syncretism reached its zenith, and, like all the currents that fed this movement, it came from the East to the West. There was even some doubt, up to the end of the third century, as to whether Christianity would survive; the world seemed just as likely to be united in the cult of Mithras. Of course, the crescendo of religious aspirations helped to prepare the soul for the reception of the Christian message; but there were dangers that the message itself might be contaminated by outside influences. Would Christianity emulate the enduring vitality of Judaism, from which it had cut itself off, and become the successful rival of the one Oriental cult which right through the ages had preserved its changeless essence? Would it find the inner strength to keep intact its original spiritual structure? Surrounded by other cults, all offering snares to trick the new faith into making concessions and yielding to expedience, it was indeed perilously placed; and as enthusiasm threatened to waver, the virulence of the ever-present sources of infection mounted.

We know from historical evidence that the fear was not unfounded. Because it embraced the wild speculations of the Gnostics and the grosser, though more popularly attractive, rites and cultural practices of the religious mysteries, the syncretic movement gave the apostles much anxiety, and they had to meet recurrent crises with unflinching resolution.

Take, for instance, the first encounter of St Peter with Simon the Magician. It raises a smile, and was perhaps more ridiculous than dangerous (Acts 8, 9). We know the vehemence with which the apostles, and St Paul himself, insisted on the faithful abstaining from food that had been sacrificed on the altars of idols, lest they should be tempted to take part, even to the smallest extent, in pagan rites. And it is important to note that whereas the first part of St Paul's ministry was chiefly taken up with the attitude towards the Jews, and the rejection of their doctrines and practices, the second part reveals him as being at least equally concerned with the pitfalls of Christian Gnosticism. We begin to perceive the extravagant speculations that here and there attached themselves to the personality of the Saviour, some- times to deny the reality of his human existence, sometimes to confuse the divine person with such a complication of nebulous 'systems' that Christ tended to be lost among the countless insubstantial beings with which these pagans populated their heaven. The epistles to the Philippians, to the Colossians and the Ephesians, and more than one passage in the pastoral letters, should be read with this in mind.

At the time of the Apocalypse, and towards the end of the beloved apostle's long life, the religious mysteries and

Gnosticism were a source of anything but remote danger. Our book makes several allusions to it, especially in the letters to the Churches. At Pergamos, for instance (2, 15) and also at Ephesus (although the Church there seems to have been more fortified in faith—2, 6) there were those Nicolaitans whose doctrine, utterly opposed to that of our Saviour, gave rise to behaviour which the Ephesians were enjoined to hate just as much as our Lord abhorred it. If we may believe Clement of Alexandria, this sect, basing their conduct on the views of the deacon Nicolas, showed their contempt of the flesh by yielding without scruple to prostitution. This sort of radical dualism is not unknown even at the present day. Many a modern Gnostic abandons the flesh and its desires to evil, without making any attempt to bring it under the yoke of morality and religion. It is quite possible that Ephesus and Pergamos were contaminated by such a sect at the time of St John.

There was also in Thyatira at that time the notorious prophetess Jezabel who, ignoring the directive from Jerusalem about the year 49-50, gave the faithful meats that had been sacrificed to idols (2, 20) and claimed, through her familiarity with suspected cults, to have access to 'the depths of Satan' (2, 24). Thyatira was not the only Church in danger of compromising itself with the pagan gods. There is a similar remark in the letter to Pergamos (2, 14) and the many anathemas in the book against back-sliding of this sort, branded by the term prostitution, prove that the danger of the Christian communities straying from the straight and narrow path was by no means illusory. Syncretism stalked abroad and was a constant menace.

As for the doctrine concerning the person of the Saviour himself, if we may rely on the evidence of the Apocalypse it does not appear at that time to have been particularly in danger of contamination by Gnosticism. It would be rather straining the text, no doubt, if we were to read into any comparison between the Lamb and the 'second beast' an allusion to Christological Gnosticism. Far more logical would be the conclusion that the 'other beast' symbolises the syncretic movement, or any current philosophy or religion opposed to truth, by which the Christian faith might be endangered. We are not justified in interpreting this as a reference to wavering faith in our Lord himself. We do know, however, that such deviations were not unknown among the Christian communities at that time; there was always the danger of false notions creeping in. Very soon the admonitions in the letters of St John prove him to be much occupied with this problem, and the last survivor of the apostolic group takes up, in his own characteristic way, the line of teaching St Paul had started, to deal with the tentative infiltration of Gnostic ideas. 'Every spirit that confesseth that Jesus Christ is come in the flesh is of God; and every spirit that confesseth not that Jesus Christ is come in the flesh is not of God, and this is that spirit of Antichrist' (I Joh 4, 2). If the Apocalypse does not deal specifically with these problems, it is because they are for the moment less urgent than those which we shall come to later on. Actually, if there had been any suspicion, or any insinuated doctrine whatsoever tending to belittle the historic, transcendent personality of Jesus, the powerful figure of the risen Christ which emerges from the inspired message of the prophet was calculated to remove such heretic deviations from the outset.

Briefly, therefore, our book is a very reliable guide to the place the Church occupied in the midst of the pagan world at the close of the first century, and the ocean of conflicting influences that lapped around it. Nevertheless, we are not justified in concluding that either the quoted instances or their relative importance entitle us to believe that the message of St John can only be understood by approaching it from the angle of Asiatic Syncretism. This applies to the principal theme developed, to which we shall return later. It also applies to most of the means of expression employed. So let us formulate a rule, which we hope the result will justify. Before deciding whether such and such a symbol or a teaching was coloured by the author's contact with the syncretic background, let us examine whether it did not derive from a Jewish source; and that means we must first explore the function of the Jewish tradition. By applying this rule, we shall quickly perceive how few of the essential elements refer directly to the Asiatic paganism in the midst of which the Christian communities, to whom the Apocalypse was addressed, had their being.

As a matter of fact, although the syncretic movement in A.D. 95-96 raised grave problems which the Apocalypse was designed to tackle, these did not spring solely, or even principally, from either Gnostic speculations or the alluring mysteries of initiation. The faith was threatened from quite another quarter. The real crisis which confronted the Christian communities emanated not from the Orient nor from Greece, but from Rome. And it was the gravest crisis the Church had ever had to face. In recognising this, we pin-point the actual historical basis of the inspired work we are now about to examine.

As has already been demonstrated, the syncretic movement was an inevitable result of events that had swept away all the religious and political arrangements of the ancient world. The conquests of the Macedonian Empire, followed by those of Rome, completely overturned the established standard of values. Uniting in their vast dominions people of many different customs and cultures, the conquerors and their successors could only keep the machinery of government running smoothly by making certain concessions to the religious sensibilities of the vanquished. Instead of imposing the cults of Greece and Rome on their new subjects, they allowed them (with a few isolated exceptions of no great importance) a certain liberty in religious matters. Tolerance on this point was, after all, a conciliatory gesture they could afford to make; it helped to keep the peace and saved a good deal of trouble.

They had nothing to lose politically by encouraging a free exchange of religious thought to keep people's minds occupied. When fusions of ideas took place they were, indeed, all in the conqueror's favour. Even if he had been in a position to enforce uniformity, the process of shackling thought would only have driven the movement underground, and would almost certainly have led to political intrigues of far graver consequence. Thus the danger of political unrest was minimised. Rome had everything to gain by allowing the subject-races complete self-determination in religious matters.

But there was another side to the picture. Up to this time, the vast political machine had derived its main driving force from the religious sentiments ranged solidly behind it. Having severed the ties that in popular belief linked it with the divine, the state ran the risk of losing that mysterious aura of omnipotence which had served it so usefully in the past. Reduced so to speak to a lay state, what authority could the Empire hope to exercise over vast populations superlatively skilled in religious argument?

With her genius for political discernment, Rome quickly sensed the danger and took steps to regain her former religious prestige. Not by forbidding the people to worship their old gods, but by setting up new ones. Because it was obviously impossible to impose whole pantheons of her own on the rest of the inhabited world, Rome simplified matters by the convenient expedient of turning her Emperors into gods. The Emperors themselves saw to this. Were they not merely following the precedent of the ancient Egyptian Pharaohs who, after exploiting for their own advantage the multitude of pantheons in their vast realm, ended by demanding not the exclusive, but certainly the obligatory adoration of their subjects for themselves? What difficulty could arise from reviving this policy, at a time when syncretism anyhow was sweeping away all kinds of out-moded scruples of conscience? After all, one more new cult could not upset anyone; it was the fashion. The adoration which Rome demanded meant no more than the official recognition of the titular divinity who now presided over the destinies of the entire known world.

Here we have the essence of the brilliant idea which inspired the cult of Rome and the Imperial cult. It was purely political. We need not go into history to trace its progress step by step. If the divinity of Rome was recognised a whole century before the Apocalypse; if the Emperors were deified subsequently, but only after their death; if Julius Caesar was the first to be the object of veneration during his lifetime; if that cult was extended, especially in the East, during the reign and greatly to the benefit of his immediate successor; if nevertheless the compulsory veneration of the Emperor did not pass into law until the end of the second or third century, all these details are of secondary importance, and do not alter in the least the essential fact that something new and important was in process of development about this time. The Empire had the power, and was fully determined to press the conscience of its subjects into its service for political ends.

Where had this movement arrived at the time of Domitian, and does the testimony of the Apocalypse agree with evidence we can obtain elsewhere?

In chapter 13 of his 'Life of Domitian', Suetonius gives many examples which point to the Emperor's obsession with his belief in his own divinity. He claimed succession by divine right before the Senate. He expressed himself in terms which left no doubt that he considered himself one of the gods. He ordered the Flavian priests to engrave his likeness, side by side with those of Jupiter, Juno and Minerva, on the golden crowns which he wore at certain festivals (Suetonius 4). And it was in keeping with the same claim that he caused himself to be addressed as 'Lord' in the amphitheatre, this being the title reserved for the divine. Furthermore, he enacted that all official documents should endorse this distinction, for he was to be addressed in them as 'Our Lord and God'.

There cannot be any doubt that an essential difference existed between the emperors who acquiesced in the cult for purely political purposes, and the sanguinary, half-mad sadist, Domitian, who—at any rate during his later years— was completely convinced of his personal divinity, and made no scruple of imposing the cult even upon his own immediate circle. He had his cousin, Flavius Clemens, executed— although he adopted this man's children. Flavius Clemens's crime was that of 'impiety'. And if this was ground sufficient for the death sentence on a near relative, can we question the fate that would befall Christians refusing to participate in the idolatrous worship? Theirs was not merely atheism in the usual sense, but treason against the Emperor as well. It was quite sufficient grounds for the persecution which followed.

There was not at that time, any more than in the time of
Nero (notwithstanding the opinion of certain historians) any
law against the Christians as such; at any rate, no known
document enables us to establish the existence of such a law.
The Christians were still numerically insignificant and not of
sufficient importance for Rome to take much notice of them.
If they were to be harassed, it was only necessary to apply
the universal rule which required every foreign cult to
obtain the Senate's recognition, which they had not done;
or that which compelled all subjects of the Empire to
subscribe to the Imperial cult. Flavius Clemens, despite his
close relationship and friendship with the Emperor, could
claim no mercy; he appears to have fallen victim to the
demand which Domitian, in his pretentions to divinity,
enforced without exception. I should be inclined even to put
these pretentions down in some measure to the necessities of
Domitian's treasury. That would explain the persecution with
which he pursued even the Jews. Their Temple having been
destroyed by Titus, his brother and immediate predecessor,
Domitian had decided that the money formerly raised by
the Jews for the support of their national sanctuary should
in future be delivered to the temple of Jupiter on the Capitol.
Now this was the one which Domitian used for his own cult.
The tardiness of the Jews in responding to this demand may
have exasperated the Emperor no less than their obstinate
monotheism. It is even possible that he looked upon
Christians as proselytes who 'lived like Jews' without
declaring themselves as such—or as persons who 'denied
their origin' with a view to evading the taxes imposed upon
Israel. (Suetonius, 12.)

However this may be, it is an undoubted fact that Domitian
appears in Christian history as the author of the second and
extremely violent persecution. Tertullian says of him:
(Apolog., 5) '*Portio Neronis de crudelitate*' and we have
quoted the chapter in which Eusebius writes to the same
effect almost within a century of Tertullian's time.

Taken all in all, it was probably a persecution less bloody
than that of Nero. That at least was the opinion of Tertullian.
But at the same time, one is obliged to recognise it was

a persecution with more far-reaching repercussions, from the point of view of the principles involved. Nero was able practically to exterminate the Christian communities in Rome, and perhaps in all Italy, by holding them up, in the eyes of the public, as the persons responsible for all the afflictions they had laid at the Emperor's door. But everyone knew that this was pure calumny, for there was nothing in the new doctrine that would encourage law-breaking. It would seem moreover that this persecution was confined mainly to Rome, and did not extend far into the provinces. Domitian's persecution, on the other hand, raised a question of principle which could not fail sooner or later to produce the most shattering consequences. Under Nero the Christians were put to the test but their faith remained unshaken. This same faith was the mainspring of the message of Patmos, and the very language the aged apostle uses to drive home his arguments gives us some idea of the appalling menace that threatened the Church, through the pretensions of Domitian and the power of Rome.

What sort of communities were they, to whom the apostle addressed his communications, and what were the precepts he wished to impress upon them? It is worth noting that, of the seven towns mentioned, five are known to us as having possessed a sanctuary for the imperial cult; Ephesus, Smyrna, Pergamos, Sardis and Philadelphia, and it is more than probable that Thyatira and Laodicea were equally equipped. Ephesus, which is mentioned first, was doubtless more important than all the others, if not already earmarked as the future metropolis of the heirarchy emerging in the Christian communities from apostolic origins. But we must not lose sight of the fact that the Imperial cult, introduced into the celebrated temple of Artemis of the Ephesians (Cf. Acts 19, 28 ff.) also flourished here. The cult was similarly entrenched in Smyrna, where the holy bishop Polycarp, less than a half-century later, suffered martyrdom for refusing to declare 'Caesar is the Lord' (Eusebius, H.E. IV, XV, 15). We need have no doubt that the problem was also a very real one at the time of Domitian. As for Pergamos, we know that worship of the Emperor-god had been going

on there for more than a century, and had reached a point
of fanatical zeal. The particularly vivid passage in which the
Apocalyptical letter to the Church of that town praises
Antipas, the faithful witness of Christ who gave supreme
proof of his faith even at 'the very seat of Satan' (2, 13)
brings the conditions in Pergamos right home to us. Let
there be no mistake about it; even without proceeding to
the main teachings of the book—and we shall see that they
all combine in the same sense—this was the fundamental
problem the heavenly message aimed to answer. It was not
this, that or the other persecution that struck at the root of
the Christian faith; the faithful had been warned by their
master that they must be prepared to suffer. And they were
prepared for martyrdom. But this was a different kind of
persecution. For the first time it came, not as a challenging
dramatic climax, but as a detail of day-to-day existence,
confronting their faith in Christ and in the Church with the
question of their whole future. Faced with a trial which
proceeded not only from the brutality of a tyrant actuated
by self-interest, but also from the relentless compulsion of
the political machine, what were they to think? Not, certainly,
of the question of worshipping Caesar, which they could
but refuse, but of the ultimate issue of the unequal struggle
with the whole power of the State on which the Church had
manifestly embarked. Obviously there could be no possible
compromise between Christian conscience and the demands
of Caesar-worship. But would this state of affairs go on and
on, endlessly, and in that case would the Church be strong
enough to survive the trial? It seemed reduced to a mere
question of survival; and what then became of all the
prospects universal evangelisation had opened up, to say
nothing of the Messianic triumphs, hope of which the
Christians had inherited from their Israelite ancestors?
Either Rome would have to give up deifying itself—and
Domitian seemed headed in quite the opposite direction—
or the Church would have to vanquish Rome; but when, and
in what way? Such were the problems that rocked the very
foundations of Christian faith in Asia, and that prompted

the seer of Patmos to throw inspired light on the future of Christianity.

Now that we have located the message of Patmos in general history, let us take a look at the religious atmosphere in which the people to whom it was addressed were living. History has given us a rough idea—a very superficial one, incidentally—of the object in view when the Apocalypse was written. Closer examination of the recipients leads us to certain conclusions on the class of literature to which the work belongs, and the actual manner in which the message is expressed.

Useful—indeed, indispensable—as it is to have an intimate knowledge of ecclesiastical history, and especially that of the syncretic movement, in studying the Apocalypse, this approach, it cannot be denied, has often been abused. Many commentators have tended to overlook the fundamental truth that applies to all problems concerned with the origins of Christianity, namely, that it grew out of Judaism and was nurtured to maturity in this native environment. This applies both to its doctrines and to its spiritual aspirations. It is also true of the first Christian communities and of Christianity's collective institutions from the earliest days. It sounds like a platitude; but very often the most obvious truths, based on common sense, tend to be forgotten in practice. Let us pause for a moment and ask ourselves how much we should understand of the gospels; of our Lord's progress on earth and of his apostles; of the difficulties they encountered in first spreading the doctrine of Christianity throughout the Mediterranean world, if we knew nothing of the Old Testament, nor of contemporary Judaism in our era, nor of the part it played in the Roman Empire and especially in the great trade centres of the Mediterranean. Need we remind ourselves that the great majority of apostolic teachings, not excluding those of St Paul, the apostle of the gentiles, were first launched in the synagogue? Or that Jesus Christ represented the Messianic tradition which of all others was most essentially Jewish? We also know of some exceptions to this initial method, some attempts to make direct contact with

the pagan world, which were not conspicuously successful—
St Paul at the Areopagus, for instance. Born on the spiritual
soil of Israel, Christianity took its first faltering steps in the
shadow of the synagogue. It was not until later that it
penetrated effectively into the pagan world.

Consequently—and so many works on Christian origins
seem to overlook this—all questions concerning these origins
should take the Hebrew spiritual background as their
starting point. Only in this way will the historian discover
the best means to clarify the problem he has set himself. He
should not attempt to extend his investigations to the pagan
religions which, at the beginning of our era, impinged on the
lives of quite as many Jews as Christians in the Mediterranean cities, until he has thoroughly dug over this field.

This applies especially to the care with which one should
approach the study of the Apocalypse. Before exploring the
most remote and unexpected connections with Grecian,
Oriental and far-Eastern religions, we ought to recognise
that here we have a book that is linked with the Israelite
tradition by a thousand literary and religious ties. Although
its major themes—which we shall deal with more particularly
in the ensuing chapters—may be dressed up in the Grecian
mode and coloured by allusions to paganism, the Apocalypse
is quite a typical Hebrew-Christian product. This is all the
more remarkable because it shows how much, in the first
century, Christianity was still dependent on the Hebrew
tradition—at a time when unquestionably the majority of
the communities in Asia Minor must have sprung from
gentile circles. The Apocalypse goes back to Jewish sources
both for its manner of presentation and for its basic religious
themes. Let us briefly run over the points which most clearly
reveal this derivation, and which it is most important to
recognise if we are to understand this inspired book. From
mere externals we can penetrate to the most fruitful sources
of inspiration.

The style of the book—so disconcerting to the uninitiated
modern reader—places it unmistakably in the class of
Jewish Apocryphal literature. In the Old Testament the book
of Daniel is the best example of this style, though one can

trace many other prototypes, in the Wisdom books, for instance, in the collection of the Psalms, especially in Prophets, and even in some passages of the Pentateuch. Many Apocrypha, both in Judaism and in Christianity, have exploited this style. Although the Apocalypse of St John has become the most widely-known and the most representative of this class of literature, it is by no means the first of its kind ever to have been written. It derived its rules and its essential mode of expression from precedents established centuries before. We need only stress that it is the *chef-d'oeuvre* of its kind, and that the essential characteristics are here found in a development of perfection no other book of this class known to us has attained.

The style continually falls back on allegorical illustrations. Celestial thrones, Elders, the Four Beasts, the Dragon and the Beasts, horsemen in different colours, opposing armies, the Temple which the prophet measures, and the City which he sees descending from heaven—all these make no sense, and have still less interest, if one takes them literally. They are symbols of other realities, which we are expected to discover for ourselves.

In the allegorical language of apocalyptic literature it is especially important to note the recurrence of numbers. All these have a symbolic value, and it is sheer waste of time to calculate them by the rules of arithmetic. Number 3 is readily recognised as divine; 4, which recalls the four winds of heaven or the four corners of the earth, is often of cosmic significance; 7 indicates abundance, perfection, and it also contains both four and three, which opens up great possibilities, the author exercising his ingenuity on sevens in two series, composed respectively of three-four units. Three and a half, seven divided by two, and six (seven minus one) are considered to be less than perfect; six can even be stretched to suggest a ridiculous pretence of perfection, a perfection which is unattainable. Using another method, whereby a name is expressed by the number-values of its letters, the adventure may end in a succession of six (666), and here is a means of ridiculing the pretentions of Nero, the persecutor. Twelve also falls short of complete perfection and it is a favourite number with our author when referring to the Church; there are twelve doors in the celestial Jerusalem, just as there are twelve tribes of Israel, twelve apostles of the Lamb—and when it comes to hinting at the countless multitudes of the elect, he speaks of one hundred and forty-four thousand, which is equal to the square of twelve multiplied by a thousand—an incalculable total. He uses the same method for indicating the immensity and divinity of the holy Jerusalem, which he sees in three dimensions, each of twelve thousand strades—three, twelve and a thousand therefore make up the total, which defies imagination but is rich in doctrinal suggestion. The number of times certain characteristic expressions are used in the book, obviously intentionally, is another matter that should not be overlooked, quite apart from the study of numbers, to which I have referred. Thus 'Christ' recurs exactly seven times, three times accompanied by 'Jesus', which is itself used fourteen times (twice seven). Sentences commencing 'blessed' are seven in number. One might also wonder if it is by mere chance that there are twenty-eight (four times seven) mentions of 'the Lamb' against twelve of the Dragon; that seven passages prophesy the sovereignty of Christ and his saints, seven others the lamentations called forth by the punishments of the ungodly, while the 'inhabitants of the earth' are mentioned six times, and there are ten kings, and so on. These examples will suffice to warn the reader unaccustomed to this class of literature that numbers in our book are meant to be accepted for their symbolic value—their arithmetical significance is negligible. The symbol holds the clue. Now this is not peculiar to the Apocalypse of St John. It fits perfectly into the mould of Jewish apocalyptic literature, to which by its characteristic style it actually belongs, although there may possibly be an earlier connection with Pythagorean speculations on the subject of numbers.

What is true of numbers applies even more forcibly to the apocalyptic metaphors or allegories. The author follows his Jewish predecessors in his complete disregard for coherence in the images and comparisons he uses. It is just as futile to seek consistency here, as to calculate the proportions expressed in numbers. The same fact and the same teaching may be conveyed, sometimes on the same page, by two metaphors having no possible connection. On the other hand, the same metaphor may illustrate two completely opposite truths or mysteries. Thus the Church is turn-by-turn a woman, a temple, a city, a bride; but again the image of a woman may successively be evoked to suggest the divine mystery of the Church, and prostituted Rome. We must not therefore expect coherence on the imaginative plane, but look for it only in the ideas or teachings which the illustrations express. It is easy to lay down this rule but not so simple to follow it, especially for the western type of mentality, confused and readily put off by this rapid succession of scintillating, disjointed metaphors. Systematic reading, especially aloud, will help to overcome the difficulty. One gradually begins to appreciate the evocative power which this somewhat lavish use of allegory conveys. Even the occasional redundance which one is inclined to criticise at a superficial reading becomes less irksome when the mind, skipping the allegorical illustrations which at first make it stumble, follows the prophet of Patmos into the human and divine mysteries which are offered for contemplation.

So much for the elements of style. There is no need to dwell on the question of rhythm, although in my opinion the Apocalypse has a very definite rhythm of its own. In the original text, declamation is often marked by the almost arbitrary repetition of the conjunction 'and' and the very conscious use or omission of the definite article, by its repetition before certain adjectives or participles qualifying the principal nouns of the phrase, or by a collection of genitives. Noticeable, too, is the frequent use of a sudden parenthesis which, holding the flow in suspense for an instant, underlines the rhythm. Occasional grammatical errors, due to the author's semitic background, make many an apocalyptic phrase more vivid, even if not more refined. Here, too, reading aloud helps one little by little to enter into the swing of the inspired poem.

The development of a literary composition is a long process, and to trace it step by step requires much exploration. Let us lay down just a few simple rules, which we must be aware of in order to follow the author's train of thought without too many stumbling-blocks. There is no need to underline the septenaries; these are quite obvious. Indeed, in some quarters there is even an inclination to regard this feature as the guiding principle of the book, dividing it into seven successive septenaries. Four of them are explicitly mentioned by the author; the determination of the other three is open to argument. Anyhow, every hypothesis requires an all-over frame, embracing the succession of precepts communicated rather than a hard-and-fast principle of interpretation.

The law of antithesis is more dependable. It applies as much to the major doctrinal teachings of the book as to its literary method. Thus we can line up a long parallel series of antithetic facts and mysteries or phenomenal manifestations that run right through the book. The Lamb and the Dragon, the inhabitants of the earth who have erected their tents with God in heaven, the Church militant and the Church triumphant, pagan Rome and the Christians who are persecuted by it, the two witnesses and the two beasts—all these illustrations which represent fundamentally the same mysteries of good and evil, or, more often, truth and falsehood, are brought together from one end of the book to the other, and, in the details of the visions and allegories, they give it a profound unity. As this applies to the whole, it is also very often true of the substance of a pericope—the triumph of good conjures up the agitation and the overthrow of evil. Father Allo is very insistent on this point.

Another characteristic consists of the frequent repetition at the commencement and end of a teaching; we meet a typical illustration in the opening lines, and it comes up again at the conclusion. Father Allo traces this trick right through the book. It is worth noting that the titles of Christ, figures of speech like the Tree of Life, the fountains of living waters, and so on (borrowed, by the way, from Genesis) or again, the announcement of the imminent coming of the Lord, figure almost identically in the foreword to the letters on the one hand, and the epilogue on the other. Many of the pericopes furnish further examples of the same method. Most of the letters to the Churches also endorse it; the first words he addresses to them correspond with the exhortation at the end. For example, in the scourge of the fifth trumpet, the author mentions, in the beginning, the bottomless pit which is opened by the fall of the mysterious star from heaven (9, 2) and then at the end he tells us that the scorpions are for the king of the angels of the Abyss (9, 11). Once one knows what to look for, countless examples will crop up in the course of one's reading.

More important still, and more original, is the method which Father Allo calls 'jointing'. This is how he defines it: 'While a vision is in progress, and generally towards the end, the seer suddenly suspends the action, in order to build up a new revelation later. I said revelation; but more often it really explains a point in a vision that preceded it, and strikes the reader all the more forcibly on that account. His imagination is quickened. He is held breathless with expectancy until God and the prophet see fit to give further explanation.' (*L'Apocalypse*, p. LXXXV.)

Two points arise here. If on the one hand a septenary, or a description of the fifth or the sixth element, is contained in a vision, generally there is a bait which can be made the subject of the vision or the teachings that follow. If on the other hand such a foretaste is lacking, the teachings given will round up others given on an earlier occasion. Let us look at one or two examples. In chapter 6, when the Lamb opens the fifth seal, the martyrs, impatient for just vengeance, are persuaded to wait a little 'until the number of their brethren, who should be killed as they were, shall be fulfilled' (6, 11). When we come to the opening of the sixth seal, and the cosmic cataclysms that precede the end of time, the action is suddenly suspended, and we pass on to Chapter 7, where we are told in detail the numbers (innumerable!) of the elect whose presence proclaims the deferred justice of heaven and their salvation by the blood of martyrs. Another instance. In the course of the vision of the infernal battle started by the sounding of the sixth trumpet (9, 13) John sees the mighty Angel carrying the little book

(10, 1). In Chapter 11, 1-14, he briefly describes the contents of the little book, before the sounding of the seventh trumpet, which links up with the events of the previous chapter, and foreshadows again the impending end. In reality the tit-bit about the little book is just a foretaste of the whole prophetic section that follows (11, 19) which takes up in detail the various elements briefly hinted at in the first announcement.

By this method, which he applies with the greatest freedom, the author keeps all the aims of his book closely knit. And this, we may be sure, was quite deliberate. It was carried out with the greatest calculation, passing from diminishing generalities to considered facts. After a somewhat abstract glance at the whole of human history, he gradually narrows the field. At the same time, whatever may be lost in the process of contraction is amply made up by the increased intensity of vision that plays upon successive developments. Step by step the prophet passes in review concrete and actual historical facts, even bringing details into the picture, such as references to living personalities, and Roman emperors associated with the persecution of the Christians.

And here is the most important point—one also completely in accordance with the apocalyptic style of writing. Every new prospect opened up invariably finishes in the same way, namely, with the end of the world. Even when he is dealing with contemporary affairs, or with the past, the prophet always has an eye to the future. Thought is prophetically directed to the great ἔσχατον. Of this traditional technique our book is a very typical example. It emerges from the very first vivid lines of prophecy (1, 6-7) as well as from each of the septenaries (of which the fifth or sixth element conjures up the last great trials of sinful humanity prior to the last judgement and the triumph of Christ and the saints). It also characterises each of the great divisions, and the general trend of the book, which links the successive divine judgements in the course of history with the final judgement and the heavenly Jerusalem. It must never be lost from view that this theme dominates the whole of the book's message. All its teachings, all its prophecies, hinge upon the end of the world. The progression, let us hasten to add, does not take place in strict chronological order. The successive elements in a septenary do not necessarily correspond with any given period of time as we know it. But in this one respect the visions or revelations all agree; they end in full ἐσχατον. The apocalyptic style cannot be separated from exhortations, visions and eschatologies; they form the basis of the pre-conceived picture, and of this class of literature our book is absolutely typical.

Here we perceive the basic distinction between books like this one, which are prophetic in the correct and limited sense of the term, and those which represent what we nowadays call a theology of history, because they confine themselves to the concrete march of events, and remain aloof from dealings with the future. Clearly, the teaching conveyed, for instance, in the breaking of the seven seals of the Book of the Lamb, although it ends in the usual apocalyptic style with a delineation of cosmic catastrophes (sixth seal) cannot be identified with actual historical events. The rider on the white horse, and the four malignant riders, are in action simultaneously, and not one after the other, throughout the whole of history. It soon becomes clear that it is the first rider, recognisable as evangelical truth, who will have the last word. The same applies to the trumpets, the judgements, the cups, and so on. For although the object throughout the whole series is to conjure up the end of the world, we are not justified in relating this repeated climax to actual facts in the sequence of historical events.

But it would be equally wrong to deny the book's prophetic function, looking at it from the angle of progressive history. How then can we be sure of the correct line to take? It is not possible to make the climax our starting point, because this invariably has a bearing on the end of the world. So we are forced back to the beginning. If this yields general, and to some extent abstract, pointers to any period of time, one is justified in applying it to history as a whole. The information thus given remains as it were outside the future, considered as such, and applies, though perhaps not quite equally, to all its phases. If on the other hand the start of a new prophetic series concerns an exact period in the historic future, the prospect opened up remains entirely within that future itself, and, linking within other series of events in the march of time, points to important stages in the ultimate fate of the human race. The message of Patmos then takes on a real prophetic significance. This is our view, and we shall explain in our last chapter that the whole of 17, 1-20, 15, opening with the prediction of the judgement and condemnation of the persecuting Roman Empire, offers the most stupendous clairvoyant prophecy on the progress of history since St John's time, making our Apocalypse the most important prophetic work in the whole of Judeo-Christian literature.

Having discovered how to distinguish between that which is prophetic in an exact sense, and the general principles governing a true interpretation of Christian history, can we combine the two? We believe it is possible, and to demonstrate it is the purpose of this book. Taken all in all, the prophetic predictions only spring from the general affirmations expressed in the visions with which the message opens. And inversely, thanks to the method of procedure which we have outlined, these first visions will shed their divine light on concrete realities of history from which at first sight they may seem very far removed. One can imagine that the faithful had a similar experience, when the message of Patmos was read to them in their assemblies; mysteriously but unmistakably they were led little by little to recognise existing conditions and approaching events in the history of Rome, which revealed the resurrected Christ to them as an irresistible conqueror. The Apocalypse, which derived its penetrating light from heaven, revealed plainly the hard realities of their struggle; but it also threw its heavenly light on the outcome, and gave them the courage to see themselves as they were in Christ—as unvanquishable victors.

The foregoing, we hope, has been sufficient to establish the message of St John as belonging to the prophetic and apocalyptic class of Israelite literature. But it should also be clear that in this class it has reached a magnitude and a perfection never before known. Only two characteristics have been mentioned to establish that style and superiority: prediction and eschatology. One may briefly touch upon a few others. For instance, the passages connected with God's judgement, or the day of his wrath, or the celestial acclamations that approve his decrees, or even the holy city of Jerusalem. Why did John, who wrote his gospel in a totally different style, choose precisely this one for his message of comfort and encouragement at the time of persecution? It is hardly necessary to ask this question because the answer is so obvious. It was the traditional style the prophets used when they wanted to spur God's people on to believe in their destiny, foretelling the defeat of the nations ranged against God. In fact one could go so far as to say it was the only style the writer of the Apocalypse could have used to convey this particular message. Furthermore, this was not meant to be a book of evangelical catechism, or, in spite of its opening letters, an apostolic epistle like those which were sent by St Paul and which St John himself would soon write; it was not to be a didactic treatise like the epistle to the Hebrews. It was to be above all a prophecy against impious nations, and in favour of the new chosen people, that is to say, the Church. We shall have to go into this more precisely in analysing the internal and doctrinal structure of the document itself. But even at this point it must be clear that anyone wanting to make real progress in the understanding of this mysterious book must seek help from analogous literature, like the books of Daniel, Ezechiel, certain passages of Isaias, the minor prophets and so on, as well as the eschatological discourses and the synoptics; these, rather than anthologies of pagan cults, will yield illuminating information. Only by this kind of study will he perceive, little by little, in their right setting the derivatives and originalities of John's message, for the apostle chose this very characteristic style of writing to express the particular theme he had to convey in the religious tradition of his fathers.

This brings us to the concluding remarks. We have penetrated beyond the literary character of the work to the very source of St John's inspiration, which reveals where the great book links up with the religious tradition of Israel. I want to say something about the use made of the Old

Testament. For my part, I know of nothing in the New Testament, with the possible exception of the epistle to the Hebrews, which borrows so freely and with such pertinence from the old authors. This is so marked that certain passages of the Old Testament called to mind by quotations from John actually serve as a clue to their interpretation. It is perfectly plain that these quotations do not arise by mere chance. There is nothing haphazard about them, such as there might be if mere echoes of old writings had been recalled at random. Each one of them is taken from the book, or that section of the book, which best matches the theme the seer of Patmos happens to be developing at the moment. Sometimes the references even seem to suggest, through a thin disguise, things with the whole of which the listeners might already be familiar—a method doubtless chosen because it would be foolhardy to speak of such things without wrapping them up in mystery. Thus the symbolism of the world's spreading sores, that of the two witnesses, or that of the Beast, would not escape listeners versed in the Judeo-Christian tradition, harmless as they might appear to un-initiated public officers on the watch for any menace to Caesar's prestige, and eager for pretexts to distinguish themselves by the alertness of their vigilance.

Be that as it may, there are quotations from the Old Testament all over the book. The Apocalypse might be likened to a cloth of purely Jewish weave, on which are embroidered the visions in which St John provides the essentially Christian revelation. Suppose a start were made with Daniel and his recital of the triumphs of the Son of Man over the empires of the people of Jahveh and over the potentates of Nabuchodonosor. That would make an excellent prelude for the message of encouragement to the persecuted Christians who perhaps had begun to lose faith in the power of the Messiah to emerge victorious from the struggle with Rome. Then, following Ezechiel, already there would be Jahveh seated in glory amid flashes of lightning, and the apparition of the Son of Man judging the nations, with the mysterious book presented to John, just as Ezechiel of old was permitted to know the prophecy. Exodus, with its memories of the liberation from Egypt, and the plagues which heaven sent to punish Pharaoh, has its counterpart in the apocalyptic sores showered upon the world at the opening of the seven seals and the sound of the seven trumpets. There we have the whole blue-print.

As for the actual realisation of it, here the Old Testament provides even more precise models of procedure. The mystery of the Church is already foreshadowed in the temple of Ezechiel and its symbolic measurement by means of a reed. The candlesticks of the sanctuary described in Exodus forecast the communities of the heavenly temple which is the Church; and Ezechiel also gives us a pre-view of the holy city which comes down from heaven. Daniel paves the way for the great central revelation of the two Beasts, just as Isaias reveals the fall of Lucifer and the triumphs of the Son of David. We find the solemn beginnings of the terrible judgements on the nations and on the great Roman prostitute in Isaias's prophecies against Tyre, Jeremiah's against Babylon, Ezechiel's against the great town (Tyre) and Joel's against the kings. Amid all this the Psalms sound their praises around the throne of the Lamb. And if it is true that the Jews 'preferred nourishing their religious appetites on the Pentateuch rather than the Prophets',[1] not only the liturgical codes of Exodus and Deuteronomy serve as a frame for the celestial liturgies, but also Genesis, at the very beginning of the book (letters to the Churches) and at the end (vision of the heavenly Jerusalem) give a foretaste of promised beatitude through the Tree of Life and the fountains of living water to be found in heaven with Jahveh. Leading sources of John's inspiration will be found in the reference list at the end of this book, and we shall return to the subject repeatedly in succeeding chapters. There has been no attempt to make a servile compiling of references. John added to the ideas he borrowed from the Israelite tradition the infinitely greater inspiration he derived from Christianity. Whatever originality he introduced, however, we are still forced back to his point of departure in order to understand the full meaning of his message.

[1] M. J. Lagrange, 'Le Judaisme avant Jesus Christ.' Paris 1931. p. XVII.

No other author in the New Testament, not even St Paul,
used the Scriptures more precisely or to better purpose. One
might say that every quotation betrays a definite intention
and conveys a deliberate lesson. The revelation rests on
truths already expressed earlier by St Paul and the first
Evangelists. It may be said that the last book of the Bible
pre-supposes all the others. In a way it recapitulates in a
dazzling synthesis the whole history of a world, the origins
of which are related in Genesis. Genesis and the Apocalypse
are inseparable, the Alpha and Omega of the Judeo-
Christian revelation. This should warn us, if we are inclined
to forget it, that we must approach our book with a determination to penetrate to the very heart of the revelation,
with a deeply religious conviction that it is inspired from
beginning to end, and with the perception that only daily
reading of the holy Scriptures can give. The Apocalypse was
written by a Christian prophet of Jewish extraction for
Christian communities to whom the holy books of the old
synagogue retained all their authority, all their day-by-day
doctrinal influence. These facts take precedence of all the
superficial effects the syncretic movement may have had
upon it in Asia Minor.

Was this book which today seems so full of mystery to
readers who are not initiated (and, in more than one detail,
to others besides!) more intelligible to the Christian communities that received it towards the close of the first century?
Did they understand all its allegories? Evidently we have no
exact information on this point, and it is difficult for the
historian to answer these questions precisely. One can only
come to the general opinion that the answer is 'Yes'.

Certainly these communities were infinitely closer to
Jewish writings than we are today. The essential themes, the
symbolism, the literary style, would cause no perplexity to
first-century hearers. To be convinced of this, we should
re-read not only the inspired writings of the New Testament
but also other documents relating to the early days of
Christianity. A course of this kind of reading makes it
easier to embark upon the Apocalypse.

It is fairly obvious, too, that the constant use of allegory, though it makes things more difficult for readers of a later period, has great advantages in times of persecution. Allusions to contemporary events would have been infinitely easier for those who first received them to understand than they could possibly be long after these events had passed. If despite the lapse of all these centuries we are able to identify with practical certainty the name of the beast as that of Nero, or to recognise this or that Emperor under the horns of the beast, or to detect in the second beast the current Gnostic ideas that were partial to the worship of Caesar; if, further, we read (Domitian, 12) Suetonius's description of the Flavian priests' golden crowns, and automatically remember the golden crowns of the beast with the name of blasphemy on his seven heads (13, 1) how much more easily must St John's contemporaries have accepted and understood these allusions! The letters to the seven Churches also strike one as being full of inferences which must have been crystal-clear at the time, but which completely escape the reader of to-day. Obviously, too, it must have been a great advantage in times of persecution to have at one's command expressions which would be quite unintelligible to interlopers, like Romans, who were not initiated in the literature of that tradition—especially when the book spoke of God's judgements reserved for Rome and the gentiles. Here and there one even seems to detect passages of symbolism which appeared to St John so easy to interpret that he suddenly wrapped them round with more mystery. Thus he formulates the number of the beast (13, 18), suggesting Babylon, that is to say, Rome; and the great prostitute (17, 5) is another instance. We need have no doubt that this book of encouragement was written in such a way that its recipients—and they alone—would understand it perfectly.

It seems indisputable that the first generation of Christians looked upon the message of Patmos as the great book inspired by God to give his Church wisdom and strength during its time of trial and persecution. In proof of this, one need only recall the attention it received even as late as

177 in the letter written to the Churches of Asia by the Church of Lyons during the persecution of Marcus Aurelius (Eusebius, H.E., V. 1ff.). Later, as time rolled on and the historical details alluded to receded from popular memory, the book little by little lost its significance. Its mystery deepening, it began to be looked upon as a timeless message and was made the object of the most fantastic speculations. The march of events developed other resources, and the revelation came to be regarded as an esoteric work having no connection with the concrete realities of history. Still, Christians in all ages did find that they could still return to it and profit by the rich inspiration which sustained their predecessors under the persecution of Domitian. That inspiration has lost none of its value.

CHAPTER II

THE 'KINGDOM OF GOD' OF THE SYNOPTIC GOSPELS AND THE 'KINGDOM OF CHRIST' OF THE APOCALYPSE

We pass from the literary and historical aspects to the doctrinal context. The question arises: which particular stage in the development of early Christian thought does the Apocalypse represent? To what extent does St John's message merely continue the tradition of the past—and in what respect is it an entirely new departure? To answer these questions and to obtain a clearer understanding of the revelation of Patmos, we must first trace the stages by which it was compiled. Without entering into too many details of the historic background, which would need to be very thoroughly studied to bring out all its subtle lights and shades, let us concentrate on two main phases; that of our Lord's own teachings, which the gospels permit us to examine, and that of the first apostolic precepts, particularly those of St Paul.

To understand the immediate import of our Lord's carefully chosen expressions—and the echo they produced in the minds of his audiences—it is necessary to examine them in conjunction with the historic background against which they were uttered. In other words, that of the Jewish people as they then existed, under the dominion of Rome.

Whatever might be the occasional lapses and lack of faith among these people, there can be no question that a great religious and patriotic dream lay dormant in their souls, ready to become imperative the moment some outside stimulus should re-awaken it. This dream embodied the long-awaited kingdom of God. It was an intellectually involved

31

idea, because the people looked upon this kingdom as the ideal and ultimate structure of human society. An organisation uniting Israel and the gentiles forever under the government of divine law. Emotionally it was also complicated, because in this ideal the two strongest sentiments man is capable of reinforced one another—religion and patriotism. The rising of the Machabees proves how powerful an insurrection springing from such driving forces could be. If only the leaders could have claimed descent from David, what a messianic 'push' it would have been! Even in Jesus's lifetime, the Zealots, in the face of Roman domination, showed to what heights of religious and patriotic fanaticism Israel could rise. Their exasperated nationalism fomented many a revolt. Remembering this, we can appreciate in their proper light certain of the gospel episodes, in which the crowd wished to proclaim Jesus, who himself belonged to the royal house of David, the long-awaited Messiah-king.

It is easy to see that the kingdom of God which Israel dreamed of was a great communal organisation, national, and at the same time what we might call international. It was a theocratic dream, religious and at the same time political, embracing the inhabitants of the whole world in a global union under an institutional charter, the Law of Moses carried to perfection. By persuasion or by force, every section of human society was to be brought under this law. If the wishes or the welfare of the individual received any consideration at all, they were presumed to follow automatically from the healing salvation divinely granted to Israel, and extended by her to the whole world. No one would be able to share in the blessings of the kingdom except by becoming identified with the chosen people of God. It would therefore behove everyone to subscribe to, and observe, the Law of the Jews; to submit to circumcision, to pay the required dues, to keep holy the Sabbath and the feast days; in short, to obey the Law punctiliously. Then they would be entitled to participate in the happiness promised to Israel.

All this, naturally, could add up to a great religious ideal. We need only re-read Psalm 118 to be convinced of this. But even at the highest estimate, it would make religious values dependent not only on conformity with a law exterior to man, but also on the vicissitudes and misfortunes of the political group of which this law was the charter. The door stood perpetually open for the confusion of political and religious ideas, not to mention the deviations of formal Phariseeism so vigorously denounced by Jesus, and legislation which St Paul had occasion to oppose because it was so crippling to internal liberty.

The kingdom of God could only be defined as the active principle of the Messiah himself. He appeared in it as the invincible champion. As to the prophetic characteristics handed down by tradition concerning him, these were either left wrapt in their mystery, or interpreted in the light of personal trials which they foretold. Not much time was wasted over the sufferings of the Servant of Israel. Much more popular were the glorious and proud titles, Son of David and King of Nations. He was to be the great champion and defender of the Law; but, still more, in the service of that law and its universal extension, he was to be the glorious and unassailable King of Israel. After having liberated the chosen people, he was to extend his dominion to the very ends of the earth. With him, Israel, the saints, the Law, would reign forever.

This is the way the prophets, inspired or not, chose to visualise the future prospect, and to emphasise their dreams —dreams which expressed the hopes of the people as a whole. Let us glance at a list of traits of the Messiah compiled by the author of 'The Psalms of Solomon'.

He would judge the people and the nations in wisdom and in justice.

He would have the people under his yoke to serve him.

And they should give glory to God in the full view and knowledge of the whole earth

He would purify Jerusalem and restore it to its original holiness (. . .)

He himself is above all men like a just king, instructed by God, And in his time there is no injustice among them,

For all are saints and their King is the Lord Messiah (. . .)

The Lord himself is their King, hope of him who is strong through trust in God,

And he shall give grace to all the nations that fear him
For he will smite the earth by the word of his mouth, for ever.
He will bless the people of the Lord, living in wisdom and
    happiness
(. . .) Such is, in God's design, the noble aspect of the King
    of Israel
To raise him on the house of Israel so that he may be its restorer. [1]

The vast compass of this role of holiness and triumph led
the most inspired of the prophets of the Messiah to depict
his transcendence vividly. Isaias recognised in him the fulness
of the spirit of Jahveh (Is. 11, 2ff.), and David gave him the
truly divine title of Lord (Ps. 110, 1, cf. the utilisation of this
text in a rabbinical discussion of Christ with the Pharisees,
Matt. 22, 23 ff.). But even with all this, the real grandeur of his
personality can only be fully perceived in his combined role.
While he had the functions of legislator, judge, king and even
priest, it was abundantly clear that he belonged above all to
the group, and it was this that gave him definition. Each
member of the group depended only upon him in submitting
to the laws which he dictated to all. There was nothing to be
seen of his acting as direct intermediary between the
individual and God. All the more reason for presenting the
kingdom of God which he would inaugurate as being in a
way dependent on the mystery inherent in his personality.
How could one suspect that this transcendent mystery of
his being lay hidden in the very structure of the kingdom,
when that kingdom was already approached only from its
external point of view? If Christianity had developed along
the lines of the Jewish conception of the kingdom of God, it
would have led to only an elementary Christology, to a
purely juristic-ecclesiastical organisation far removed from
any doctrine analogous to that of the Mystical Body.

It is hard for us to imagine the emotion aroused when
John, son of Zacharias, appeared among the people down
there on the banks of Jordan, baptising and announcing
in urgent accents: 'Repent, for the kingdom of God is at
hand!' (Matt. 3, 1-2) and foretelling the imminent approach
him who 'shall baptise you in the Holy Ghost and fire'

[1] M. J. Lagrange, 'Le Judaism avant Jesus Christ.' Paris 1931. pp. 155 ff.

(Matt. 3, 11). As to the messianic character of this double message, none, not even the most illiterate, could be in any doubt. Inevitably it aroused the deepest religious sentiments, coupled with the re-awakening of lively aspirations towards national independence. The intensity of these feelings could only be increased when Jesus himself appeared on the scene, and was recognised by John in a spiritual transport, the crowd listening with gathering excitement as he took up with even more urgency the theme of his fore-runner: 'The time is accomplished and the kingdom of God is at hand. Repent and believe the gospel' (Mark 1, 15).

From this point on, we notice the growing rift between the old notion of the kingdom of God and the precepts conveyed in the sermons of Jesus. The kingdom of God was of course the foundation of the whole edifice he intended to build; it was also the focal point on which all thoughts centred. Every one of his listeners ardently desired this long-awaited kingdom of God; and to realise the place it occupied in our Lord's preachings we have only to recall the number of parables that begin: 'The kingdom of God is like unto ...' [1]

We need not enter into all the details here. It is nevertheless necessary to say a few words on the one hand to underline the points of agreement, and the misconceptions which our Lord slowly and patiently set himself to dispel, and on the other hand, how these developments themselves posed a new question, to which it seems to us the Apocalypse gives the most explicit answer.

In the minds of the Jews, as we have said, the kingdom of God was a concept certainly religious, but at the same time political, so that the majority took the religious domination of the Law to be co-incidental with, and dependent upon, the political triumph of their nation. This was a point of view with which our Lord totally disagreed, and from the very outset rejected. The long-awaited Messiah was expected in the role of invincible herald of the holy Law and victorious king leading his nation to political domination of the whole

[1] P. A. Lenoyer has suggested a classification of them in his 'Theology of the New Testament'. Paris, Blond and Gay, 1928. pp. 33 ff., 43 ff.

world. This was the second confusion our Lord set himself to clear up.

We have to look at the teachings of the gospel from this dual point of view. Then we are better able to understand certain things on which our Saviour insisted, and also certain of his attitudes—towards his family, for instance—in which the transition stage between the entirely new understanding of the kingdom, and the old conception of the Messiah, stands out very clearly. We will underline just a few salient points.

First of all, let us agree on terms. One word in the Greek of the gospels may have two or three different corresponding words in a modern language. Hence kingdom (or realm) also sometimes conveys the sense of reign and royalty. We have seen that in Israel, what was primarily expected was a kingdom, that is to say, a collective institution of which the Messiah would be the head—a kingdom that would extend its tentacles to the very ends of the earth. The kingdom which Jesus Christ was about to inaugurate was a reign or a kingship of God over the souls of men. Only from this starting-point would it have any influence on external matters.

Bearing this in mind, it is profitable to re-read the great programme which St Matthew outlines for us. Here the contrast is immediately obvious. It clearly shows that Jesus is promulgating a message he had brought from God; by the tone of the synoptics as they describe it, we can still get an impression of the solemnity of the occasion. Now what did Jesus say to this crowd, standing all worked up and ready to support him in the effort they expected him to make in the interests of political independence—ready, in fact, to press for a holy war of conquest on the world? The very first words strike a note of discord; this was not what the crowd expected. They and he spoke a different language. All the aspirations were reversed. There was no question of the restoration of David's kingdom. Very soon the new prophet showed that the kingdom of God has its origin in the most secret heart of man. 'Blessed are the poor in spirit, for theirs is the kingdom of God. Blessed are the meek; for they shall possess the land,' etc. The whole of the Beatitudes pursue this contrast (Matt. 5, 3 ff. and para. 11) to the point of paradox. The kingdom of God is promised to those most denuded of the normal outward signs of success and power. Nevertheless, it is a kingship, a reign of God installed in the innermost soul. And precisely here, Jesus begins to stress his demands. In these very depths, the foundations of the new and final alliance, which will be the outcome, must be laid. The work of God among men has really nothing directly to do with the fate of laws which are collective and quite external. These external acts are conditioned by the inner intention, the choice by free will in the personal soul of each individual. Only by these secret options can a man enter the kingdom of heaven here on earth; and mankind's whole progress depends on this choice.

Here, and here only, is where any disagreement exists between the Old Law and the New Law. Let us re-read St Matthew in his great statement of comparisons which succeeds the Beatitudes. 'You have heard . . . but I say unto you'. In this résumé of the whole evangelical doctrine, it is immediately obvious that the Law of Jesus does not differ in essentials from that of Moses, either in content or in its objects; these remain the same. The difference lies in the way they affect men's actions, in the way he looks at things. The New Law is concerned with the first inception of the impulse, even before any external act, which could come under a collective law, has been committed. 'You have heard that it was said to them of old: Thou shalt not kill' (here we have an external act). 'But I say unto you that whosoever is angry with his brother' (in the secrecy of his own heart) 'shall be in danger of the judgement'. 'You have heard that it was said to them of old : Thou shalt not commit adultery' (external act fully covered by the external law). 'But I say unto you that whosoever shall look on a woman to lust after her hath already committed adultery in his heart. Again you have heard it said to them of old : Thou shalt not forswear thyself; but I say unto you not to swear at all, but let your speech be : Yea, yea. No, no '—that is to say, confine yourself to words which you yourself, and God within you, know to be strictly true. Briefly, when our Lord

began his work for the kingdom which he was to inaugurate
among us, his first task was to persuade his followers that
religion and salvation spring from the direction of the heart,
and only come under the laws regulating outward acts,
even religious acts, of human society in a secondary sense.
If the salvation of society, and of all human values, can only
come from God, and therefore from the religion which God
ordains, then we are warned that divine order in the world
depends primarily on the acceptance—or the refusal—which
men accord in their hearts to this morality and to this inner
religion which Jesus taught.

Do not misunderstand me. This is not a matter of
Christianity being a purely 'inner' religion, taking no account
of external effects which also form part of our collective life
and are necessary to our well-being. To think so would be
to leave out of the reckoning charity, which is the first law.
Charity's demands are as imperative in the intercourse of
men with one another as are the secret relations of each
individual with God. Nothing in Christianity can be pleasing
to God if it does not also include love of one's neighbour.
How then can the kingdom of God in the secrecy of men's
hearts be organised into the kingdom of God on earth? Our
Lord took care of this by establishing the organisation of
the Church, himself laying the foundation of the essential
hierarchy on which is based the visible structure for the
external expansion of the kingdom of God. If there is no
longer a chosen people in the sense of a national and political
group, there is still an elect body of believers, the holy race
of the baptised, the new Israel which is the Church, and
which, inheriting the ancient promises of Abraham, must
invisibly extend to the ends of the earth under the direction
of St Peter and the apostles, to offer everyone a chance of
entering the kingdom of God. All this is clear, and cannot
possibly raise any difficulty. What one must stress here is
that all these external expansions, as necessary and obligatory
as they may be, are but secondary phenomena, and presuppose the essential preliminary which our Lord never
failed to preach, and which indeed is the essence of all that
is new in his message. The realm of God cannot be truly

born except through personal choice, moral and religious. All the rest, salvation and the progress of temporal society included, are so many additional gifts vouchsafed to mankind.

While our Lord was engaged in the task of correcting the popular notion of God's kingdom, he had also to transmute the notions his audiences had hitherto formed of the Messiah, not only as to his actual role, but more especially in regard to his mysterious personality.

He did not call into question the characteristics attributed to the Messiah by Jewish tradition. Son of Man, Servant of Jahveh, King of Israel, Liberator of the Chosen People, New Moses, Emmanuel—all these he accepted and endorsed, together with the prophetic promises; and both in speech and conduct he appeared careful to vindicate these messianic titles.

To his audiences and even to his apostles, the logical conclusion was that he had come to re-establish the kingdom of Israel. Let us recall the apostles' question on the eve of the Ascension (Acts 1, 6; cf Lk. 9, 11). And again the request of the mother of James and John (Matt. 20, 21): 'Say that these, my two sons, may sit, the one on thy right hand and the other on thy left, in thy kingdom'. All this belongs to the same outlook, I would almost say the same impatience, religious and at the same time patriotic, which prompted so many tentative feelers on the part of the crowd as to the proclamation of his kingdom by Jesus, the son of David —even if it meant a rising against the Romans and a march on Jerusalem.

In the face of these feverish outbursts of messianism, the attitude of Jesus remains always the same. On the one hand he does not trouble to repudiate the titles the crowd bestow upon him. When one day the Pharisees remonstrated and tried to prevent the people from acclaiming him as King, he said that if the people were silenced, the very stones would cry out (Luke 19, 38-40). Doubtless the royal title was not so often applied to him as that of Son of David. Nevertheless he consistently rejected the conception of royalty which was commonly entertained. Whether it came from Satan during the mysterious Temptation in the desert (Luke 4, 5) or from the crowd after the miraculous distribution of the loaves and fishes (John 6, 15) or after the triumphant entry into Jerusalem (Matt. 21, 1 etc.) or finally before Pilate at the trial, Jesus always categorically denied any pretensions to political power, and would never permit his cause to be confused with political issues. That was not the best way to establish the kingdom of God which the prophets had promised and which he himself had come to inaugurate. In rendering unto God that which is God's—that is to say everything—the first essential is to distinguish between God's cause and that of Caesar. And furthermore Caesar must also get his due (Matt. 22, 21). In order to bring all human values into line with the divine scheme, one must go to the very roots; that is to say, to the most spiritual essence of man, and politics are powerless on this ground-plan of emotion, thought and desire. Therefore Jesus would not be a king, neither would the apostles after him. The kingdom of God would be no theocracy, of the kind the Jews had so long awaited. The universal and perfect realm which he, the Son of David, was to establish would not follow the lines laid down by Samuel, nor without resistance (1 Sam. 8, 5 ff.) as imagined by the Jewish people. Every attempt to adjust the perfect kingdom of God which Christ was establishing to the dimensions of a political cause would call forth the same rebuke which the mother of James and John received, and even St Peter himself, in the Garden of Olives. Christian politics must above all respect the first laws of the kingdom of God, of which indeed they are only one aspect, and abide by the discrimination of the Master in his reply to the Pharisees on the rights of Caesar (Matt. 22, 21) or in that which he made to Pilate in his palace as Roman governor (John 18, 36-37).

But at this point a problem arises. If the kingdom of God is not first and foremost a temporal organisation, if Christ does not exercise a regal authority on an equal footing with the princes of this world, what are its means of action? Is there anything more powerful than political pressure that he can employ to establish the perfect order in human affairs that was forecast by the messianic promises? The new kingdom of God must be something quite different in character. Can it be that we must look for the explanation in the equally mysterious character of the Messiah who will establish it? This turns on the transcendent personality of Jesus, and the nature and efficacy of his intervention among us. And this ultimate kingdom of God which he came to inaugurate —would it be the continued out-working, the companion, as it were, of its predecessor, so that we can trace the dependence of the two latter mysteries directly to the first?

Suddenly new light on the message of his forerunner and that of Jesus, and their close connection, dawns upon us. The kingdom of God is at hand, St John the Baptist had said; receive the baptism of penitence and be converted. When he first began his ministry, Jesus took up the same theme, adding: believe in the gospel. (Mk. 1, 15). But from then on, in all circumstances, he never failed to demand faith. Throughout the long tradition of doctors and prophets of Israel such a thing had never been known before; it was an entirely new requirement, and absolutely characteristic of his message. We have pointed out that all his teachings concern the kingdom of God. We might add that all his teachings, like all his miracles and all his acts of mercy, aim at awakening faith. Actually these do not run parallel; they are most often inter-related. Until Jesus came, the religious and patriotic yearning for the kingdom had rested on wishful thinking. But with the coming of Jesus, it was made plain that the kingdom which he was inaugurating could be entered by faith. Just as a temporal monarch conquers and holds his kingdom by force of arms, Jesus would establish his by the preaching of faith. When, after his Resurrection, he declares that all power is given unto him in Heaven and earth, the first use he makes of that power is to send forth his apostles to preach, converting all nations to faith. Their salvation or damnation is made a direct consequence of their acceptance or rejection of this invitation. (Matt. 28, 18; Mk. 16, 15-16). The inter-relationship of the kingdom of God and faith is a gospel axiom too obvious to require emphasis.

But we must go a little farther into the mystery of the new

revelation. What actually is faith? Unquestioning belief in the teaching of Jesus, of course. But that is a thing every prophet requires of those who listen to him. Our Lord never figures as the leader of his people, like his ancestor, David, or like Moses, in his role of legislator, bringing his people in the name of God the charter of a temporal constitution. No; his is a religious message, a message of truth revealed to the innermost heart of all men of goodwill. It is in this role, played first by himself, and continued by his apostles to the end of time—even though it led him to the Passion and his apostles to martyrdom—that he gradually inaugurates and realises the kingdom of God among men. That is why he demands, first and foremost, not obedience to laws, nor submission to a power, but faith.

Of course one might say that in a way this was true even of the other prophets and teachers. But there is more to it in the case of Jesus, as we shall see if we try to understand how the kingdom of God is entirely based on, and owes the manner of its expansion to, the personal mystery of Jesus, a doctrine indispensable to any understanding of the Apocalypse. This surrender which the prophet of Nazareth demands is not only, or even chiefly, adherence to his doctrine but, in the most profound sense, to his own person. It is a surrender which cannot be avoided, and must be absolute. 'This is the work of God, that you believe in him that he hath sent' (Joh. 6, 29). And again: 'For if you believe not that I am he, you shall die in your sin' (Joh. 8, 24). And there are many other texts which insist on the connection between faith and the mysterious person of Jesus. It is not just faith in God—I am speaking of real Christian faith, and not of rationalistic dabbling—which never figures in the gospels except in conjunction with that faith which primarily has Christ as its object. 'No man hath seen God at any time; the only-begotten Son who is in the bosom of the Father, he hath declared him' (Joh. 1, 18; 9, 45). 'No one knoweth who the Son is, but the Father, and the Father, but the Son and to whom the son will reveal him.' (Lk. 10, 22). It is not a revelation in which the Son remains a kind of stranger; it is rather that, in seeing him, as he said to Philip, one sees the

Father (Joh. 14, 9). Christian faith in the mystery of God acts through the person of Jesus, as St Peter so vividly learned at Caesarea (Matt. 16, 16).

There is another and still stronger reason for Christian faith. Whatever particular object it may centre upon in the revelation, Christian faith must first accept the mystery of Jesus and surrender to it. Perhaps this is not always sufficiently insisted upon. Certainly there is no misunderstanding the insistence of Jesus in the gospels when he demands of his disciples a faith which must accept not only what he says, but also himself as speaker. We can easily check that none of the ancient prophets proceeded to this length. But we seem too often to look upon the mystery of Jesus as one among many, and not as a thing at all singular in itself. In reality, it is the one thing that conditions all the rest. Reading the gospel carefully, one soon perceives that its whole morality, the laws of which are the very laws of the new kingdom of God, presuppose a Christology and always go back to it. It is impossible to follow the rules of that morality, in so far as they are characteristic of the gospel, if one does not recognise in them the continuity of this, that or the other aspect of the mystery of Christ. One could quote many examples, and even say that there is not one of the requirements of the New Law which, so far as its original inspiration and evangelical context are concerned, does not appear to be linked with the personal mystery of Jesus Christ, and is not definitely based on Christology.

If, therefore, faith, by which one enters the kingdom of God, or, inversely, by which the kingdom of God is extended on earth, consists above all in surrender to Christ's personality, we begin to see how that mystery could well be the foundation on which the kingdom is based. In the sense that the laws of the latter's structure depend entirely on the former. Far from visualising the Messiah in the role of ruler, as the Jewish tradition did, Christian thought must little by little recognise the true characteristics of the kingdom and their true out-working, both so radically different from those of any political structure, even if theocratic. In this sense, the personality of Jesus is at once seen to dominate both the

kingdom's methods and its powers of expansion. This power
and these methods are not those of the political order, as we
have seen. To which order, then, do they belong, and what is
the royal power exercised by Jesus? It is made clear in many
episodes, and particularly in the scene before Pilate. 'Thou
sayest that I am king. For this was I born and for this came
I into the world; that I should give testimony to the truth'
(Joh. 18, 37). His kingdom, his means of action and of
domination, his power, are those of truth, for he is himself
the Truth. And now we can understand the final commandment: 'All power is given unto me in heaven and in earth . . .
going therefore, teach ye all nations' (Matt. 28, 18-19). The
propagation of faith will be the instrument of Jesus Christ's
universal domination, the actual way in which he will
exercise his regal sway.

But here a problem which did not exist in the Jewish
conception of the kingdom begins to raise its head. Would
the nations accept the truth, and if not, would their refusal
prove a set-back to the perfect kingdom of God? We know
that the Jews thought in terms of force and political pressure
when picturing the establishment of God's universal domination. These means being discarded, what chance had truth
alone of winning through? This question must occur to us.
And we may be sure it occured still more forcibly, if somewhat
confusedly, to the Jews in Jesus's time, who were less capable
than we are of conceiving a kingdom other than in the form
of a theocracy pressing political power into the service of
religious truth. Even among the disciples there were several
who often found the somewhat indifferent and complaisant
tolerance of Jesus towards constituted powers disconcerting.
His friendly attitude towards the gentiles and to the Roman
Empire was not at all shared by the average Jew. They could
not help speculating on the possible relationship between the
new kingdom of God and the temporal order of society, and
it seemed questionable whether such methods could eventually lead to the fulfilment of the old prophecies concerning
the universal domination of the Messiah over the nations.
One can understand the feelings which produced such

expressions of current ideas as 'Lord, wilt thou at this time restore again the kingdom to Israel?' (Acts 1, 6). That dream continued to persist.

One can look at the matter from another angle and ask how the nations themselves, accustomed to order their temporal affairs to an established pattern, would fare under the new dispensation. Having once distinguished between the realm of Caesar and that of God, and having established the latter, individually and collectively, on the foundation of faith in Christ, would the former cease to hold any interest and to share in the divine blessing? The kingdom of Israel and of the chosen race being at an end, such at least as it was in the centuries of preparation, would the political order as such be excluded from the kingdom of God, without hope and without any right to count on the resources of salvation, a stranger forever to the definite alliance between God and man? Would Christians not only be required to give preference to the kingdom of heaven, which indeed was not difficult, but even to abstain from any interest in the world, abandoning it beyond all redemption to the powers of evil? Without doubt, the second coming of Christ, anticipated at any moment, simplified the problem for a great many in the early days. Nevertheless, there was still a problem which sooner or later the disciples would have to face. If it be necessary to distinguish in order to straighten things out, our Lord had with the utmost precision distinguished the kingdom of God from that of Caesar; but it was less easy to see how the two could be brought together, even if one wished to do so. And if the two could not be reconciled, what sense was there in the messianic prophecies foretelling universal domination over the nations?

Did St Paul and the other first apostolic writers offer any solution to this problem? It is clear that from the start all the teachings of Jesus centred round the kingdom of God. Those of St Paul and the apostles, on the other hand, hinged from the beginning on the mystery of Jesus Christ. What we have already said dispenses us from showing that despite this apparent displacement of the centre of perspective, there is undeviating continuity between the two first stages of doctrinal Christian history. Examining the gospel message as a whole in its original characters, it seems inevitable that Christology should have become the centre of Christian doctrine, as it is in St Paul.

Now, what we must underline here is that this Christology is in line with the preachings of our Lord himself in all essentials, I mean, in being not greatly concerned with the sphere of temporal and political values. The Pauline mystery of Christ is certainly of great importance for the public at large—but the community of which it is the very foundation is none other than the Church, and nothing new is said about the relationship existing between this and the political order. What a contrast between the Pauline mystery of the Christ and the Church, and the role which Israel assigned to the Messiah dominating the nations in the midst of his people! And this in such a short space of time, and in the very same circles! St Paul's mystery of Christ is quite beyond the man of politics, and furthermore, at least at first sight, has no aspect that might cause him anxiety. It can only be shared by the essential courage of faith; faith which quite clearly has no traffic with any nationalistic aspirations whatsoever. The more St Paul studies the mystery of Christ, the more he—the one-time zealot for the Law of Israel—leaves the temporal order of things behind him. Whether we speak of the presence of Christ, by faith, in the Christian soul; of the mystery of the Son of God which is communicated to us in Christ; of participation through the sacrament of baptism or Holy Communion in the salvation of the Passion and the Resurrection; of the all-embracing unity of the Body of Christ in which all Christians are one—all these seem to leave the realities of the collective temporal order altogether on one side. The community which began to be constituted around the new doctrine was purely religious in character; here all were alike, and the distinctions Jew, Greek, pagan, slave and freedman were no longer recognised. Despite the sad attachment which his patriotism maintained for it, St Paul from now on speaks of Israel only in order to underline the benefits conferred on Jews, Greeks and gentiles alike when they formed part of the New Israel, Israel not according to the flesh (1, Cor. 10, 8), but according to the promise (Rom. 9, 6 ff.). The time had arrived for the universal inheritance of the children of Abraham, father of believers, a heritage which knew no frontiers and was governed by no particular political law. All men of faith were from now on the true sons of Abraham (Gal. 3, 7), the only authentic heirs to the benefits of God's promises made in earlier times, and of the perfect alliance which came into being with the advent of Jesus (Gal. 3, 39 and the whole of the epistle to the Hebrews).

Up to the year 70 or thereabouts, a Jewish community certainly still existed. One of the greatest difficulties of primitive Christianity was to establish that its cause had nothing in common with that community. Many crises had to be passed through, though they were concerned more with practice than with actual divergencies of doctrine. From the first days of the apostolate, St Peter spoke of the Holy Spirit and of the wonders that accompanied the conversion of the centurion Cornelius, showing that it was not necessary to be a member of the Jewish community in order to enter into the religious community of Christ (Acts 10, ff.). The gifts of the Holy Spirit were not reserved for those who had come from Jewry; the chief of the apostles repeatedly stressed that it was the will of God that the gospel should be announced to the gentiles (Acts 15, 7-9). Now here was a new problem: would believers who sprang from the gentiles have to fall in with the laws and customs of the Jews—to constitute, in short, a sort of larger Jewry? There was the affair at Antioch where Paul (and Barnabas) defended the legality of Jews and gentiles in Christianity, in arguing the manifest will of the Holy Spirit in the apostolic campaigns already conducted. The congress of apostles at Jerusalem in 49 or 50 also broached this question, at least in principle. With the reserve of some concessions aimed at preventing the scandal which even the semblance of participation in pagan cults might cause the Jews, it was clearly laid down that Christian communities no longer came under the authority of the Law (Acts 15, 23 ff.). In religious, and still more in political

matters, Christianity thus finally severed its connection with
the national and religious destiny of the Jewish community.
And if this sorting out of relationships between Christians
and Jews took some time in the early communities (see
the epistles to the Galatians, Romans, etc.) it had nothing
to do with the practice or religious inspiration that caused
their differences. Loyalty to the national traditions of
Judaism, and, it seems, even to the royal family of David, did
not long survive; at most, it was kept alive for a time among
the Christian communities of Jerusalem, then at Pella
beyond Jordan. Hegesippus tells us that, precisely at the
epoch of the Apocalypse, Domitian took umbrage at the
claims of some of the relatives of Jesus to be descended, like
him, from the race of David (Eusebius, H.E., III, XIX-XX).

But this was only a local and strictly limited episode on
the outer fringe of the great Christian movement. If the
political authorities were still liable to confuse Jews with
Christians under Claudius (*Judaeos impulsore Christo assidue
tumultuantes Roma expulit*: Suetonius, Claudius, 25) under
Nero this confusion is already no longer possible. It even
appears that the former diverted the tyrant's fury to the
latter, along with that of the populace (Tacitus, Annals XV,
44; Eusebius H.E. II, XXV). And even if Domitian, at the
time of the Apocalypse, found it convenient for financial
reasons to pretend once again that the two were identical,
soon (under Trajan, for instance) their complete independence
of one another could no longer be in any doubt. From a
totally detached standpoint Christianity clearly had no
connection whatsoever with any political or national cause,
and least of all with that of Jewry. Christianity was a purely
religious amalgamation of people.

Relationships with other political groups apart from the
Jews—which, practically speaking, covers the Roman
Empire—proved even less of a problem. Between Rome and
the new religion there might at first have been some local
conflicts or personal misunderstandings, but they did not
involve any question of principle. Pilate, who among the
first believers reaped all the odium of condemning Jesus,
could never have seriously thought of the king of the Jews

being a menace to the Empire. A few other magistrates were able to misuse the power they derived from Rome against the apostles or against the early communities. Paul and Silas could be imprisoned and beaten, the Churches of Ephesus or of Asia Minor could be persecuted; but these were only local incidents and personal injustices, and it would not be right to read into them any opposition in principle to the new religion on the part of the Empire at that time. Furthermore, how could the Empire at that early period be at all concerned about any threat to its own political aspirations by the universal pretentions of a new sect which had come obscurely out of Palestine? So insignificant was the movement that it took a long time to discover any potential menace, and then the discovery aroused distrust rather than fear.

The apostles on their part do not appear to have caused the political authorities in gentile circles any trouble. There is every evidence that the faithful submitted meekly to the established authorities; that they respected the laws, the impartiality of which they had no reason, moreover, to suspect. By their exemplary conduct they entered into no conflicts; they even prayed for the Emperor and for the heads of constitutional government. But in their secret hearts, the first care of their lives was directed to quite another plane (cf. Rom. the whole of Chap. 13). *Praeterit figura hujus mundi*! (1 Cor. 7, 31). No need to let fugitive incidents detain us! Our Lord alone counted! Soon, perhaps, he would re-appear in his glory to inaugurate the ultimate order of all things. While waiting, and from now on, the Christian's real loyalty, his citizenship and nationality, was fixed with him in heaven (Philipp. 3, 20). They had something better to do than to trouble themselves with earthly matters.

St Peter never speaks in any other terms. 'Dearly beloved, I beseech you as strangers and pilgrims, to refrain yourselves from carnal desires which war against the soul. Having your conversation good among the Gentiles; that whereas they speak against you as evil-doers, they may, by the good works which they shall behold in you, glorify God in the day of visitation. Be ye subject therefore to every human creature for God's sake; whether it be to the king as excelling or to governors as sent by him for the punishment of evil-doers and for the praise of the good. For so is the will of God, that by doing well you may put to silence the ignorance of foolish men; as free and not as making liberty a cloak for malice, but as the servants of God. Honour all men. Love the brotherhood. Fear God. Honour the king. Servants, be subject to your masters with all fear, not only to the good and gentle but also to the froward. For this is thankworthy; if, for conscience towards God, a man endure sorrows . . .' (1 Pet. 2, 11-19). Briefly, a consistently correct attitude towards social and political authorities, an attitude loyal but indifferent, because the vital interest of the soul was centred elsewhere.

And anyhow, what exception could be taken to the methods of the Roman government? They insured justice and tranquillity at home and abroad; were not these dispensations providential? Paul had no difficulty in reconciling his loyalty as a Roman citizen (and we know with what vehemence he could on occasion claim his rights in this respect (Acts 22-25)) with his religious faith, however monopolising the vital force of his spirit. There was nothing of a revolutionary about Paul. In contrast with what was to come at the time of the Domitian persecutions, there was not one problem of any importance, above all, not a single doctrinal problem, that could entangle the Christian communities in their relations with the political powers of the Roman Empire. Their position was even simpler, more detached, in this respect, than that of the Jewish synagogue before A.D.70. The mystical Church of Christ, in which all believers were incorporated, had less trouble than the synagogue in avoiding an equivocal position; even its recruitment, since it made no distinctions, was proof against any suspicion that it might have political or nationalistic motives. As for the apostles, they were so much occupied in preaching the mystery of Christ and in organising the new-born Churches everywhere, that they appeared not to visualise the immediate universal domination of the Messiah except so far as that domination was in line with the development of the Church. (Cf. Rom. 16, 24, Eph. 4, 7-16, etc.)   The

Christology of St Paul leaves scarcely any room for the characteristics by which the Israelite tradition had forecast the universal reign of the Messiah over the nations, and in this the contrast with the Apocalypse is very striking (cf. farther on). The problem of the nations remains quite outside the orbit of the first apostolic preachings, just as it seems to have given very little concern to the Saviour himself. Now this silence is nothing less than remarkable. Let us reflect for a moment on the development of other points in the Christology of St Paul. The first Gnostic speculations, for example, give him the opportunity to present the mystery of Jesus in its cosmic, super-temporal dimensions and therefore properly speaking divine; but although he speaks of the kingship of Jesus, he says nothing of the rights which this royalty will give him among the other kings of this world. God, he writes 'who hath delivered us from the powers of darkness and hath translated us into the kingdom of the Son of his love; in whom we have redemption through his blood, the remission of sins; who is the image of the invisible God, the first-born of every creature, for in him were all things created in heaven and on earth, visible and invisible, whether thrones or dominations, or principalities or powers. All things were created by him and in him, and he is above all and by him all things consist. And he is the head of the body, the Church, who is the beginning, the firstborn from the dead, that in all things he may hold the primacy; because in him it hath well pleased the Father that all the fullness shall dwell, and through him to reconcile all things unto himself, making peace through the blood of his cross' (Col. 1, 13 ff.). The same brilliant delineations occur in the epistles to the Ephesians and the Philippians, the same affirmations of the absolute primacy and dominion of Christ, but also the same vagueness, the same omissions, in all that concerns the actual manner of that terrestrial reign. And it is quite possible that if the great apostle had been pressed for his views on that reign, or the exact part it would play in the temporal order of human affairs, he would have brushed the question aside as being unworthy of attention. The Roman government was favourable to the dissemination of the Christian doctrine;

why bother about anything else? As long as no one fell foul
of the established authorities, and lived in peace with others
according to the rules of the Republic, he was satisfied to
give temporal affairs no more thought than they deserved.
The transcendent mystery of Christ, which is the true object
of Christian faith, is infinitely worthier of attention than all
these things.

Thus, even while they attempted to define the mystery of
Christ and the Church in all its magnitude, St Paul and the
other witnesses of the first apostolic generation saw it more
as a kind of cosmic and supernatural matter than a thing
directly affecting the nations of the earth and their temporal
history. In this they differed completely from the Israelite
prophets, whose messianic forecasts, on the other hand, were
always made with prospects of actual domination in view.
Even the epistle to the Hebrews, which is so Jewish in
context, depicts Christ clearly as the heir of all the promises
made to Israel, but even these bear no imprint of the traditional views on Jewish nationalism. Christ, here introduced
in the fulness of his rights by virtue of his own sacrifice, is
shown more in the character of priest than king. If there is any
suggestion of kingship, it is nearer to the Melchisedech
conception of it, that is to say, the role of Priest-King, whose
sacerdotal function entails all power. Nevertheless, the author
maintains, if all the rights of the earth follow as a consequence
of the promise made to the Jews, it is by faith that these
rights are acquired, and clearly this refers not to mundane
realities, but to the invisible and celestial realisation of our
hope. In which, to the very end, the Pauline doctrine, while
affirming the absolute primacy of Christ and his right
without reserve to the heritage of the old promises, remains
absolutely faithful to the care our Lord himself took in
proclaiming the kingdom of God's radical independence of
the collective realities of this world, whether they bear the
name of Kingdom of Israel or Roman Empire.

But see how these temporal and political realities, which
seemed capable of being regarded as negligible, suddenly
force us to be aware of their existence—not only in local
conflicts of limited importance, like those that could crop up

in Ephesus or in Corinth, or even in Rome, under the cynic Nero, but in a clash of principles which the most clear-sighted could perceive at once to be irreducible. Domitian, who represents the incarnation of the Roman political order, laid claim to the divine title of Lord (Κυριοσ), which the Christians reserved exclusively for Jesus and God—for Jesus because he was God. Loyal to Caesar in all other respects, the Christian believer had no choice but to refuse this homage, even at the cost of his life. Thus at Pergamos, where there was at that time a temple to Caesar, Antipas, the faithful witness (2, 13) made the supreme sacrifice. Persecu-tion little by little spread over the whole Empire. The political order of Rome began to take arms against the Church. Who could foresee the end of this conflict in which, obviously, neither side could give way? Rome could not, because she regarded this adoration of Caesar as the only means of assuring the unity of her immense Empire; neither could the Christians, because they could not lend themselves to this idolatry.

In basing itself on principle and in gathering such momen-tum, the persecution faced believers with a new difficulty. Although, since the founding of the Churches, they had encountered nothing more than local limited opposition, they did know something of these persecutions which their founder had foretold (Matt. 10, 17 ff.), but concerning which he had also told them they need not trouble themselves, because he had overcome the world (Lk. 11, 22; Joh. 16, 33). These trials, they might think, were of short duration, and soon the Churches also would demonstrate, if only in their peaceful development and the increase in their numbers, the triumph of the Resurrection over the gentiles. Now, not only was this progress brought to a sudden halt, but a new and greater persecution faced the Church, not merely from this remote synagogue, or that local carver of idols, but from the whole vast resources of the Empire which had at first appeared to favour the propagation of the truth. Now that the Empire had in its turn become the enemy of Christ, how could one go on talking about the victory of the Resurrection, which had so enchanted the faith of Christians, and of which they

were constantly expecting renewed manifestations? Were not
the actual facts a cruel denial of this very triumph? Or should
one, facing these concrete facts, counter them by political
action, and revolt against the tyrannical pretensions of
Caesar by force of arms?

As can be seen, it was in reality the problem of the kingship
of Christ that Domitian's persecution raised confusedly in
the minds of the Christians. At least we are justified in
thinking so, if we refer to the Apocalypse, which is the
principal Christian document affording an insight into this
crisis, and the great inspired book dealing with that kingship.
Let it suffice for the moment to recall that the description of
Christ, in this great book, is essentially that of a triumphant
king, dominating the nations, if necessary, with a rod of iron.
From the address (1, 5), from the first prophetic evocation
(1, 7), from the first vision (1, 13) he appears as the Son of
Man triumphant over empires, as the Judge before whom all
the tribes of the earth are made to tremble. And then, in the
unforgettable passage which is the culminating point of St
John's message (19, 11-16) he is solemnly declared King of
kings and Lord of lords, his name at last being mentioned
without mystery (19, 16). Thus the Apocalypse, at the end of
the New Testament's revelation, abruptly and with manifestly deliberate intention goes back to the great traditional
messianic themes, and the domination of the Messiah over
the whole earth.

That this domination posed difficult problems, we shall
see. Once the radically spiritual and religious notion of the
kingdom of God inherited from Israel had been transformed
by the Master; once the super-national and super-temporal
precedence of the Church over all temporal and national
institutions had been made clear (and with what firmness and
insistence!); once the heritage of Israel had been transformed
into 'a chosen generation, a kingly priesthood, a holy nation,
a purchased people' (1 Pet. 2, 9) what became of the prospects
of a universal order realised here on earth, under the leader-
ship of the Messiah—the kingdom of God? Would human
communities, those of Israel or of the nations, races and

people, rich and poor, powerful and humble, subjects and kings, all or any of them escape that imperial domination of Christ? (I am not speaking here of the secret religious life of the individual, but precisely of their condition as members of collective society.) All the messianic promises made for centuries had foretold the universal kingship of him whom the chosen people expected. Would they now need to be transferred, making this kingship a matter confined to the inviolable secrecy of the individual conscience of men who gave their faith to Jesus, and postponing to another world, or to his final re-appearance, the redemption of collective values?

It can easily be seen that here was a problem that went beyond the particular crisis of Domitian's day and struck at the very nature of Christianity. It is a problem posed to human thought in every age. Our own age has seen things done against the Church, and promulgated among the masses, not unlike those which were launched among our fathers in the faith when persecutions began. By seeking your salvation in a future life, people have been told, and only fixing your desire on heavenly realities, you are depriving human society of the dynamics and the resources which are within you. The complaint is no new one. It was already being formulated at the time of Domitian against that high personage of royal blood, Flavius Clemens; he showed himself disinterested, it is said, in public matters (Suetonius, Domitian 15). On the other hand, by one of those contradictions that abound in antichristianism, as soon as the Church, appearing to take the preceding complaint seriously, recalls to Christians their responsibilities and their duties in human affairs, there is no lack of critics to protest against what they call the interference of religious authorities. Some even accuse the Church of betraying its founder and the spiritual character of the kingdom of God which it is their duty to preach. Stay in your sacristy, we are told, prepare your discourse for those who are interested in the hereafter, but leave the state to organise mundane society and life here on earth without any interference from you.

Even leaving polemics aside, the dilemma is a serious one,

and can be met with at every turn of Christian history. It forms the real reason for the persecutions of the first three centuries . . . It runs right through the history of the Byzantine Empire, from Constantius II, Constantine's successor, to Photius, and from Michael Cerularius to the collapse in 1453. It was responsible for innumerable crises in the Middle Ages, and a whole library of literature, from Gregory VII to Boniface VIII, illustrates the theme. The English schism, the Gallicanism of France, Febronianism in Austria, and various contemporary 'isms' all spring fundamentally from the same uncertainty. In the great social phenomena of modern times or in the great moral problems which precede them in economic history, the presence of the Church is promptly suspected of intolerable interference, and its absence quickly followed by moral decadence and sanguinary conflicts. When the Church recalls Christ's rights over human society, and the teachings of his morality, which are the only saving grace, it is accused of wishing to install a theocracy which would in fact be contrary to the leading of Christ in the gospel; when nations and society cut themselves adrift from the tutelage of Christian laws, they soon suffer the first disastrous consequences. These then are the recoils of civilisation and what the Christian formed in the school of the Apocalypse must, as we shall see in the following pages, recognise as the sanctions inherent in Christian truth or the judgements of Christ in history. In societies deprived of the only possible salvation, pseudo-messianisms must inevitably be born, expressing the yearning of masses of men and the spirit of the times for a saviour and a king to extricate them from their distress. How the Christian must deplore these aspirations and these religious movements, knowing by his faith that they are blind alleys! Because there is only one Saviour, the one and only King of kings and Lord of lords, for the individual or for society as a whole. But it is necessary for the believer to know the exact nature of that kingship of Christ, and how it operates for the redemption of mankind. In short, the Christian must know how Jesus Christ, ceaselessly preaching by his Church that the kingdom of God is within us, while rendering unto God that which is God's and unto Caesar that which is Caesar's, is actually the King of kings and Lord of lords. The Apocalypse, of all the books of revelation, is undoubtedly the one which contains the Christian answer to these questions which, in one form or another, have been arising ever since Domitian's time. It is the great theological authority on the universal kingship of Jesus. It is the answer of the New Testament to the prophecies of the Old concerning the domination of the great king, Son of David, over all the nations.

CHAPTER III

THE MYSTERY OF CHRIST IN THE APOCALYPSE

'Revelation of Jesus Christ.' These are the first words of the message of St John to the persecuted Churches. No doubts need arise over the genitive; it is Jesus Christ who, through this revelation, 'makes known to his servants the things that must shortly come to pass' (1, 1).

All the same, there has been no lack of commentators to hold the view that St John's intention was to present a 'revelation of Jesus Christ', that is to say, one having Jesus Christ as its object. In order to admonish and encourage the Churches in their time of trial, the exile on Patmos would have wished to give the Churches instruction which, if not quite new, would at least throw additional light on the person and the role of Jesus, 'the faithful witness, the first-begotten of the dead, and the prince of the kings of the earth' (1, 5). In order to fortify their courage, John set out to prove the complete mastery of the Resurrected one within the framework of contemporary history. The very first doxology shows the preponderance of Christ in the visions which the exiled Apostle will describe.

He who hath loved us
And washed us from our sins in his own blood
—And hath made us a kingdom and priests to God and his
    Father—
To him be the glory for ever and ever. Amen. (1, 5-6.)

The first vision (1, 12 ff.) still further confirms the impression that the book as a whole is dominated by the personality of Jesus, and that all the rest of its contents are like mere rays emanating from that blinding focus of light.

In the foregoing chapter we dealt with the historic circumstances arising out of the relationship between the resurrected Messiah and the impious nations. It seems to us that this is the angle which gives us the best chance of penetrating the mystery of Christ as it was given to John to reveal it in his revelations.

But it would be a mistake to limit one's curiosity to the incidents which impinged upon the great book at that particular period of primitive Christian history. In reality it presents the elements of a genuine Christological synthesis, sometimes by inference, sometimes explicitly formulated. One may even go so far as to say that, of all the writings of the New Testament previous to the fourth gospel, it presents Christology in its most developed form. It derives its major theological contributions from St Paul and the early catechism. The fourth gospel goes little farther than to gather up the various new strands that first appear in the Apocalypse, commencing with the doctrine of the Word. All this amply justifies us in approaching the book by way of its Christology. The Christian vision that comes to us from Patmos is primarily this: a vision of Christ, and a delineation of the invisible but positive part he plays in history. Let us proceed in the manner of the book itself, by successive and complementary evocations, starting with the near and very real presence of the Resurrected one and his universal mastery as king and judge of the nations, by way of the divine mystery of his origin and his person.

The very first impression we get from the opening vision as well as from the letters to the churches is that of his mysterious but very real and immediate presence.

I, John, your brother . . .
I heard behind me a great voice, as of a trumpet . . .
And I turned to see the voice that spoke with me.
And being turned I saw seven golden candlesticks
And in the midst of the seven candlesticks one like the Son of Man
Clothed with a garment down to his feet
And girt about the paps with a golden girdle
And his head and his hairs were white

As white wool and as snow
And his eyes were as a flame of fire
And his feet like unto fine brass, as in a burning furnace
And his voice as the sound of many waters
And he had in his right hand seven stars
And from his mouth came out a sharp two-edged sword
And when I had seen him I fell at his feet as dead.
And he laid his right hand upon me saying
'Fear not . . . ' (1, 9 ff.).

And again the opening of the first letter, that to the Church
of Ephesus, which shows him coming and going in the midst
of the Churches (symbolised precisely in 1, 20 by the golden
candlesticks):

> 'These things saith he who holdeth the seven stars in his
> right hand and walketh in the midst of the seven golden
> candlesticks . . .' (2, 1).

And above all the insistence with which he repeatedly
stresses his resurrected life:

> 'And behold I am living for ever and ever, and
>
> Have the keys of death and of hell' (1, 18; cf. 2, 8).

The very tone of the letters drives home the impression of
the resurrected Christ's almost tangible presence in the
midst of the Churches. Of course it is not only the Apocalypse
that deals with the Resurrection of Christ; we know that this
was one of the main objects in the preaching of the faith to
the first generation of Christians. We already find in St Paul
this expression, 'first-begotten among the dead' (Col. 1, 18),
which is one of the Apocalyptic titles of Christ (1, 5). But the
characteristic thing about St John is the frequency with which
he insists on the actual presence of our Lord among the
communities of believers who depend upon him. It is here on
earth, and not in some distant heaven, that he sees him and
shows him (1, 12; 1, 20). We notice that the passage which
suggests this is very closely related to the impression the
fourth gospel will give in the chapters devoted to the
appearances after the Resurrection. Here, as there, Christ
appears and disappears, and either makes himself known
immediately, or on the contrary simply suggests his mysterious presence, in a progressively unmistakable manner.
Briefly, those who share in the experience are aware of an

unmistakable, exciting personal presence which is somehow not in conformity with the laws of the material presence of ordinary human beings. Moreover, in all cases, the awareness of that presence is only shared by the disciples and those who, coming after them, shall be capable of believing without seeing. This is how it was at the time of the Apocalypse. He 'walked' in the midst of the Churches (2, 1), ready to dispossess this one of its primacy (2, 5) or to intervene 'quickly' in the affairs of another (2, 16) threatening the woman Jezabel and those who are led astray by her with punishment (2, 22 ff.) or lingering behind the door, ready to sup with any who will have him (3, 20). The Acts of the Apostles also give this impression of the vivid presence of the resurrected Christ, operating either in his own person, or in that of the Holy Ghost, to further the apostolate. But no other book in the New Testament stresses this so emphatically as the Apocalypse. The most illuminating passage on this theme is to be found at the end of St Matthew's gospel, in which our Lord says: 'Behold, I am with you all days, even to the consummation of the world' (Matt. 28, 20). Before revealing the apotheosis of Jesus and his Ascension to the mysterious heaven of his divine glory, the revelation of Patmos paints in vivid relief his quickening presence among the Churches. We can see how comforting such an idea must have been. When a fighting regiment knows that its commanding officer is there, sharing the smoke and the heat of battle, that awareness has a far more tonic effect than a message of encouragement conveyed to the fighters by a general seated in glory in some distant palace headquarters.

It is by no means sure whether we Christians of today have been able to keep alive the realistic faith our forefathers had in the Resurrection of Christ. It certainly gave them tremendous power. For the want of it we may fail to grasp the full meaning of the message of St John. If we examine ourselves honestly as to our faith in the Resurrection of Jesus, we may find that our attitude towards it scarcely differs from our attitude towards our own dead—by this I mean that it has scarcely more significance for us than our belief in the immortality of departed souls. We are not at all excited by it, and we scarcely ever think of dwelling upon its effect on the evolution of world events. Certainly we do not deny the survival of Jesus, any more than we doubt the continued existence of our own departed after death—but we go very little farther to distinguish their case from his. Like them, we picture him in a dis-incarnated, cosmic state, divine, perhaps, but beyond our horizon of imagination, where death puts men with whom, apart from remembrance and prayer, we have no contact until we are all re-united in our Creator at the end of time. There is no communication between the two worlds; they cannot return to help us in our affairs, whatever deeds they have left behind them, or whatever prayers they may offer to God on our behalf. Our dead are no longer personalities playing a part in history. Life goes on without them.

It is to be feared that nowadays we have a similar conception of our Lord's position in regard to our human affairs, and thus we practically deny the Resurrection. Like the women whom the Angel reproached on Easter morning, we go on obstinately looking for 'the living among the dead' though he has already gone before us into Galilee (Lk. 24, 5-6)—that is to say, into the very heart of the world which is our living environment, the 'here' which the Resurrection has enabled him to re-enter triumphantly. By this we reduce the Resurrection to a mere episode of some vague tomorrow, which may perhaps inaugurate a personal triumph for the Crucified one, but has nothing whatever to do with the external progress here on earth of the work he came to do. The Apocalypse teaches us that the real triumph of Jesus's work commenced by virtue of his victory over death, the absolute mastery which gave him the keys of death and hell (1, 18)—and this he has brought back with him into the world. For this reason the resurrected Christ, now present, though invisible, is the foremost and the most active personality in human history.

By what title could he inherit this power? Undoubtedly by his sacrifice. In the Apocalypse, as in the whole of the New Testament, the Passion is inseparable from the Resurrection.

'I was dead. And behold, I am living.' A fleeting but adequate reference to conjure up the Passion. Obviously, this is no new teaching. And at once one gets the impression that St John can scarcely go on without driving home a lesson with which all are already familiar. It might almost be St Paul who is writing the message. For example: 'He who hath loved us and washed us from our sins in his own blood' (1, 5), is from the same workshop as the following from the epistle to the Galatians: 'And I live, now not I: but Christ liveth in me. And that I live now in the flesh: I live in the faith of the Son of God, who loved me and delivered himself for me' (Gal. 2, 20). It is clear that the redemptive Passion is at the heart of all New Testamental Christology and one cannot regard the Apocalypse as being at all singular in this respect. But we very soon become aware that whenever the Passion is mentioned there, it is linked with the idea of the mastery Christ achieved through it. Thus, the King of kings and Lord of lords appears in Chapter 19 'clothed with a garment sprinkled with blood' (19, 13) just as in the apotheosis of Chapter 5 he is depicted as 'a lamb standing, as it were slain' (5, 6). It is precisely in his sufferings that the message of Patmos shows Christ triumphant, and what could have been more heartening to the persecuted churches?

We presently perceive that it is the author's intention to present the Passion of our Lord as his supreme act of testimony. Jesus Christ, in our book, is above all the 'faithful witness' (1, 4), the 'witness faithful and true' (3, 14) who has proved up to the hilt the messianic prophecies of a psalm (Ps. 89, 38). He came in order to bear witness to the truth, as he says before Pilate. He did this even unto death as did Antipas, also a faithful witness, after him (2, 13) and all those who by similar testimony earned the title of overcomers (cf. the ending of each of the letters). Until the end of time, the two mysterious witnesses who represent the Church, and of whom we shall speak later, will be both sacrificed and victorious (11, 3). 'Faithful witness,' 'Lamb as it were slain,' 'First-begotten among the dead,' these three first titles of Jesus in the Apocalypse are directly dependent upon one another and in strict continuity. We shall soon see that the special lessons the message of Patmos strove to drive home all fit into the frame of the testimony rendered by Christ to truth.

Let us return to the first vision, in which Christ appears to St John to give him his assignment. Perhaps we are wrong in not underlining the one thing which must have struck the original recipients most forcibly, filling them with both terror and consolation. They cannot have failed to recognise in the mysterious being 'like unto the Son of Man' the very same personage in whom Daniel saw the vengeance that could be taken on persecuting and idolatrous empires (Dan. 7, 13) —the vengeance inseparable from the triumph of his people. He, too, is dressed in a white garment, denoting his sacerdotal office, adorned with the regal girdle of gold. His white head and his penetrating glance (Dan. 7, 9) prove that the Ancient of Daniel's day was a divine personage, just as his brazen solidity, contrasting with Nabuchodonosor, and the terrifying sound of his voice, made his domination irresistible to his enemies. In this way, Christ is presented from the start as the triumphant hero who will lead the people of God to victory over the great pagan empires, just as Daniel had prophesied, and no reminder could have been more welcome to the persecuted Churches.

It must certainly have been a thought capable of striking terror into any religious soul schooled by the Old Testament to familiarity with a vengeful God. Inasmuch as we have to some extent become insensible to the mystery of God, it is difficult for us nowadays to realise the full force of such suggestions. The effect of the vision upon St John himself gives us some idea of the hold the old awe had upon him. Although he was the one whom Jesus loved—

'And when I had seen him,
I fell at his feet as dead' (1, 17).

Then, by one of those sudden transitions which abound in this great work we get, side by side with this awesome terror so reminiscent of the Old Testament, the moving evidence of Jesus's gentleness and comfort—

'And he laid his right hand upon me,
Saying "Fear not" ' (1, 17).

This contrast is maintained right through the book. There are countless instances of the infinite delicacy with which our Lord expresses his tenderness for his own (3, 19-20; 7, 17; 21, 3-4; 21, 7; etc.). Even when it is necessary to show him in the role of judge, we are permitted to detect his solicitude for the elect (14, 14-16) while he leaves to the Angel of Wrath the necessary execution of divine justice. And the whole ends with the sublime peace and intimacy of the marriage of the Lamb, and the holy Jerusalem which is impregnated with his divine light. But, on the whole, the figure of Christ in the Apocalypse has much in common with the vengeful divine manifestations of the Old Testament. Which is none the less reassuring for those who are undergoing the trials of persecution.

The central portion of St John's prophecies opens with an apotheosis of Christ in that great vision of the thrones in heaven which is inspired by Ezechiel. 'The things' (4, 1) are entirely dominated by the omnipotence of God, which is inseparably associated from now on with the omnipotence of the Lamb. So the prophecies do definitely concern the progress of history, or rather the future which will follow contemporary events in the lives of the prophet and his correspondents. But it had first to be shown very emphatically that God and Christ are entirely in control of that future. This is the object of Chapters 4 and 5. We cannot pause to consider each individual characteristic; moreover none of them gives rise to any major difficulties. The incomparable art with which the inspired prophet has touched in the reliefs and colours of this great fresco rouses our admiration. The majesty of the Creator (4, 1) radiates the whole story with a supernatural glory. Naturally, no description is given of him. Out of respect for his transcendence, his name is not even mentioned. The Apocalypse, so prodigal in its imagery, deliberately avoids any attempt to personify God, leaving his majesty to the imagination. The book suggests this by the symbol of a flame throwing out fiery rays—a suggestion vividly borne out by the scintillation of gems, or

the rainbow, a synthesis of the richest colours. In his efforts
to convey an impression of the divine mystery, he chooses
the most delicate, iridescent shades.

God from his throne of majesty reigns irresistibly over the
whole creation he has made. It is linked with him by the
symbols of the twenty-four ancients and the living creatures.
Many explanations of these two major symbolisms have been
suggested. To us it seems that the twenty-four ancients in the
garments and crowns of victory are intended to represent the
march of time—not, perhaps, time in an astronomical sense,
so much as a sense of the progress of human history prior to
'these things', that is to say, the period represented by the
Old Testament, and the saints whose lives have left imprints
on the different stages. The fact that they are garbed in white
and have golden crowns signifies that they have been
victorious in the great fight for truth and now share the
triumph, though not perhaps completely, in the manner that
the elect share the throne with the Lamb. For the time being
their prayers rank with those of the angels supporting the
world, that is to say, the living creatures (4, 9-10; 5, 8-14).
In these it is hardly possible to avoid recognising ancient
signs of the zodiac, since they call to mind astral evolutions
and the immense stretch of time these evolutions take. The
angels lead the cosmic paean of praise, and, unlike that of the
ancients, their sight already penetrates to the throne itself
(4, 6) and they praise God day and night in terms which make
it absolutely clear that he is master of time. 'Holy, holy,
holy, Lord God Almighty, who was, and is now, and who is
to come' (4, 8) 'for ever and ever' (4, 9)[1]. Thus in John's
vision it is the whole of creation, space and time, that
celebrates the glory of the Creator in praises, led by the

[1] Let us seize the opportunity offered by the first of these titles to give an
example of the meticulous care with which the Apocalypse is composed.
When, at the beginning of the book, he expresses the hope of grace and peace
to his correspondents, he uses the elements of the title in the following order:
'He who is, who was and who will be' (1, 4; 1, 8). God was then visualised in
the present, so the present comes first. Here, on the contrary, when God is
visualised from the point of view of duration in time, the past logically comes
before the present or the future, so it runs: 'He who was, and who is, and
who is to come.' Finally, at the consummation, when the future has to be
made plain, the same title becomes 'O Lord who wast' (11, 17).

angels who preside over the world's evolutions, and taken up
by the twenty-four witnesses of earlier human history.

Now it is at the moment when the twenty-four ancients
enter into the sequence of human history with their contribution that the cosmic continuity of the vision is suddenly
interrupted, and the apotheosis of the Lamb unfolds. (Cap.
5). In order that the praise which history owes to God shall
be complete, it is necessary that the Lamb shall intervene.
A book appears out of heaven, but it is a scroll, the ancient
form of a book, and it has the peculiarity of being written on
both sides, so that it can only be read by unrolling the whole.
No commentator has ever questioned that this book is the
clue to the meaning of human history. By reading it the
persecuted Churches will better understand the reasons for
their trials, and they will also get an insight into subsequent
events. But alas, 'no one, either in heaven nor on earth nor
under the earth' can open the book or look into it. The
bitter disappointment of John at the inability of anyone to
understand, much less control, the march of events, is
augmented by the anxiety of the Churches in the face of
persecution. But the ancients are not perturbed, no doubt
because of the knowledge of the way in which God has led
their people throughout the whole of their long history, and
because they have learnt to wait with confidence for the
coming of him who is at the centre of history. One of them,
in whom we are tempted to recognise Jacob (so much is the
blessing of choice which he gave to his son Juda recalled
here [Gen. 49, 8-12]) reminds John of the lion of the tribe of
Juda and informs him that the root of David is successful in
opening the book (5, 5; cf. 22, 16). Then the triumphant
conquerer of the world and of history, the 'lamb standing'
appears in all his resplendent divinity, 'as it were slain' (5, 6).
And the same ancients fall down before the Lamb and sing
in his praise the new canticle, celebrating his mastery over
that history which is to fulfil the glory of the Creator.

Thou art worthy, O Lord
To take the book and to open the seals thereof;
Because thou was slain and hast redeemed us to God
In thy Blood
Out of every tribe and tongue and people and nation.

And thou hast made us to our God
A kingdom and priests
And we shall reign on the earth (5, 9-10).

From this point onwards, the Lamb having now appeared, the song of praise can swell into a canticle of all creation, space and time, throughout the length of history, a canticle which will no longer distinguish between God and the Lamb, for all ages of ages (5, 11-14). Thus we know, at the end of this great vision of Chapters 4 and 5, that it is through Christ triumphant that history renders glory to God, and from now on we are as impatient as the Churches were to hear the message and understand how this triumph of Christ in history will come about and also how those whom he has purchased with his blood for God shall become a kingdom of priests reigning on earth.

Let us run over the major teachings which this great vision gives us on Christ and, completing them by the other Christological visions of the book (particularly 1, 12-20; 14, 14-20; 19, 11-16) pick out the main lines of this Christology in the Apocalypse.

To start with, it is perfectly clear that the prophet of Patmos had no doubt whatsoever of the divinity of Christ. We have already seen that, at the climax of the opening vision (1, 12-20) Christ appears to him with all the attributes of God himself, in the true prophetic and apocalyptic tradition. His pre-existence is already affirmed here. But that is not all. Many essentially divine titles are used for him, besides that of 'Lord' which is used for Christ throughout the New Testament. We have, for instance, Alpha and Omega (1, 8; 21, 6; and 23, 13); the first and last (1, 17; 2, 8; 22, 13); he, living for ever and ever (1, 18; 4, 9; 10, 6, etc.). The throne of God is also interchangeably that of Christ (22, 1-3) etc.; furthermore, there is the same wrath (6, 17). In the final vision which depicts the eternal life of the elect, God can no longer be distinguished from the Lamb: THEY are one; the same homage is offered to THEM; their united name is written on the foreheads of the elect (22, 3-4; compare also 21, 23 and 22, 5). Furthermore, the symbolism of numbers, so dear to our author, gives further testimony of the divinity of Christ by the repeated use of the figure seven. The word Christ is used seven times (1, 1, 2, 5; 11, 15; 12, 10; 20, 4, 6) of which three are in company with Jesus (1, 1, 2, 5) which is used fourteen times besides (twice seven).

The Apocalypse is primarily concerned with enlarging on the mystery of Christ's divinity, and it anticipates the gospel in giving us an insight into this intra-divine relationship. Especially the relationship existing between the Father and the Son. This is stressed not only by texts where God is specifically named, as in the synoptic gospels and in St Paul, with almost an excess of simplification, the Father of Jesus Christ, (1, 6; 2, 18, 28; 3, 5; 3, 21; 14, 1) but by to some extent new side-lights on the mystery of that paternity. This is one of the most profound lessons of the book, and forms the best introduction, a kind of prologue, to the fourth gospel.

Who, first of all, is the mysterious pregnant woman whom St John sees in the first of the seven visions of heavenly signs, clothed in the sun, with the moon at her feet, and crowned with twelve stars? (12, 1 ff.) No doubt this symbolises the Church, bringing forth her offspring in pain and sorrow (2) and we shall have to return to this point in a later chapter. There is also no doubt that the Church embraces the whole of the Old Testament, that the issue of Jacob, the chosen people, are symbolised by the stars and astral figures which Joseph, the prototype of Jesus, had already seen bending before him (Gen. 37, 9). But the woman right down the ages who gives birth to the elect is also above all the Mother who brings forth the male infant which the Dragon cannot reach, and this is evidently Jesus Christ. Every Christian takes this illustration as a reference to the Virgin Mary, and a traditional interpretation in legitimate continuity with the literal sense has also recognised her as that woman. Jesus, Son of Man, is for all races and for all time the 'terrible fruit' as regards Satan. But I should be willing to think that there is something more in it, and that there is also in this great heavenly vision of the woman a reference to the mystery of the eternal generation of the Son of God. We should not

lose sight of the fact that we are concerned here with the first
of the 'signs in heaven'. This Chapter twelve is characterised
by the emphasis it lays on locating its visions in heaven before
the descent of the Dragon and the commencement of earthly
history. As we see in the sequel, for example, the combat
between Michael and the Dragon, the starting point of these
visions, occurs before the creation of the world, even before
the appearance of the Dragon. We are at the very inception of
all creation (2, 14; cf. Pro. 8, 22) in the closest possible
proximity, in fact, to the eternal mystery of God himself.
Now, why not recall here that other great symbol of the
woman in the Wisdom literature of the Old Testament, she
who is the wisdom immanent in God before all creation?
*Dominus possedit me in initio viarum suarum, antequam
quidquam faceret a principio'* (Pro. 822; cf. Wis. 6, 22; 7, 12;
7, 15 ff.; 7, 25 ff.; 8, 2-3; 9, 10, etc.—Eccl. 1, 4; 15 ff., above all,
Chapter 24). Wisdom of God, self-generated; created and
creating; the virgin motherhood of Mary; the Church in all
ages bringing forth the elect; these are the three mysteries of
generation which the Holy Spirit never ceases to show in
continuity, the first giving root to the two others in the very
reality of God. The same texts could be indiscriminately
applied to the three mysteries by the Christian liturgy, and
especially that with which we are now concerned. How then
can we reject the idea that this opens up a new vista on the
intradivine fertility from which issues the male child, whom
the Dragon pursues but can never reach?

   If this is too agitating a line of thought, and one prefers to
limit the symbolism to the temporal birth of Christ, there is
another passage of the revelation dealing with the transcendent
origin of Jesus which we cannot possibly evade. 'And he had
his name written, which no man knoweth but himself' . . .
And his name is called the Word of God (19, 12-13). This is
the first time St John formulates the doctrine of the Word, the
foretaste of that long dissertation of the mystery of the
incarnation of the Word of God among men which opens the
fourth gospel: 'In the beginning was the Word; and the
Word was with God, and the Word was God . . . and the
Word was made flesh and dwelt among us, and we saw his

glory, the glory as it were of the only begotten of the Father'
(Joh. 1, 1-14). This identification of Christ with the living
Word of God is not here a matter of secondary importance,
as if it had slipped in by accident; it is the key to the whole
Christology of the Apocalypse. All the other attributes of the
figure of Christ in the book refer back to it—the sword
issuing from the mouth, the faithful witness, the white
horseman who rides across the world, proceeding from
victory to victory. It is as the Word and as truth that Christ
proceeds eternally from God, and it is also as the Word and
as truth that we watch his triumph in creation and in history.
The mystery of Christ is that of truth expressing itself, the
former revealing the personal character of the latter, the
latter explaining the irresistible character of the former.

We must now take a look at some other aspects of the
Apocalypse referring to the mystery of Jesus Christ. They
are those concerning the Holy Ghost. Just as instruction on
the divine origin of Jesus Christ is given indirectly by means
of his manifestation and radiation in the world, equally the
action of the Holy Ghost is suggested by the omnipresence
of the living spirit which is in God. Thus, on the very first
page of the book, we get this formula of the Trinity:

Grace be unto you, and peace
From him that is and was and that is to come;
And from the seven spirits which are before his throne
And from Jesus Christ who is the faithful witness . . . (1, 4-5).

It is from the throne of God that the fulness of spirit
proceeds—and Jesus Christ in his humanity was only the
most decisive divine manifestation of that fulness; and he is
named here after the seven spirits which distinguish the
Holy Ghost, and, in a way, as the fruit of their perfect
mission. For the same reason, when Jesus wishes to give a
message for the Churches to the prophet of Patmos, the
latter, in his letters, attributes the message both to Jesus
himself, who made it known, and to the Holy Ghost who,
by these letters, will in his turn make it known to the Churches
(2, 7; 2, 11; 2, 17; 2, 29; 3, 6; 3, 13; 3, 22). Thus the whole
book is a testimony of Jesus and a prophecy of the Holy
Ghost (19, 10). But inversely, when, all at once, in Chapter

five, we are shown the Lamb in his apotheosis, he appears to us having, like his Father, the fulness of spirit, and can therefore also send it into the world (cf. 4, 5). Again, we must turn to the fourth gospel for further enlightenment of the action of Jesus and of the Father by the Holy Ghost (cf. J. 14, 17; 14, 26; 16, 3 ff. etc.). We must recognise the Holy Ghost in that fountain of living water which is shown to us, in the holy Jerusalem, flowing from the throne of God and of the Lamb (22, 1; 22, 17). Is not this a prelude to the passage in the fourth gospel, in which St John expressly identifies the Holy Ghost with the rivers of living water which give grace to the soul? (Joh. 7, 38-39.) As the river flows from the one throne of God and the Lamb we should have here, in addition to a new delineation of the mission of the Holy Ghost by the Son, explicit information on the later dogmatic formula regarding the Holy Ghost proceeding from the Father and the Son (the *Credo* of the Latin Church).

This, then, was how the prophet of Patmos saw the truly divine transcendence of Jesus of Nazareth. Nevertheless, instruction on that transcendence was not the primary object of the message addressed to the Churches at a time when they needed encouragement. He was certainly convinced of the divinity of Jesus Christ, and that conviction expressed itself plainly whenever he spoke, but it was not on this ground that he wished at that particular time to demonstrate the mastery of Jesus since his Resurrection over the progress of human affairs. To the ordinary believer, the resurrected and omnipotent Christ was more easily recognisable in continuity with the historic figure of Christ than in the eternal and transcendent divine Word, and this divine origin was only touched upon to drive home the idea of Christ's omnipotent and invisible action. St John makes the Word his starting point for the fourth gospel; in the Apocalypse, however, he is more concerned with the royalty of Christ and the kingship which he would extend over the nations.

We have already seen how the very first vision, borrowing its illustrations from the prophecies of Daniel, shows the Son of Man reducing the empires of the world to subjection.

Undoubtedly the two characteristic features of priesthood (long garment, 1, 13) and royalty (golden girdle), as given in this vision and in those that follow, belong inseparably to the figure of Christ. Actually, his role of king is much more strongly emphasised than that of priest. In the New Testament, the epistle to the Hebrews is the one which most clearly brings out the sacerdotal qualities of Christ. The Apocalypse is the book of his universal kingship (14, 14; 19, 12) and this regal sway is formidable. When, in the vision of Chapter nineteen, St John gives us what is undoubtedly the most powerful picture of Christ in the whole of the New Testament (19, 11-16), he shows him to us as a king exercising irresistible domination. Even then Christ appears in a priestly vestment sprinkled with blood (19, 13). The mention of the Word likewise reminds us of his divine origin; but when it is desired to use a word which will more simply express the mystery of Jesus, his domination over the world is summed up under the titles 'King of kings and Lord of lords' (19, 16; cf. 17, 14). The meaning of this is sufficiently clear, especially when we turn up the passage of Daniel from which it is borrowed (Dan. 2, 47). Nabuchodonosor himself in all his power had bowed before this King of kings and Lord of lords.

One might wish that Christian artists would more frequently consult the Apocalypse in attempting to visualise Christ—and all believers likewise! This would reduce the number of crude representations of the God-Man scattered about, many of which would no doubt have scandalised the Son of Thunder (Mk 3, 17), that admirable witness of Jesus! John, the disciple whom Jesus loved—the one who more than all others has revealed to us the love of Jesus for all mankind—is also the author who, in the Apocalypse, has given us the most formidable portrait of Christ. Rather like Jahveh in certain passages of the Old Testament, the Christ of the Apocalypse is first and foremost King of kings, conqueror, avenger and judge. We ought to guard against an over-hasty judgement on the terrible Christ of Michelangelo's Last Judgement in the Sistine Chapel as lacking Christian inspiration. Are we ourselves being quite true to the

Christian message when we adopt this critical attitude? For my part, I know of nothing more awe-inspiring than the accumulation of genitives used by the prophet of Patmos to express the overwhelming torrent of avenging justice bringing God's punishments to the impious nations, through Jesus Christ in his role of irresistible judge.

'And he shall rule them with a rod of iron

And he treadeth the winepress of the fierceness of the
    wrath of God the Almighty' (19, 15).

And this is not an isolated note, expressing only one accessory aspect of the message to the Churches. It is quite often in the role of stern ruler dominating the nations that St John shows Jesus Christ, for the comfort of the faithful persecuted by Rome. When the woman is in labour in Chapter twelve, this is precisely how he depicts her male child:

'And she brought forth a man child

Who was to rule all nations with a rod of iron' (12, 5).

There was nothing new about this. St John borrowed very deliberately from psalm two, which clearly prophesied the rising of the nations and their kings against God and his Christ.

Why have the gentiles raged,
And the people devised vain things?
The kings of the earth stood up
And the princes met together
Against the Lord and against the Christ . . .
He that dwelleth in heaven shall laugh at them
And the Lord shall deride them
Then he shall speak to them in his anger
And trouble them in his rage
But I am appointed king by him over Sion, his holy mountain
Preaching his commandment.
And the Lord hath said to me 'Thou art my son
This day have I begotten thee
Ask of me, and I will give thee the gentiles for thy inheritance
And the utmost parts of the earth for thy possession.
Thou shalt rule them with a rod of iron
And shalt break them in pieces like a potter's vessel' (Ps. 2, 1, ff.).

The comforter whom the Apocalypse presents to the persecuted Churches for their encouragement is exactly like this formidable Son of the psalm. In the last inspired book of the Christian Canon, the theme of the Messiah's rule over the nations is thus resumed in a really imposing manner by the new religion. For although it belongs more than any other to a style of literature inherited from the Old Testament, the Apocalypse is primarily concerned with human society. The explicit purport of its most characteristic texts and the historic circumstances they illuminate with the light of Christian thought forbid the interpreter to dismiss these references to the domination of Christ over the nations as merely symbolical. The Apocalypse presents the mastery of the resurrected Christ as being actually in operation over the nations whose turbulent activities make up the sum total of human history. All we need say now—and we shall return to this later—is that the nations described as being brought under the dominion of Christ are enemy groups that make war on God and his Christ.

But then the question arises: how can this domination be brought about? Is the last book of the New Testament a flat contradiction of the most positive teachings of our Lord himself and how can this kingship be reconciled with the kingdoms of the earth from which, in his lifetime, he so carefully remained aloof? Is the historian of Christian origins justified in regarding this as a tentative call on the Christians to rebel against Rome?

The answer to this question permits us to go deeper into the mystery of Christ as it is explained by this great book. No, the prophet of Patmos was not untrue to the teachings of Jesus Christ as to the nature of his kingship. He does not incite the Churches to armed rebellion. Since we shall return to this in the chapter on the Church, for the moment we need only prove this by quoting the passage which exhorts Christians to submit patiently to their trials, thus echoing the words of Christ himself to St Peter: 'All that take the sword shall perish with the sword' (Matt. 26, 52).

'He that shall lead into captivity shall go into captivity;
He that shall kill by the sword must be killed by the
                                                        sword.

Here is the patience and the faith of the saints' (13, 10). Neither the sword of war nor political insurrection will further the victory of Jesus and his people over the nations. History teaches us how often real values are lost amid the ephemeral gains of aggressive intervention, even when it succeeds. The victory of Jesus will be total and irrevocable; so where is the mystery?

The answer falls into two parts. First, we notice that the domination of Christ over the nations is habitually expressed in a context where mention is made of a mysterious, sharp, two-edged sword which issues from his mouth. It appears in the first vision which struck such fear into St John (1, 16); and we get another reference to it in the letter to Pergamos, which was precisely the town in which the idolatrous cult of Rome and Caesar offered most resistance to the invincible royalty of Christ (2, 12; 2, 16). And the great vision of Chapter nineteen defines to perfection the use made of it by the King of kings and Lord of lords.

'And out of his mouth proceedeth a sharp, two-edged sword

That with it he may strike the nations.

And he shall rule them with a rod of iron' etc.   (19, 15).

What, then, is this sharp-edged sword which Christ wields so terribly in the Apocalypse, and which is not to be confused with the lethal rapier, the arm political force more commonly employs? There is no doubt about the symbolism of this obscure passage. St Paul had already called upon the Ephesians to arm themselves with the sword of the spirit, that is to say, as he immediately explained, the word of God (Eph. 6, 17). The allusion was a classical one. Addressing the nations, for instance, the servant of Isaias says:

Give ear, ye islands
And hearken, ye people from afar;
The Lord hath called me from the womb,
From the bowels of my mother;
He hath been mindful of my name.
And he hath made my mouth like a sharp sword;
In the shadow of his hand he hath protected me
And hath made me as a chosen arrow.
In his quiver he hath holden me
And he said to me: 'Thou art my servant Israel
For in thee I will glory' (Is. 49, 1-3).

The sharp sword which issues from the mouth of Christ in the Apocalypse, and by means of which he wields his irresistible power over the nations, brings us back to the mystery of his transcendent personality itself, to the mystery of that living Word which is God, and of which the epistle to the Hebrews has already told us it is 'living and effectual and more piercing than any two-edged sword reaching into the division of the soul and the spirit, of the joints also and the marrow, and is a discerner of the thoughts and intentions of the heart' (Heb. 4, 13).

This, then, is the formidable weapon Christ makes use of in securing dominion over human history, the weapon of the Word of God and of truth. 'My kingdom is not of this world', he said before Pilate. 'For this I came into the world; that I should give testimony to the truth.' With the Resurrection, this triumph was accomplished, and the whole of human history is but a further unfolding of it. The testimony which Jesus made with his blood has been succeeded by unquestionable mastery. This is the lesson the Apocalypse makes clear. In stating this we are following the fourth gospel, which says: 'Have confidence. I have overcome the world', and in the first epistle of St John: 'Whatsoever is born of God overcometh the world. And this is the victory which overcometh the world: our faith' (1 Joh. 3, 4)—with this difference, nevertheless, that the Apocalypse concerns the personal victory of Christ, 'Word of God,' and 'King of kings, Lord of lords,' but also, in consequence of this first victory, the triumph of the gospel throughout history, which the prophet of Patmos so vividly suggests by the white horseman leaping forth and riding through the world at the breaking of the first seal.

There is another difference. It introduces us to a second essential quality of Christ's dominion over the nations and is linked to some extent with the class of literature to which the whole book belongs. It is that this dominion also appertains to a judge of imprescriptible judgements. In this class of literature, the eschatological evocations show the judgements of God and Christ unfolding irresistibly in human history. One must therefore speak of justice and not only of truth, although, as we know, these two concepts are coincident in the tradition of prophecy. Conforming to this long tradition, John therefore presents Christ as

'. . . faithful and true,
And with justice doth he judge and fight' (19, 11).

All the properly prophetic part is full of these irrevocable judgements of Christ, including the Last Judgement (of which more later). Of course there are reminders, amid all this rigour, of the mercy which is the essence of the Christian message. The tenderness of Christ towards the Churches and towards faithful Christians (see the endings of the letters), the protection with which he surrounds them and which shelters them from the punishments he will inflict upon offending nations; even the corrections which will fall to their lot, and in which they must see nothing but a further proof of his love (3, 19; 2, 10; 3, 10); the eternal consolations held in reserve for the day when he will lead them to the source of life and illuminate them with his own light in the holy Jerusalem (7, 17; 19, 14; 21, 22; etc.); all these, as we have said, contrast admirably with the manifestations of divine wrath which occupy the larger part of the book. It must be insisted, however, to avoid misunderstanding, that Christ most often appears in the revelation of Patmos as the avenging monarch exercising over hostile nations the prerogatives of Judge traditionally associated with the Messiah. It is not without reason that, from the very first lines, St John shows Christ to the Churches arriving already on the clouds of judgement (cf. Dan. 7, 13; 7, 26), sowing terror among the tribes of the earth when they recognise him (1, 7). For just as the kingship of Christ over the nations is already in progress and we need only wait for its consummation (11, 15; 22, 16, etc.), in the same way his judgement and his wrath are already overtaking us. The final judgement (described in 14, 14-20) can only consummate that which has already mysteriously fulfilled itself in history. And while the messianic psalm and other prophecies of the Old Testament telling us of the triumphs and reprisals of the Son of David only prophesy an intangible future of which nothing is to be experienced at present, the prophecies of Patmos show us

the conquering action of Christ already in progress, through
the extension (which we do not always perceive) of his saving
truth, and in the afflictions with which God in his wrath
punishes the nations. It will be the object of the following
chapters to sort out these teachings. Some of the visions of
Christ's anger yield nothing to the descriptions of Jahveh's
terrifying wrath in the Old Testament.

To sum up, then, this is how Christ appears in the
Apocalypse. Clearly the detailed explanation of the texts
introducing St John's imaginative delineations will throw
penetrating light upon them, to reveal their finer shades, and
the following chapters will also offer important suggestions
on the way in which the domination of the resurrected
Christ finds expression in the pursuit of divine justice and
retribution so that truth may be established. Many may find
this Christ of the Apocalypse forbiddingly severe, preferring
the gentle Saviour whom St John reveals in the discourse
after the Last Supper, in the fourth gospel. Personally I do
not feel that the two should be set up in opposition. They
are actually very much alike, not only in their methods of
expression but even more in the deep religious inspiration
that runs through both delineations. It is the same adorable
figure, human and yet divine, historic yet supernatural,
attractive yet awe-inspiring, that St John conjures up, and
I am not sure whether the powerful manifestations of the
Apocalyptic Christ are not calculated to have a more tonic
effect upon the Christian soul than the unfathomable
kindness and condescension he shows towards his disciples
at the Last Supper or in the feet-washing scene. It is clear, at
any rate, that the thought of his book possibly having a
depressing effect upon the persecuted Christians to whom
it was addressed never entered St John's head. It is true that
the face of Christ which gradually emerges from his powerful
testimony could at first glance inspire fear by its expression
of divine wrath and vengeance. Soon, however, one is struck
and then attracted by his absolute and incomparable majesty.
Certainly there is silent and indescribable compulsion in his
glance—that 'flame of fire' (1, 13; 19, 12, etc.), but obviously
this compulsion, whether for individuals or for groups, is

immanent in the very nature of truth. Falsehood and injustice are intolerable to him, and in his presence they receive the punishment they deserve; but, like truth, he reaches with gentleness and irresistible power into the very depths of the soul that believes in him, and will one day become, with him and like him, a son of God. So he radiates, not the cold light so terrifying to malevolent shadows, but the warm love of a living person immediately accessible to his own. He sacrifices himself for all, and offers to all the mercy of truth, even when, as the faithful witness, he defends to the last gasp the rights of divine truth, which is himself, and which is destined in the end to be triumphant for all time.

Such is the mystery of Christ in the Apocalypse. From beginning to end, from Alpha to Omega, it is a mystery of light and truth. Word of God in his eternal pre-existence (19, 13); faithful witness even unto death in his historic existence among us (1, 5; 3, 14; 19, 11); king of the nations, ruling and judging them with an inexorable sword (1, 16; 2, 12; 19, 11) and scoring incessant victories (6, 2) by his truth in this triumphant resurrected life which he leads invisibly here on earth and will lead until the end of time; and finally, in the consummation of all things, in the holy Jerusalem; the candelabra illuminating the elect with the very glory of God (2, 23), the mystery of Christ in the Apocalypse is from one end to the other that of the truth of God made manifest among men, and radiating irresistibly in accordance with the prophecy of Isaias:

'So shall my word be, which shall go forth from my
mouth.

It shall not return to me void, but it shall do
Whatever I please and shall prosper
In the things for which I sent it' (Is. 55, 11).

All in all, one scarcely knows what to admire most in this Apocalyptic doctrine of Christ—the courage with which, taking up the traditional theme of the Messiah's dominion over the nations, it attempts to show Christ realising this promise in the very midst of a most trying period of history —or the integrity with which, having done this, it keeps strictly to the gospel line in distinguishing between the religious and the political order—or the profound teaching it conveys on the mystery of God-incarnated or, finally, the consolation, the fervid zeal and the fidelity it could not fail to inspire among the Christians persecuted by Domitian, or, for that matter, by impostors of all times.

CHAPTER IV

THE CHRISTIAN VIEW OF HISTORY ACCORDING TO THE APOCALYPSE

It is essential that Judeo-Christian religious tradition should be presented both as doctrine and as history. Man is a spiritual being living in time. His consciousness of truth is conditioned by his experience in a concrete conception of time as duration. The Judeo-Christian tradition takes this into account. It offers him instruction by means of facts which succeed one another through the centuries by a progression which is continuous, and guarantees the authenticity of higher truths which move on the same plane although they may be outside human control. These are justly called the facts of revelation.

It follows that the inner significance of the doctrinal message of that revelation is affected by its historic compass, and inversely, the message itself, by its superior inspiration, throws light on the history of which it forms a part. The believer, having encountered God in history, learns to recognise his hand at work behind important events, just as it is at work in each individual destiny. The only difficulty that arises is that he may err in his interpretation of history from the religious standpoint, and in coming to conclusions as to the divine intention. It is therefore important to discover whether the Apocalypse provides appropriate guidance for this kind of study.

The historic character of the revelation in the Old Testament, and also the religious significance of that history, are too obvious to need stressing. So systematic is its structure that when we attempt to describe it, we can only follow the order of the sacred books themselves, for they are in historic order. We have to begin with the creation of the world and that of the first man, at the beginning of time, and then follow the chosen people stage by stage on the devious route through their history. Moses himself, when he drew up the code of Laws which would seem only to be concerned with the present, opened with a résumé of the origins of all things, drawing from the facts of that distant history the essential points for his legislation: monotheism, the Sabbath, patriarchal control, and so on.

Because of its rigid religious aspect, as, for example, the alliance with Jahveh, this history is essentially that of a race, a chosen people living in the distant past among other races. The whole of Genesis is thus conceived to mark the progressive steps by which these elect people gradually distinguished and separated themselves from other races. The remainder of the Torah explains to the last detail the Law which characterises, and must characterise, these people in order that the alliance which Jahveh has concluded with them may be maintained. The historic books then describe the wanderings of these people, considered as such, in their secular life, even the great heroes of Israel deriving their glory less from their personal qualities than from the role they played in Jewish nationalism. It is for the race as such that the prophets, at given moments, recall the compulsions of the past, or lift the veil from the future. In order not to interrupt this great current of history, they galvanised the religious and national consciousness of these people living surrounded by other nations. When victories were scored and prosperity reigned, they fervently called on them to exalt Jahveh, the king of the world who had singled them out from the rest of the nations. When, on the other hand, adversity overtook them, and drove them into captivity, the prophets admonished them to repent the sins which had called forth such condign punishment; but they also reassured them with the comforting promise that the future would bring renewed victories over their enemies, victories as mysterious as they were brilliant, for truth itself and the honour of Jahveh demanded this; his cause was so linked with that of his chosen people that their defeat was tantamount to the defeat of God and the triumph of evil (cf.Ps.

115, 1-2). It is necessary here to read the many prophetic oracles, of Isaias and of Jeremias, of Ezechiel and Daniel, of those who are called the Minor Prophets, in order to form some idea of the stimulating pictures of Israel's future triumphs, the glory of Jerusalem, and the punishment of any nations oppressing them, constantly held before the chosen people.

Which brings us to an important observation touching the Jewish conception of history, which differs entirely from the Christian conception which was to develop later. When we analyse the Old Testament to discover how the Jews regarded the progress of history, we find their views were entirely coloured by messianic hopes. The good Israelite implicitly believed that the future would culminate in a Golden Age. Whether under the influence of fervent and otherwise admirable religious aspirations centred on the ultimate and perfect manifestation of Jahveh, as with the prophets and the upholders of the Ancient Law; or under that of an inflamed imagination, as with the licentious authors of the later Apocrypha, the future which Israel counted upon was one in which God would definitely intervene in her favour. A future filled with the splendour of a new order, combining the glory of religion with temporal prosperity by a cosmic regeneration in which messianic and apocalyptic expectations of the justice of God met. Even after all these centuries have rolled by, we can still sense the burning enthusiasm which these prospects opened up by the prophets must have aroused among the masses.

'I beheld therefore in the vision of the night' says Daniel in an oracle from which, as we have already seen, the Apocalypse borrowed freely, 'one like the Son of Man came with the clouds of heaven. And he came even to the Ancient of days: and they presented him before him. And he gave him power and glory and a kingdom; and all peoples, tribes and tongues shall serve him. His power is an everlasting power that shall not be taken away; and his a kingdom that shall not be destroyed' (Dan. 7, 13 ff.).

And again another text in which, after speaking of the empires that will attack the people of God, the prophet foresees the glorious revenge these people take, and the establishment of their universal dominion:

'And that the kingdom and power and the greatness of the kingdom, under the whole heaven, may be given to the people of the saints of the Most High. Whose kingdom is an everlasting kingdom, and all kings shall serve him and shall obey him.' (Dan. 7, 27.)

In this future triumph of Israel, as we have said, all messianic and eschatological prospects merged. The coming of the Messiah, son of David, would coincide with the end of the world, the Last Judgement. The last Jewish apocalyptic works before the Christian era expressed all this expectation of divine vengeance, and even those Jews who no longer believed in the political triumph of their people without renouncing for all time the triumph of Jahveh's cause, took refuge in the terrible judgements at the consummation. 'After so much ephemeral success,' writes Father Lagrange, 'they had lost all faith in the world here below, where they were menaced by the irresistible onrush of enemies exerting all the powers of evil. This is the state of mind we recognise in the apocalyptic writings, one which would call into being a new hope, of an Israel that could only rise from the debris of the world, thanks to a Saviour from on high.'[1]

Even in the prophets this piling up of messianic prophecies and eschatological prospects is to be found. Witness this passage of Joel, which I have chosen among many because of three things: messianism, eschatology and judgement, here found in conjunction, but also because we shall presently see St Peter using it in preaching the Christian gospel.

And it shall come to pass after this that I will pour out my spirit upon all flesh:
And your sons and your daughters shall prophesy:
Your old men shall dream dreams
And your young men shall see visions.
Moreover upon my servants and handmaids
In those days I shall pour forth my spirit.
And I will show wonders in heaven: and on earth,
Blood and fire and vapour and smoke.
The sun shall be turned into darkness
And the moon into blood:
Before the great and dreadful day of the Lord doth come.
And it shall come to pass that everyone that shall call
Upon the name of the Lord shall be saved

[1] M. J. Lagrange. 'Judaism.'

For in Mount Sion and in Jerusalem
Shall be salvation, as the Lord hath said,
And in the residue whom the Lord shall call (Joel, 2, 28-32).

Thus, turned towards the future, the souls of religious
people were already caught in the enchantment of the holiness
the Messiah would radiate as he called this new world into
being. How can we help quoting Isaias:

And there shall come forth a rod out of the root of Jesse
And a flower shall rise up out of his root.
And the spirit of the Lord shall rest upon him:
The spirit of wisdom and of understanding,
The spirit of counsel and of fortitude,
The spirit of knowledge and of godliness.
And he shall be filled with the spirit of the fear of the Lord.
He shall not judge according to the sight of the eyes,
Nor approve according to the hearing of the ears.
But he shall judge the poor with justice
And shall reprove with equity the meek of the earth . . . etc.
(Is. 11, 1 ff.).

Here again, in thoughts closely related to those we find in
St John, the primarily spiritual character of the Messiah's
domination of the nations is very marked.

And in the last days
The mountain of the house of the Lord
Shall be prepared on the top of mountains,
And it shall be exalted above the hills;
And all nations shall flow unto it.
And many people shall go and say:
Come, and let us go up to the mountain of the Lord,
And to the house of the God of Jacob;
And he will teach us his ways
And we shall walk in his paths.
For the law shall come forth from Sion;
And the word of the Lord from Jerusalem.
And he shall judge the gentiles,
And rebuke many people:
And they shall turn their swords into ploughshares
And their spears into sickles.
Nation shall not lift up sword against nation;
Neither shall they be exercised any more to war.
Oh, house of Jacob, come ye!
And let us walk in the light of the Lord (Is. 2, 2 ff.).

Not all the texts have the same admirable spiritual content.
Jewish apocalyptical writings, for example, the Jubilees and

the Testaments of the Patriarchs, take more pleasure in describing material pleasures which the Golden Age will bring—length of years and the fabulous fertility of a land flowing with milk and honey, as well as cosmic and astral wonders which mankind will see. It is waste of time to pause over these literary productions, the emphasis and the grandiloquence of which contrasts strikingly with their doctrinal poverty. We only mention them here because their style, like that of all the most beautiful oracles and prophecies, proves that the history of Israel, like its religious aspirations, always lay in the future. This was a progressive conception of history, the progress here being understood in the sense that it finds its fulfilment by the intervention of new developments and the installation in all spheres of a new order of things different from those in which the people then lived, which the Messiah would bring with him, and to whom the soul of Israel turned as its history marched towards him.

'When the fulness of the time was come,' writes St Paul to the Galatians, 'God sent his son, made of a woman, made under the law; that he might redeem them that were under the law' (Gal. 4,4). Elsewhere he says that it was the design of God in the fulness of time to 're-establish all things in Christ, that are in heaven and on earth, in him' (Eph. 1, 10). Again the same conception of history's evolution is expressed by St Peter in his first epistle (I Pet. 1, 20), and in the admirable way the epistle to the Hebrews opens: 'God who, at sundry times and in divers manners spoke in times past to the fathers by the prophet, last of all, in these days, hath spoken to us by his son . . . ' (Heb., 1, 1).

For the first generation of Christians, this was the certainty on which they based their ideas of the progress of history. With the birth of Jesus, the 'end of time' foretold by the prophets had arrived. We are now in the last age of human history. Jesus himself opened his ministry by emphatically declaring: 'The time is accomplished and the kingdom of God is at hand. Repent and believe the Gospel' (Mk. 1, 15). None of the apostles spoke in any other strain. This, indeed, was an indispensable condition of their adherence to Christ.

In that Jewish environment in which they propagated their message, to recognise Jesus as the Messiah was to proclaim that the last days had arrived.

This is the substance of St Peter's speech to the Jews of Jerusalem after the miraculous descent of the Holy Ghost on the day of Pentecost: 'All were astonished and said to one another: "What meaneth this?" But Peter, standing up with the eleven, lifted up his voice and spoke to them: "Ye men of Judea and all you that dwell in Jerusalem, be this known to you, and with your ears receive my words. For these are not drunk, as you suppose, seeing it is but the third hour of the day (about 9.0 a.m.). But this is that which was spoken of by the prophet Joel: And it shall come to pass in the last days (saith the Lord) I will pour out my spirit upon all flesh: and your sons and your daughters shall prophesy",' etc.—the text of Joel already quoted then follows (Acts, 2, 12 ff.).

From that time onwards, this is the habitual theme of apostolic preaching. The time has come; cease, therefore, your straining towards the future for essential things, the kingdom of God has already been inaugurated, and is only waiting for you to enter and claim its inexhaustible riches.

But, by the same token, history and revelation entered upon a new relationship, and one which was to raise many a problem! Christian revelation, to be sure, rested, like that of the Jews, on sacred history, for it depended entirely on the historical fact of Jesus Christ, apart from whom the necessary access to God could in no way be gained. But whereas Jewish history leant towards the future with all the force of its messianism, Christian history, recognising the Messiah in Jesus, became centred in him, and will forever remain so, having nothing essential to expect of the future. This is fully understood; nevertheless the last day will come, when all creation will reach its destined end in 'the new heaven and the new earth' of the prophets and of the Apocalypse (21, 1). But this will embody only the ultimate extension of a principle, all the essentials of which came into being with the birth of Jesus Christ. For the true Christian, there is no gift of God that can ever take precedence of him whom he gave to the world in Christ. Mankind, therefore, cannot hope for any principle of salvation more effective than that which was given to them with the New Adam. Here, then, was a Christian eschatology directed towards the 'consummation of time'; there was no longer a Christian messianism. The Messiah had already arrived, bringing with him the ultimate alliance between God and man. It only remains for individuals and nations to enter into this alliance. Men may reject Christianity as the Jews rejected it; nevertheless, this stone remains the only corner-stone possible, 'neither is there salvation in any other' (Acts 4, 11-12). This was, and must always remain, the most positive conviction of Christians.

We shall soon see that this new turn in the significance of history could not fail to involve the religious soul in a number of problems. Let us leave on one side, for later examination, the difficulty of completely reversing the religious sentiment inherited from Israel, by substituting the actual possession of Christ in faith for the messianic expectation of his coming or of his return. This involved the whole problem of the coming, to which we shall return. It was not a matter of what Christians could still expect of the future, since by their faith they recognised the coming of the Messiah in Jesus of Nazareth. That being so, the main question was the interpretation they should place on that future, and, above all, what should be their attitude towards the present. Their messianic hopes being henceforth fulfilled, what became of the triumph of the Messiah which they had expected—his promised domination and that of his people over the whole universe? Certainly Christ himself, after having been humiliated in the Passion, had proceeded to the glory of the Resurrection and the Ascension, which had for the early Christians an importance probably no longer accorded to them by the faithful to-day. The manifestations of the Holy Ghost also added their testimony to the invisible triumph of Jesus. But what other evidence was there? By what signs could one recognise the mastery of Christ over the nations? Or that of his people side by side with him?

Of course there were at first undeniable spiritual victories. They were obvious to everyone in the days following the Ascension and Pentecost, and could not help causing some

sensation. The gospel looked as if it was actually on the way
to conquer the world. 'All power is given to me in heaven
and in earth,' our Saviour had said after his Resurrection.
'Going therefore, teach ye all nations' (Matt. 28, 18). The
programme was as precise as it could be: the teaching would
commence with Jerusalem and Judea, then extend to
Samaria, and then go on to every corner of the earth (Acts
1, 8). This was the plan as mentioned in the Acts of the
Apostles, and, profiting from the unity of the Roman Empire,
which seemed nothing short of providential, St Paul
journeyed from East to West, sowing Churches everywhere;
he even got so far as Spain, that is to say, to the outermost
limit of the world then known, pursuing his apostolic labours.
In his letters he describes the conquering ardour of the first
Christians, roused by this rapid propagation of the faith.
'I give thanks to my God, through Jesus Christ, for you all,'
he writes, 'because your faith is spoken of in the whole
world.' It was spoken of in the Churches, from Jerusalem
to Rome, from Corinth in Macedonia, across the whole of
Asia Minor, in Alexandria as in Athens; and this visible
progress of God's reign, in such a few years, as well as the
intensity of the religious life it awakened in so many souls,
not in any narrow circle of deep thinkers, but among people
of all sorts and conditions, seemed sufficient explanation of
the delay in the spectacular manifestation of Christ's return,
with which he was expected at any moment to crown his
work on earth.

    And now here was Domitian with his decree, shattering
not only the hope of the Church's extension but also the
spiritual reign of God which was to be established in this
world by the Church. This was no minor disaster, affecting
only a few local communities; it struck at the very root of the
Christian Church itself. Far from going on, step by step, to
culminate in a final sensational victory, the kingship of
Christ seemed to have been brought to a halt, its force
scattered more and more by the grim realities of life in the
material world, to take refuge in men's secret hearts, where
this check, in more than one case, raised doubts, and an

attitude of 'What is the use?' In assuming such vast dimensions, the problem of the trial and persecution within the Christian set-up to some extent changed its nature. Christian faith was no longer blind and unquestioning; it demanded to know how the expected glorious Second Coming of Christ, in a way decidedly different from what they had been imagining, ought now to be awaited, amid all the misfortunes which had overtaken the Church; indeed, did it not look as if the powers of evil had, after all, gained the upper hand? With the first coming of Jesus, or, more strictly speaking, with his Resurrection, the 'last days' had arrived; that no one doubted. Neither was there any doubt about the personal triumph of our Saviour, by his Resurrection, over death and hell. But what they could not understand was why, now that the last days were definitely in progress, evil apparently retained all its old power and virulence, just as it did before the coming of Jesus—and why should God's chosen people, the new Israel, be just as much at the mercy of impious nations and their persecution as they had been in the past?

To these questions the Apocalypse gives the answer of Christian revelation. The previous chapter has shown us that by the evidence of human history, the Apocalypse proves Christ to possess complete mastery in the glory of his Father. Again by the concrete realities of history it goes on to demonstrate how Christ actually exercises that power, and in what way we must weigh up the progressive events of that history as it is now governed by him. Chapters six and seven constitute the first stage of that progression, the former showing how we can recognise what may be termed the major essentials of history, and the latter their object or raison d'être.

What, actually, are the real component parts of this history, the Christian meaning of which we desire to understand? What is St John's notion of this perfect mastery, which he describes in Chapter five? Do we speak the same language, or, at least, allowing for different shades of meaning in different vocabularies, can we be quite certain of the facts on which St John bases his notion? It may be that there are certain facts in human history we have overlooked, and we are ready to be enlightened concerning them. At least, we are entitled to examine the information offered us, to see if it agrees with the conclusions our own human experiences enable us to arrive at. We have to ask ourselves whether Christ does possess the mastery according to this analysis and if so, to what interpretation of history does this lead?

The Book of the Lamb is sealed with seven seals (5, 1), that is to say, not only is it completely indecipherable until the seals are broken, but the actual unfolding of the events which it contains will depend on the one who is able to break the seven seals. In every respect the author indicates that the sacrificed Lamb, and he alone, is master of the book. He alone therefore, has the complete mastery over the elements of history, and he also is the only one who can reveal the mysterious meaning of each of them. The Apocalypse, the revelation of Jesus Christ, teaches Christians to believe that Jesus Christ has the mastery over war, plague, and all the recurrent visitations that occur in human history. 'And I saw that the Lamb had opened one of the seven seals' (6, 1). This is to be repeated seven times. Despite their different features, all the visitations enumerated are shown to depend upon the Resurrected Christ. With their aid the author follows the lace-like tracery of the scroll on which is inscribed the history of human life. Christ, therefore, is in command even of evil—the particular mystery of which will presently be revealed to us—and with sovereign majesty uses even misfortune in the service of his divine ends.

We suddenly notice the division of this Chapter six. The breaking of the first four seals is accompanied by the intervention of the four living creatures, which, as we have seen, represent the four corners of our earthly world. Each of them launches in history a symbolic horseman. The historic factors symbolised by these four horsemen, all of them under the command of Christ, are therefore the realities of this world, and we can all easily figure out their activity in the realm of our own experience (6, 1-8).

The breaking of the fifth seal, on the other hand, although equally dependent on Christ, brings us face to face with a reality which is outside our human perception, for it is located in heaven. This tells us of the prayers of the saints, considered particularly in their relation to the march of events in human affairs (6, 9-11). Here is something which the Apocalypse repeatedly throws into bold relief.

Finally, the breaking of the sixth seal brings with it (6, 12-17) the cataclysms and cosmic disturbances which are the traditional prelude to the Last Judgement and to the establishment of the new order which the breaking of the seventh seal (8, 1) will inaugurate.

We shall return to all this before long.

We have, to begin with, as the first component of history under the command of Christ, the white horseman. His colour, the crown which belongs to him, the dashing impetus with which he leaps forth, bow in hand—all these indicate an invincible hero galloping forth to victory. In history, the conquest is already his, and it belongs to him only. Or, if he does share it with anyone, it is with the Christians (see the ending of each of the letters, 2, 7; 2, 11; etc.), even as they share it with Christ and the armies that follow him (19,14), white being the colour of victory. Actually there is no distinction between the causes; evangelical truth is symbolised by this horseman, too. Christian commentators tend more and more to agree that this figure, like that in Chapter nineteen, represents the Word of God personified, as it will be in Chapter nineteen, rather than in its impersonal aspect as evangelical truth disseminated throughout the world and throughout history; but the two points of view are in perfect continuity, as we pointed out in the previous chapter. This is a matter we shall frequently have further occasion to mention.

Thus, from the very beginning of this explanation of history, victory is promised to the truth of the gospel, and to it alone. One finds an analogous certainty in what is already said of the Word of God in the Old Testament. For example, This beautiful text in the Book of Wisdom:

While all things were in quiet silence
And the night was in the midst of her course,

The almighty word leapt down from heaven
From thy royal throne
As a fierce conqueror
Into the midst of the world of destruction
With a sharp sword, carrying
Thy unmistakable commandment (Wisdom, 18, 14).

The first of the four apocalyptic horsemen expresses a similar idea. To the persecuted Christians he represented the start of a great prophetic message, the victory of evangelical truth sent forth into the world by Jesus, and the responsibility for which rested upon them in their present crisis. Moreover, this victory was depicted to them as being already won from the start. There is no doubt about the horseman being destined to conquer, which carries our thought towards the future; but he is shown as a victor from the start, from the very moment we see him leaping forth. The victory of the resurrected Christ, whose true personal name is Word of God (19, 13) is already the victory of the same Word of God spread throughout the world and throughout history by the preaching of the gospel. Whatever progress it may make in the course of time will not, properly speaking, represent new victories, but merely the necessary continuation, the irresistible expansion, the inescapable manifestation of the all-important fact which began on the day of the Resurrection. This is a victory which has no possible alternative.

There is no need to underline the optimism to which this apocalyptic conception of the evolution of history since Jesus Christ gives rise. Just as the word of God, in its impersonal form, triumphed in Jesus Christ on the day of his Resurrection, it will triumph in the course of time under its impersonal guise as evangelical truth. Of course, we want to know how. But the assurance is given. No doubt because of this assurance and of this great mystery, Christians in the Apocalypse receive the title and the quality given here to the first horseman, here called 'the overcomer' (see endings to the letters). What a stimulation, what a comfort to those whom Domitian's persecution had already reduced to trembling fear! The truth would conquer, even if Christians had to prove it with their own blood; it would triumph eventually!

And now come the other three horsemen, the dark horsemen of death, spreading their malevolence on earth even as
the white horseman rides to the victory of truth. Obviously
they represent the three great scourges which alas, after
nearly twenty centuries, we may take to be characteristic of
the major portion of human history. War, symbolised by the
red horseman (6, 3-4), is armed with a great sword, and all we
know of him is expressed in one shattering sentence; simply:
'It was given that he should take peace from the earth: and
that they should kill one another.' No need to describe the
scientific techniques and the cruelties which are sown by war.
To my mind, no description could call forth a more shattering
human echo than these lines suggesting the hecatombs men
make of other men in this hard human life where men seem
incapable of breathing the same air in peace with one another.

And then famine, black famine (6, 5-6). A few simple
strokes suffice to define this misery. It is accompanied at all
times by a disproportionate rise in the price of necessary
food—not forgetting grain—and by the hoarding of things
which in the East are as common as oil and wine! No other
comment is necessary; we know from the experience of our
own lifetime that famine is never slow in following the
footsteps of war.

And when everything on earth has been devastated,
plague in its turn takes possession (6, 7). Plague, and all
similar epidemics, are brought by the cavalier who rides
recklessly among men mounted on a dark horse, a horse the
colour of decay. Judging by the name which is here given
to them, these epidemics claim more victims than either war
or famine. We have only to consult the history of eastern
races to discover how true this is, and even though the
sanitary measures taken keep these afflictions in check to
some extent in the West, there is no knowing whether there
may not be some disastrous experiences in store for us in
course of time. But there is no point in comparing the evil
effects of the three scourges. They combine with one another,
and their ill-effects are felt over 'a quarter of the earth'.
And on this it is necessary to make a few remarks.

The first is that these three dark horsemen represent

traditional scourges in Jewish apocalyptic works.   It is almost certain that St John borrowed the idea from Ezechiel (Ez. 6, 11; 7, 15). If there was any necessity to prove this, the 'beasts of the earth' (6, 8) would provide that proof. If, then, what we said in our first chapter of the use our inspired author made of Old Testament is true, we must conclude that he looked upon the three plagues as punishments sent as a result of the direct intervention of God's wrath in the history of mankind. It is thus, in fact, that they appear traditionally in Israel's past. Thus Jahveh, wishing to punish David for the haughty census he had imposed upon his people, sent Gad to give him the choice between 'seven years of famine, three months of enemy pursuit in battle, and three days of plague (II Kings, 24, 13). In Ezechiel, who seems here to be the immediate source of St John's inspiration, the scourges also signify punishments (Ez. 5, 17; 14). This, then, is also the way in which the history of communities is controlled by Christ, according to the Apocalypse. I mention 'history of communities', for this is not a matter concerned with the destinies of individuals. Visitations which, in each person's destiny, might correspond with the collective misfortunes these sinister horsemen symbolise, are to be judged by the ordinary Christian teachings on the trials of that individual life. These are imposed by the Father as a means of acquiring greater perfection (Heb. 12, 4-12) and accentuating the resemblance to the crucified Son; or as a warning, to impel the sinner to conversion; or, alas! in some cases as the beginning of the punishments merited by obstinacy in evil.   Individual conditions, under a common trial, may vary infinitely. But for communities as such, great afflictions must always be regarded by Christians as divine punishments for the sins of mankind. Christians are not permitted to regard them as conjunctures of circumstances that by some chance have escaped the mastery of Christ, who is possessed of the book of history. Whatever secondary casualties the scourges may bring in their train, or however we may attribute them to the powers of evil (see farther on, in Chapter five) the Christian faith teaches us to believe that the ultimate sanction of their descent upon us lies in the supernatural but positive will of God through Christ, and this will is the will to chasten. Chastisement of whom? And for what? The breaking of the fifth seal begins to answer these questions, and from that point onwards the book proceeds to give more detailed explanations. We now perceive the firmly established principle that God's judgements and his punishments are already being carried out, and the whole of history since the Resurrection is nothing but the unfolding of this justice, which will go on until the Last Judgement. When a St Vincent Ferrer sets the West ablaze with his fiery eloquence, the people affected are not merely the crowd he converts: his message is a reminder to the whole of Christianity that the justice of God is revealing itself perpetually in history, and the failure of the mass of mankind to recognise this only makes its sternness more menacing. At first we might almost be put off by St Vincent Ferrer; but the Apocalypse helps us to understand where his message links up with the most profound Christian revelation. One could wish that in these days of neo-paganism God might vouchsafe us the grace of a witness equally capable of seeing and stressing his salutary justice throughout the course of centuries.

The second remark I should like to make—and how the twenty centuries that have passed since the book was written emphasise it!—is that the Apocalypse really is human history. The whole record of human existence throughout these centuries illustrates the uninterrupted progress of truth, and of the Church which presents it—also, alas! the epidemic scourges of war, famine and infection which have attended this progress as the prophet foretold. Let us leave the victorious advance of the Church and the gospel for the time being; we shall return to these points later. Who would dare to contend—even, and indeed especially, in our own time—that the conception of history revealed by St John from the very start, in order to explain its meaning to the Christian communities, has not proved to this very day singularly and sadly prophetic? We should not think only of that tiny fragment of history in which we happen ourselves to be playing a part. We should look at history from the

angle of the world's total population. Then the tragic
constancy of the scourges which the prophet of Patmos saw
piling up as the years rolled by will be perfectly obvious.
Wars in the West, famine in the East, epidemic diseases in
China and the tropics—dark horsemen ceaselessly riding
over the earth and scoring victories which, at first sight, seem
at least equal to those of the white horseman. This is real
history. Real history, I say, and not the anecdotal kind to
which we have grown accustomed and which, neglecting
the actual condition of the human masses, tells us only of
picturesque personalities playing their part in the forefront
of the stage, with the limelight full upon them. If anything
could justify the prominence historians give to such trivialities,
surely it could only be the benefit derived from them by the
masses as a whole, through the advancement of truth among
these anonymous brothers by men dedicated to their salvation, and the removal of the constant causes of war, famine
and disease, which goes hand in hand with it. If the traditional
illustrations of the Apocalypse seem too elementary; if the
words, through excess of use, seem to have shed some of
their terror—though the Church does not disdain the age-old
supplication: *a peste, fame et bello, libera nos Domine!*—let
us be worldly-wise and speak of politics which, in the setting
aside of evangelical truth as a guiding principle in human
affairs, seeks to establish some sort of balance, yet cannot do
so without resorting to continual wars; let us speak of
economics, which somehow have not yet put an end to
slumps and depressions and famines, as evangelical truth
might have done, if left to itself; let us speak of public health
measures (not forgetting the degeneration of multitudes of
human beings who can no longer be described as civilised)
which would have everything to gain, in their own sphere, by
the progress of truth and the demands it makes in the way of
charity and moral tone.

But it must not be thought that the history of mankind, in
refusing to yield to the conquering white horseman, will
escape the mastery which the resurrected Christ has acquired
throughout history. The punitive scourges of war, famine
and plague are also within his disposition. Their release on

mankind depends entirely upon the seals which he alone can break, and if his dominion still means a certain amount of misery for the world, it is only because mankind obstinately refuses to submit to the healing salvation of truth. Although these afflictions come to us through evil agents, these agents are themselves created for the very purpose of executing the penalties divine justice demands, as the book shows us. The Apocalypse teaches Christians to recognise in these visitations the necessary chastisements of that justice which is inherent in truth, and are therefore identifiable with the victories of the white horseman himself.

My third remark should counteract, to some extent, what may seem austere and bitter in the preceding comments. By its progressive revelations the book restores the balance of the Christian conception of history which is here expounded. Of the four horsemen launched in the world, only the first, who represents the saving truth of the gospel, is certain in advance of securing the victory. The others are not described as 'going forth conquering, that they may conquer', however aggressive they may appear; this is said of the first alone. Here we have the Christian's cause for optimism; he need never despair as to the ultimate victory of Christian truth, whatever show of weapons the powers of evil may put up. We will not enter here the problem of Christian civilisation's limitless progress; in another chapter we will go into its implications, and try to discover whether the Christian's optimistic view of history is justified.

With the breaking of the fifth seal, we leave the earth, for it is in heaven that the subsequent enumeration of the factors of history takes place. In heaven those who were sacrificed—like the Lamb—are still occupied with our mundane history, because of the Word of God and the testimony by which they are linked with it. 'How long. O Lord holy and true, dost thou not judge and revenge our blood on them that dwell on the earth?' (6, 9-10).

'Those that dwell on the earth'—a phrase which, in our book, has a very distinctive meaning. It does not refer to all the people who live on earth, good and bad, but only to evil persons. Between these and the witnesses of Jesus, who have already erected their tents with him in heaven, there is eternal antagonism. Their names are not written in the book of life (17, 8); they adore the Beast (13, 8, 12, 14) and commit fornication with the great prostitute (17, 2). On them will fall the three great curses put upon the earth—the curses against which the disciples of Jesus are protected (3, 10). And they are the sinners concerned when we hear the prayer of Jesus's martyrs at the breaking of the fifth seal. Thus the prayer of the saints constitutes a demand for vengeance against the inhabitants of the earth, that is to say, the opponents of Jesus and the Church. We get a similar passage in the book of Enoch (Cap. 22) which shows Abel praying in Sheol to secure the punishment of Cain and his descendants. Here the petition is less denuded of mercy, for it only concerns sinners who are obstinately unrepentant.

Here again we must be on our guard lest an anaemic form of Christianity mistake the point of this teaching. There are believers who resign themselves far too easily to the apparent triumph of evil in our midst. Their faith affirms the omnipotence of God, exalts the rights of his holiness, and the predestined purpose of all things to share in the praise and glory which the elect shall offer at the throne of God, yet they creep through the world like poor relations, more as if they were apologising for their faith than giving fervent testimony of its victory over the world. Perhaps they imagine that by this attitude they are prolonging the Passion and its attendant humility (we may have doubts as to whether this is the best way to set about it); but certainly they are not giving evidence before the world of the clear, triumphant morning of the Resurrection! St Paul was one of the first to criticise this kind of thing. 'Know ye not that the saints shall judge this world?' he wrote to the Corinthians. 'And if the world shall be judged by you, are you unworthy to judge the smallest matters? Know ye not that we shall judge angels? How much more the things of this world!' (I Cor. 6, 2-3). The prophet of Patmos developed a similar theme. The elect whom at the opening of the fifth seal he heard 'crying in a loud voice' (6, 10) made a similar emphatic demand. Even though they knew that the temporary triumphs of evil would one day be avenged, they were shocked to see them lasting for such a long time on earth, and practically insisted on the Lord settling up the account. 'How long dost thou not judge and revenge our blood on them that dwell on the earth?' Once again it is a demand for justice which they formulate in this call of vengeance. Looking at things in the light of God, it is not normal, from the Christian standpoint, that evil should go unpunished.

In this way, therefore, the saints in heaven intervene in our earthly affairs. For this prayer is considered here as one of the factors in history, over which Christ exercises sovereign mastery. We shall return to this prayer of the saints in the following section, that dealing with the trumpets which launch the judgements of God here below (8, 2 ff.) as the text itself invites us to do (8, 3-5). This will confirm that the judgements of God have been in process of execution right through history, to some extent in response to the prayers of the saints and the objective demands for justice formulated by them. The saints, and more especially the martyrs whose blood has been spilt in the cities on earth, may thus be regarded as the agents, by their prayers, of our human history. They contribute effectively to the victory of truth, to which they have already given testimony at the cost of their lives —*sanguis martyrum semen Christianorum*—but also to the confusion and the punishment of the 'inhabitants of the earth' who bear the responsibility of their apparent and temporary defeat. More and more, as we shall see, through Christ and with Christ, they reign on earth, even though invisibly (5, 10). In the end, when justice has been accomplished, we see them still applauding its sternness (see 16, 5-7; 19, 1-2, etc.). It is always the same teaching that John gives to the persecuted Christians. Do not be discouraged, he seems in effect to say: hold your heads high. Your cause is just, and not only just, but destined to be victorious and very terrible for your enemies. Every new blow that you receive is another and more terrible punishment in store for those who injure you. The whole of heaven, which knows the requirements of true justice, will not cease demanding of God and his Christ that these demands be satisfied.

Why, then, is vengeance delayed? We can see that actually it is already in operation. Nevertheless, the forces of evil still continue to produce wars here on earth, and although their results may be deceptive and ephemeral, they still act as a check on the triumph of good. What can we make of this? How should we judge a chequered history in which evil seems to lay down the law far more often than good, and in which the victory of Christ seems so slow in making its final, definite appearance? The answer of Christ and of the saints opens what is perhaps the most triumphant passage in the Apocalypse. It permits us to perceive the real Christian reason for the prolonged extension of the 'last days' between the Resurrection of Christ and his glorious Second Coming; at the same time it opens up prospects of century after century of Christian optimism touching the salvation of the human race. In truly Christian souls it therefore quietens the agitation that has been roused regarding the fate of so many generations of human beings by reminding them of the inexorable demands of divine justice.

And it was said to them that they should rest for a little time
Till their fellow servants and their brethren,
Who are to be slain even as they,
Should be filled up (6, 11).

'When the number of the elect shall be complete' is therefore the reason for the prolonged continuance of these last days separating the Resurrection of Christ from his glorious Second Coming. This is the first lesson these visions teach us about the meaning of history in the Christian sense. Whatever misfortunes and injustices may mark this temporal duration, the end which dominates and justifies the whole unfolding is that of salvation. It concerns itself only with multiplying the number of those who pass through the great tribulation, 'washing their robes in the blood of the Lamb' (7, 13-14), so that they may be worthy to stand erect before the throne of God. From the Christian standpoint, our world is primarily a machine for making God's!

Therefore they are before the throne of God;

And they serve him day and night in his temple.
And he that sitteth on the throne shall dwell over them.
They shall no more hunger or thirst
Neither shall the sun fall on them, or any heat.
For the Lamb, which is in the midst of the throne, shall lead them,
to the fountains of the waters of life;
And God shall wipe away all tears from their eyes (7, 15-17).

Here the history of mankind ends; this is the finish. Could any Christian resist this prospect of bliss, to which his brothers have been called? 'Eye hath not seen, nor ear heard; neither hath it entered into the heart of man, what things God hath prepared for them that love him.' (1, Cor. 2, 9). This is undoubtedly true! Nevertheless, the spiritual depth of this description which St John gives us enables the truly religious soul to understand that 'the sufferings of this time are not worthy to be compared with the glory to come' (Rom. 8, 18), and also to see our temporal history in true perspective. It is the crucible in which are made the precious stones which are actually human souls that little by little go towards the building of the heavenly Jerusalem (see farther on, in the chapter on the Church).

Can we form any estimate of the number of the elect— that ultimate total which is the real reason for temporal history? We cannot presume here to give an answer to this question, which has caused so much discussion and controversy among learned Christian doctors. The only possible remarks are those our book asks for. Everyone will admit that on this matter it is an unequalled authority. Its testimony appears all the more optimistic because it occurs in the middle of a message which picks out the demands of God's avenging justice in high relief. It is not without reason that the Church, desiring to incorporate in its inspired Liturgy an inkling of the number of saints who will be assembled in heaven, makes use of the great text in Chapter seven for the feast of All Saints.

This page is one that makes the most profound impression of any in the book, its powerful inspiration, even from the point of view of literature, coming through with the utmost vividness, after the lapse of nearly twenty centuries:
After these things I saw four angels

Standing on the four corners of the earth,
Holding the four winds of the earth,
That they should not blow upon the earth
Nor on the sea nor on any tree . . . etc. (7, 1 ff.).

These devastating winds, all ready to launch the decisive
vengeance of justice upon the earth, are held in check by the
intervention of the angel who is to put the mark on the
foreheads of the elect. John listens to the number of the
chosen. They come from everywhere; first the Jews of the
twelve tribes, whose enumeration begins, as it should, with
that of Juda; he was not the eldest, but as the blessing of his
father Jacob had foretold, it was he who brought forth the
lion whose victory now made possible the innumerable
crowd of his brothers who were among the elect (7, 4 ;
cf. Gen. 49 particularly verses 8-12). And the cavalcade of
Judeo-Christians proceeds irresistibly!

'Of the tribe of Juda twelve thousand signed;
Of the tribe of Ruben, twelve thousand signed;
Of the tribe of Gad, twelve thousand signed;' etc.

And we at once hear the echo in our hearts of the *duodecim
milia signati* of the epistle of All Saints, and feel again the
thrill of adoration which it occasions year by year. As
incalculable as the figure might be, it could still be expressed
by numbers. Yet still the crowd surged on. Then the prophet's
arithmetic gave out. Not even a symbolic figure could express
what he saw.

'After this I saw a great multitude
Which no man could number!
Of all nations and tribes and peoples and tongues . . '
(7, 9).

Thus there was not an empire or a nation, not a dialect or
a language, not one race that we might deem superior or
inferior which had not some of its members among the
chosen people in this crowd which assembled from East and
West to rest in the bosoms of Abraham, of Isaac and of
Jacob. Did I say rest? Think of them in their triumphal robes,
waving before the throne the palms of that testimony for
which they had given their lives, while they loudly acknow-
ledged before God and the Lamb the salvation they have

received from him (7, 10). They know the meaning of history, these chosen ones; no doubt in their minds that the Lamb knows how to lead mankind by the very best of ways!

'And I heard another, from the altar, saying:

Yea, O Lord God Almighty,

True and just are thy judgements (17, 7).'

In our haste to consider the triumph of the innumerable chosen people who are the real cause of 'time' as we understand it, we have seemed to overlook the sixth seal. The martyrs' prayer demanding justice was answered with the request that they possess themselves in patience 'until the number of their brethren' be complete—but they were not in any way rebuked for making that demand. And almost immediately the breaking of the sixth seal begins to satisfy their desires (7, 12-17). No difficulties arise over the interpretation of the cosmic cataclysms that follow the breaking of this seal. The events are quite characteristic of the prophetic tradition concerning Jahveh's Day of Wrath and more especially the judgement of the nations (see for example Isaias 13, 10; Ezechiel 32, 7, ff.; Joel 3, 3, ff.). The kings of the earth make no mistake about them.

And they say to the mountains and the rocks:

Fall upon us and hide us

From the face of him that sitteth upon the throne

And from the wrath of the Lamb.

For the great day of their wrath is come.

And who shall be able to stand? (6, 16-17).

This also will be a decisive section of temporal history, and the Lamb will be the master of it, as of the other seals. Tidal waves in Japan; whole cities flattened by sudden volcanic eruptions; disastrous floods and inundations in all parts of the world; vast regions shaken by earthquakes, to say nothing of astral conflagrations which the astronomers warn us are on the way—these are, alas, constant features of our earthly history, and science, imagining it has discovered their immediate causes, is a long way short of the truth if it fails to attribute their real sanction to that King of the Universe who is in command of all things. The prophet of Patmos, taking the traditional line, looks upon them merely as the tragic prelude to the new heaven and the new earth (6, 14; 20, 11; 21, 5) when the present world will pass away, and their terrifying nature will at the same time demonstrate God's supreme anger. We have already seen that the only reason for the delay in pouring these disasters upon the world is that the number of the elect is not yet complete (7, 1-3). When the harvest is ripe, God will use his sickle on the earth; the Angel of Wrath will empty his vials, and the harvest will be gathered in (14, 14 ff.). Thus the judgement of God, when each man will receive according to his deserts, will be fulfilled (20, 12).

These cosmic cataclysms are only the forerunners of the judgement itself, and must not be confused with it; that is the Christian teaching. The sixth seal being broken, there remains the seventh, which will introduce the actual Last Judgement. Up till now its coming has only been announced, and a foretaste given of what may be expected. And when that Judgement does arrive, we shall have come to the end of the constituents of history, set down in the book of the Lamb —the book which enables us to understand the meaning of history, as Christ unfolds its facts throughout the centuries of these final days.

Notice that, in the vision of John, the Lamb also opens this seventh seal; in the septenaries that follow, this last element will always be reserved for the final consummation. This is a direct consequence of its being a scroll-book, which cannot be completely unrolled until the seven seals that hold it together have all been broken. We know that our author had not sufficient regard for the coherence of his imagery to make this alone a principle in arriving at the interpretation of this section. If he expressly mentions the opening of the seventh seal by the Lamb it is with the idea that we have here a last essential element explaining history, and that that element is already in action. This element is none other than the judgement of God. The deadly silence which follows the breaking of the seventh seal, and which is a traditional dramatic device when prophecies announcing the intervention of God's judgement are concerned (Hab. 2, 20; Zach. 14, 17, etc.) proves that it has been going on since the triumphal intervention of the Lamb. The rest of the book confirms this.

We are now, therefore, in possession of the essential factors of the book of history: the irresistible conquests of truth, the great scourges and divine punishment that will overtake humanity, the prayer of the martyrs and saints crying for vengeance against the enemies of God, the cataclysmic catastrophies preceding the final judgement, and then the judgement itself—these are the things the revelation of Patmos invites us to recognise at work in history, while showing us through them that Christ, the overcomer, is completely in command. We also know what all this leads to, and the ultimate success that will justify this long period of waiting, so full of trials and sufferings. The adding up of the final total of the elect is the end to which this whole human cavalcade is moving.

We also know now that there is not a single event in this world which the Christian can escape making an effort to comprehend by the light of his faith, because the resurrected Christ, by his mastery, is in command of all things, and nothing can possibly occur outside his dominion. Everything in the history of mankind, good or bad, has a religious significance. Of course we have up till now only gathered the general principles of the religious meaning behind the elements that constitute history; the rest of the revelation will clarify all these things. At least we now realise that none of the great events of the world in which we live can be left out of the compass of our faith. The mastery of Christ removes the scales from our eyes, and gives us the light which enables us to interpret every event from the standpoint of his divine intentions.

We have already seen in the foregoing pages how much the Christian outlook differs from the Jewish conception of history. Both, at first sight, enlarge on the same themes, so much so that a superficial reading of any early Christian document might give one the impression that it was simply borrowed from the Jewish tradition. The scourges of famine, war and plague, cosmic cataclysms or the threat of divine judgements—the same forbidding illustrations, and hard experiences—are exploited by both Jews and Christians.

So far as the Apocalypse is concerned, however, these
derivatives are all more or less material ones—the perspectives opened up are quite different. In the Old Testament, as
we have said, everything turns on the Messianic future, but
nothing of that future is ever shown as having arrived.
Present trials may be spoken of as having a pedagogic value
in preparing Israel for this expected future; but it continues
to be the future. The 'present' which it should become is
never inaugurated. The prophet of Patmos, on the other
hand, sees the 'last days' as the present time; the 'end' has
already arrived and the great scourges which are a part of
it belong already to the cycle of eschatological events. It is
therefore necessary to look upon them as the judgements of
God already in operation. Judgements of mercy for his
people; judgements of vengeance against the 'inhabitants of
the earth'; in both cases judgements primarily of truth.
Mercy lengthens the duration of the period in history, so
that the number of the elect may be increased. Vengeance is
already being meted out to those it is bound to overtake.
But in either case divine truth itself is at work. It is that
which saves, and that which judges. That is why the breaking
of the first seal brought the white horseman—the intervention
of truth—upon the scene, as was right and proper in a
Christian vision, truth being for Christians the first factor in
history. In line with the victory of the personal mystery of
Jesus, which we have seen is the same as divine truth, there is
first of all in history the triumph of this white horseman who
represents evangelical truth. Actually, these are both the
same mystery and the same victory, since the truth is
indivisible, and from the one luminous centre spreads its
radiations through the world. This is the essential fact
concerning the Christian view of history which the Apocalypse teaches; the conviction that the truth of God is none
other than our Lord Jesus, and the created truth which God
gave to mankind in Jesus Christ is none other than evangelical
truth which, since the Resurrection, has been scoring its own
irresistible victory throughout the world. It is always truth
that carries the day and that will have the last word, whether
it be by the salvation of those who have received it and given

their testimony, or whether it be by punishment of a sort inherent in the sin of blasphemy, meted out to those who have rejected truth and are sunk in error. St John's prophecies, and the divine revelation which is offered by them, throw a powerful light on the evolution of history and the inevitable triumph Christian truth will eventually obtain in it.

These certainties, however, general as they are, do not suffice to give us the true meaning of history from the Christian standpoint. They are based on a theology which is too intemporal. Leaving the revelation aside, the persecuted Christians of Domitian's day were no doubt as perplexed as we are by passing events which appeared to compromise the work and the victory of Christ. The mastery of the resurrected Christ is demonstrated by the opening chapters. The breaking of the seventh seal defines how this mastery coincides with evangelical truth and finds expression in the great facts of human history. But for all that, a connection had not yet been established between these realities and those more limited, but more immediate problems which weighed so heavily on the Christian communities at that time—the persecution launched by the Roman Empire against Christ's Church, for example. If the great perspectives revealed had any connection whatever with the anti-Christian political move on the part of Rome, it was difficult to see that connection. In order to be effective, the message of Patmos had still to face these events and apply to them the profound teachings which it had set out to impart.

And that is how the subsequent visions developed, until they linked up again with the historic realities of the time of Domitian and the politics of the Roman Empire, until they arrived at a precision which not even the densest among the recipients of the message could possibly mistake. Which permits us once again to establish the strict sequence of the book's instructional purpose, and the process consistently adhered to in its composition. Each new stage is governed by the one which preceded it, but enriched with a wealth of new details. The Christology of the Apocalypse, centred as it is in the mystery which unifies the supernatual personality and the historic role of Jesus, concerns a view of history in which victory is predestined for the gospel truth given to the world by Jesus. At the same time, the agents at work to prevent this victory, and the fate which awaits them, must also be clearly shown. Thus the light of revelation illuminates the whole picture, picking out detail after detail, until St John's correspondents recognise the contemporary situation in all its realism, and its sense from the Christian standpoint becomes quite clear. At this point the message of John ceases to be purely doctrinal teaching and takes on a prophetic value as it unveils to the Church the broad outlines of its future in history. Then it will not be only through faith in certain great principles quite outside temporal laws that Christians will acquire a proper Christian understanding of the evolution of history over which Christ presides, but they will also be able to formulate certain rules by which to determine the course of things as it were from the inside of that evolution. Thus the principles of a true theology of history from the Christian standpoint will be built up. The chapter which we are now ending is thus inseparable from the one which follows it. Just as we cannot truly understand the Christ of the Apocalypse until we see him illuminated in the celestial clarity of the holy Jerusalem, equally we shall not arrive at the true Christian sense of history as it is shown in the revelation of Patmos until we have mastered, to the last detail, leaving nothing out and adding nothing, the 'prophecy of this book' in its entirety.

CHAPTER V

THE ACTIVITY OF SATAN IN HISTORY

The seventh seal having been broken by the Lamb, the book of history begins to unfold. The history of the last days, we must remember; that is to say, the period extending from the Resurrection of Christ to the great eschatological events which will accompany the end of time. By these are meant the human and cosmic cataclysms which will immediately precede the Last Judgement; the Judgement itself; and the glorious coming of the holy Jerusalem to the New Earth. The central portion of the book (8, 2-20, 15) offers instruction concerning this particular fragment of duration in time.

The teachings do not follow any orderly plan, each new feature dealing in chronological order with a fresh period. They either have a general application, or they single out individual aspects which complement one another, not throwing light on this or that period, but illuminating the whole of Christian history up to the end. Only in the last of these surveys (17, 1-20, 15) is a precise chronological prospect opened up as the narrative evolves. It concerns the fulfilment of God's judgements in history and, as we have already said, it applies in a truly prophetic way to events from the reign of Domitian onwards. Between the breaking of the seventh seal, and this prophetic section, in the narrow sense of the term, the general teachings little by little give point to other sections bearing upon the historic future.

There is first of all a general description (8, 2-11, 18) of the worldly condition of the 'inhabitants of the earth.' Their trials recall those inflicted upon Egypt under Pharaoh when he obstinately insisted on keeping the faithful in bondage. They therefore have the same meaning. This section which, like the others, ends by conjuring up the disasters of the

111

final days (9, 1-19), the consummation of all things (11, 15;
cf. 10, 7); and the heavenly ovation which closes the drama
(11, 16-18) also, by the dovetailing (10-11, 14), broaches the
problem of Satan's struggle with the Church, and this
problem is the real object of the following section.

Then the author resorts to a new flash-back. He traces
this struggle between Satan and the Church to the very root,
in its heavenly phase (11, 19-13). He describes the defeat of
the Dragon in heaven, amid the acclamations of the celestial
choir (12, 10-12). And only after that does he begin to deal
with the titanic combat on earth (12, 13). There Satan is seen
stirring up trouble among men through the medium of the
two Beasts. And we are now properly prepared to follow
their defeat and his, step by step (14, 20). After that it only
remains for the New Jerusalem to appear in a regenerated
cosmos, and this is fully described in the last chapters
(21-22, 5).

At the point where we now find ourselves, therefore, two
closely-related mysteries are introduced into the instruction:
that of Satan and that of the Church. We must commence by
studying the former. The latter was intended to bring
comfort and encouragement to the persecuted Christians,
and the former to make clearer the real causes and the chief
instigator of their persecution. Through it all runs the
inspiring assurance that truth will inevitably triumph, whatever apparent defeats it may temporarily suffer through the
powers of darkness. In all the agitation brought about by
these appearances, the mystery of the Church is shown, by
contrast, poised in a state of unchanging serenity—very
different from the feverish contortions of Satan as his end
draws near.

We shall define the different stages by which the progressive
advance of the mystery of evil is exposed, summing up the
lessons conveyed by each of them. Sorting out the details of
this explanation, we shall arrive at a comprehensive view of
this mystery of evil, as St John saw and revealed it in human
history.

We cannot but admire the skill with which the instruction

on Satan's activity is built up, which is in complete contrast with the way St John has chosen to present the mystery of Jesus. He conveys this mystery by the symbol of radiating light, so intense that we are almost blinded by its brightness. The indomitable personality of the resurrected Christ appears without the slightest doubt in every phase of history, as revealed from the very first vision throughout the whole of the book. Any difficulties presented arise only from the prodigal richness of the author's word-pictures. The mystery of Satan, on the other hand, is presented in a very different manner. It is very slowly developed, so that every detail may be taken in, leaving room for no misconception whatsoever. At first we almost fail to recognise him amid the wealth of created details which are the object of the visions in which he appears. He insinuates himself unobtrusively, slyly, calling no attention to himself. Only towards the end does he throw off the mask, permitting us to catch a glimpse of his hatred and ill-will. And now we cannot fail to recognise his malignance at work through the medium of his agents. There is no doubt that at this moment he is already facing his defeat; but the whole of his subterranean progress in the world is marked by the distilled essence of his malevolence.

There is no need to emphasise the art of this literary composition, the skill with which the author adapts his style to the object he desires to depict. A mystery of light is revealed in all its resplendent clarity; but the mystery of deceit and illusion is conveyed by obscure hints and suggestive undertones. At least they serve the purpose of warning us; and in reading the visions that follow, we have to pay close attention lest we should at one point or another fail to unmask the prince of darkness as he goes about his evil work.

The section from 8, 2 to 11, 18, if we except the dovetailing 10-11, 14, which is the prelude to the following section, describes the seven trumpets and the scourges that are sent to the earth at the sound of these trumpets. The two symbols of the trumpets and scourges, taken together, reveal the general meaning of the instruction they convey. In apocalyptic literature trumpets always announce the great day of Jahveh and the release of his just wrath in the judgements on that day. But with this announcement is inseparably associated the release of the elect and their triumphal reunion (cf. Father Allo, Excursus, XXIII).

Blow ye the trumpet in Sion,
Sound an alarm in my holy mountain,
Let all the inhabitants of the earth tremble;
Because the day of the Lord cometh,
Because it is nigh at hand. (Joel, 2, 1 ff.)

St John is not the first, among the authors of the New Testament, to resume this symbol of the trumpet. There is a reference to it in our Lord's eschatological discourse (Matt. 24, 31) and also in St Paul (1, Cor. 15, 51; 1 Thess. 4, 15 ff.). We are thus warned that the passage which follows will resume, under different symbolism and with a different doctrinal intention, the theme of the avenging scourges of which we have already had a foretaste in the vision of the seven seals, by means of the three dark horsemen and by the cosmic cataclysms. Whilst in the former instance these were shown as being totally within the command of the master of history, here their other purpose, namely, the punishment of evil-doers and the liberation of the elect, is emphasised.

The importance of this last aspect is further underlined by the choice of scourges which the trumpets will release. Obviously they recall the plagues which descended upon Egypt under the Pharaohs, in order that the chosen people might be released from the bondage under which they were being held (Ex. 9, ff.). Therefore these concern the liberation of the people of God. Right through this section, the author takes extreme care to point out the parallel between the disciples of Jesus, who have his mark upon their foreheads just as in Egypt the houses of the Jews were marked by the avenging angel, to distinguish them from the 'inhabitants of the Earth' (in ancient times the Egyptians) who alone were the victims destined to suffer by the avenging scourges. By which it is seen at once that these scourges, which for the first time permit the hand of Satan to be clearly distinguished, can never affect the disciples of Jesus. At the very time the disciples were enabled to recognise the test they would have to meet, a trial which might even demand the supreme testimony, they were actually already situated 'in heaven', and therefore out of reach of the scourges which the trumpets would release for the punishment of the 'inhabitants of the earth'. The book of Wisdom offers the following illuminatingly analogous passage:

For when they were tried and chastised with mercy,
They knew how the wicked were judged with wrath
and tormented (Wis. 11, 10).

Here we notice for the first time that the author attributes the unleashing of misfortune not to the sacrificed Lamb, but to good and bad angels. In the opening vision, and throughout the breaking of the seven seals, it was necessary to demonstrate the complete mastery of the Lamb over all history, even in its disastrous moments. So he intervenes alone. Now that the message is beginning to deal with precise causes and immediate agents, the Lamb is no longer shown as personally intervening except when it is a matter of salvation or of mercy. Divine justice must be satisfied, but it is left to angels to execute the judgements. There is no need to stress the fact that in this respect the book again resumes the most consistent tradition of Jewish angelology, and shows Jesus once again exercising a divine prerogative. It demonstrates clearly the supernatural supremacy of God; he only intervenes in human affairs through the ministry of angels who are themselves, whether good or bad, only the executors of the providential will.

Therefore these Chapters, eight to eleven, in which the judgements demanded by the prayers of the saints (notice by the way that 8, 3-6 takes up the theme of 6, 10-11, and 9, 14 returns to it) begin to take effect; angels, at the sound of the trumpet, actually see to their carrying-out.

In accordance with a scheme very much favoured by our author, they divide themselves into two groups, one of four (8, 7-12) describing cosmic phenomena of the eschatological type, and the other of three (9, 1-21, and 11, 11-18, with which are also bracketed the events of 10-11, 13) describing the human torments of a more moral order very familiar in this type of literature.

Now in each of these two groups a 'falling star' appears.

At the first reading this might almost escape notice. One would be wrong, however, in regarding this as merely a picturesque detail in the arsenal of apocalyptic symbols when cosmic wonders are being described. Let us compare the two texts:

And the third angel sounded the trumpet (notice the order: the *third* in the series of four, the chief place!)
And a great star fell from heaven, burning as it were a torch.
(8, 10.)
And the fifth angel sounded the trumpet (the first place, in the series of three)
And I saw a star falling from heaven upon earth.
And there was given to him the key of the bottomless pit.
And he opened the bottomless pit. (9, 1 ff.)

Considering the two texts separately, and even supposing one cannot be perfectly sure at this point as to their exact meaning, both of them, and especially the second, put one on the alert; the star which is entrusted with the key of the abyss must conceal a mystery of more than cosmic significance and bring us face to face with the spiritual world. Now it is traditional, in apocalyptic literature, to identify fallen angels with stars. Thus Enoch, in his vision of the terrifying place, sees seven stars of heaven linked together in that place, looking like great mountains ablaze with fire. And he asks: For what sin are they in chains, and why have they been put there? And Uriel, one of the holy angels acting as his guide, answers: On what are you seeking information, and why are you anxious? These stars are those who have transgressed God's law, and they are chained here for ten thousand centuries, the number of days of their sins.[1]

In Chapter eighty-six, the angels who had taken wives from among the daughters of men (Gen. Cap. 6) are likewise described as stars falling from heaven to earth.[2] Finally, in Chapter eighty-eight, during the punishment of the bad angels by the good angels, Enoch sees one of them seizing the first star which had fallen from heaven, tying its hands and feet, and casting it into the abyss which is narrow and deep, steep

[1]Book of Enoch. 21, 3-6. Trans. Fr Martin, Paris 1906. p.56.
[2]Ibid. pp. 200 ff.

and dark.[1] The Apocalypse obviously takes up the same theme.

When we compare the two texts, we have no longer any doubt that St John wished here to introduce the mystery of Satan; this is made quite clear by another text taken from the prophet Isaias. I am quoting this in full, as we shall need to refer to it again later.

How art thou fallen from heaven, O Lucifer,
Who didst rise in the morning?
How art thou fallen to the earth
That didst wound the nations?
And thou saidst in thy heart
I will ascend into heaven
I will exalt my throne above the stars of God.
I will sit in the mountain of the covenant,
In the sides of the north;
I will ascend above the heights of the clouds.
I will be like the Most High.
But yet thou shalt be brought down to hell
Into the depth of the pit. (Is. 14, 12, ff.)

To whom does this text of the prophet Isaias refer? Not directly, as one might think under the influence of the traditional Christian interpretation, to the fall of Satan and his descent into hell, but in the historic perspective which is that of Israel, to Babylon, which vanquished and oppressed the people of Israel. But we have here the case of a prophetic inspiration which is too remarkable and too important for us not to pause over it for a moment. There is hardly a better example by which we can verify all that the strictest theology has been able to say about the phenomenon of inspiration.

Briefly, the prophet Isaias, in order to fortify the people in their courage amid the trials of bondage, foretold the ultimate collapse of the Babylonian empire which then appeared to be invincible. This king of Babylon, who aspired to dominate the nations and to become like unto Jahveh, would be thrown into the bottomless pit! The intensity, if I may say so, of the divine inspiration in the prophet's vision led him to reveal this prospect in a manner at once prophetic and historic; that is to say, prophetic along the lines of future historic developments, with such a richness

[1]Ibid. p. 202.

of language that even wider perspectives could not fail to be opened up. Providentially (for it was the same spirit that inspired the Apocalypse from end to end) this was a foretaste of a still more important revelation, surpassing the case of Zorobabel, prince of Juda, and the high-priest Jesus, and one which, at the right moment and in course of time, would develop in such a way as to permit a complete understanding of providential intervention. With the Apocalypse of St John we have arrived precisely at the privileged moment in which the Holy Ghost, in order to make its message clear, takes up again the revelation of which a foretaste was given at the time of the Babylonian captivity. Notice how carefully the situations correspond in the revelation of Isaias and that of Patmos. Just as in Chapters thirteen and fourteen Isaias encourages the Israelite captives by prophesying to them, in the name of God, the downfall of the Babylonian king, 'destroyer of nations,' who aspires to raise his throne on an equality with that of God, St John on Patmos, to hearten and enlighten the Christians persecuted by Rome, the new Babylon, permits them to watch the fall of another brilliant star, like unto the king of Babylon, and, like him, responsible for the troubles of the chosen people. Here the revelation pursues its course; it is clear that the brilliant star, given the supernatural fall which casts it from heaven into the bottomless pit, and the mysterious power it possesses over that pit (9, 1)—the king of Babylon, in Isaias, was equipped with nothing like that—could only signify the Emperor reigning in Rome. The picture conjured up obviously concerns a personage of the highest importance with a spiritual orbit which could almost be described as cosmic. It is thus that, starting from the prophecy of Isaias, but rounding it off and surpassing it, St John begins to make it clear that in persecuting Rome another brilliant star, as active a 'destroyer of nations' as the king of Babylon, and even more avid than he in proclaiming itself 'like unto the Most High', must be recognised. In formally identifying Satan with the text of Isaias, Christian tradition has followed the line laid down by St John in this text of the Apocalypse, which Isaias himself had forecast by his extraordinarily prophetic evocation. For the theologian interested in the phenomenon of prophetic inspiration, this is a privileged case which deserves special mention and which furthermore leaves no doubt as to the meaning of the mysterious fallen stars from heaven which John introduces in Chapters eight and nine, pointing his teachings on Satan and the role he plays in temporal history.

The fallen star of Chapter eight torments the inhabitants of the earth with mortal venom. Here in Chapter eight it overshadows everything. Already we perceive the contrast between this and the light, the quickening peace, which flows through history from the resurrected Christ. But the smoke also recalls that which rose long ago from Sodom and Gomorrah after the judgement of God (Gen. 19, 28) or that which Joel also foresaw on the day of Jahveh's wrath (Joel, 2, 2-10). After this we are not surprised that what we have previously said about the judgement of God is already in progress at the present time. 'Woe, woe, woe to the inhabitants of the earth' was well spoken by the angel flying in the midst of heaven (8, 13). We have been duly warned that the justice of God is already being exercised against his enemies in condign punishments.

For this reason, in a still more detailed vision of the mystery of Satan, locusts wriggle out of the smoke spread by the fallen star. There is no doubt about their diabolical character. 'The angel of the bottomless pit' is king over them (9, 11). His name is then given; it confirms the interpretation we have already arrived at. In Greek as in Hebrew his name signified Destroyer. Now Isaias had already called his king of Babylon 'destroyer of nations' (Is. 14, 12). St John's prophecy goes from detail to detail.

How does the destroyer set to work? By an invasion of locusts (9, 3 ff.). Here is first of all a reminder of the plagues of Egypt unleashed by Jahveh for the liberation of his people. As before, a doctrinal definition is thus implied. These scourges which in Chapter six, in accordance with the theme, are ascribed to the direct will of the Lamb, here nevertheless are justly spoken of as being attributable to the

powers of evil, the divine master of history merely using them
for the necessary enforcement of his justice.

We should notice in passing that the locusts under which
the Egyptians suffered in Pharaoh's time simply consumed all
green things, causing famine; but those now released upon
mankind inflict such torments as to make their victims long
for death (9, 4-5). Already at its first appearance the fallen
star has introduced mortal venom into the world (8, 10).
Naturally, St John takes care to stress, all this applies only
to the evil-doers, and not to believers 'who have the mark of
God on their foreheads' (9, 4), that is to say, by faith, in their
thoughts.

We can easily understand this when we take into account
the behaviour of these locusts. How do they behave? Like
scorpions! (Another example of the way in which St John
mixes his metaphors.) A passage from St Luke at once comes
to mind; it is the one in which our Lord says to his apostles:
'Behold, I have given you power to tread upon serpents and
scorpions and upon all the power of the enemy: and nothing
shall hurt you' (Luke 10, 19). Father Allo has noted, following
Swete, that in the Old Testament the scorpion is already
coupled with the serpent as a symbol of the spiritual evil
by which man is benighted in this world.

How does the scorpion express its malevolence? In two
stages. The first is in the cunning, deceitful, lying fashion in
which he attacks. He looks you straight in the face, giving
no hint of his hidden sting; he almost inspires confidence.
Then suddenly his tail rises and strikes the unsuspecting face
that lies open before him. 'And they had tails like scorpions,
and there were stings in their tails' (9, 10). The locusts are
false as scorpions, as false as the devil himself, and they are
nourished by this same falsehood. And then, when their
sting has been driven home, what else do they do? 'And it
was given unto them that they should not kill them; but
that they should torment them . . . ' (9, 5). Error is the venom
which gnaws and gradually poisons. Its falsehood is injected
into you; your discomfort increases until you wish you were
dead. But death, says St John, flies from them (9, 6) for all
these sufferings, as in the case of the plagues of Egypt, have

only one purpose, to lead individual sinners and sinful nations to repentance. But alas! The inhabitants of the earth remain unconverted.

All this, despite the incoherence of the illustrations, makes admirably coherent doctrine. It contrasts impressively with the manner in which, at the beginning, the mystery of Jesus and his triumph over the world, is approached. From the first fall of the Angel of Light into the bottomless pit, from which he can only send forth that dense fog which obscures the light of the sun itself, to the bitterness of the waters which human beings have to drink and the venomous error-thoughts of those who have not the mark of the Lamb upon their foreheads, everything fits perfectly into the first rough sketch the author has given of Satan's activity in history. We know from now on that this activity and this mystery are false from beginning to end, and therefore are completely destructive.

Suddenly, and without a moment's pause, we are informed that this diabolical malignancy of error lasts only five months (9, 5-10). We shall have to return to this in the chapter on the evolution of history, and to define the limits, even chronologically, of this destructive malevolence of the nations.

As for the infernal horsemen unleashed by the trumpet of the sixth angel after a renewed and more pressing petition of the saints (9, 13) they are depicted in obviously eschatological terms; the reference to the river Euphrates (9, 13), as are also the 'hour, the day, the month and the year' (9, 15) and the astronomical number of the combatants (9, 16). The really infernal powers of evil (fire, smoke and brimstone) (9, 17; cf. 9,2 and 21,8) all have a bearing on the crescendo of events towards the end. As we have said, this is all characteristic of the class of literature to which the Apocalypse belongs. The whole series of teachings must always culminate in some fact or other connected with the last days. Here, the sixth trumpet (the one immediately preceding the last) already shows us that there will be a vast increase of the diabolical malignance of error and deceit towards the end. We shall have to return to this, also, in our last chapter.

In verse seven of Chapter eleven, the famous Beast of the
Apocalypse makes its first appearance. It occurs in the
passage concerning the two witnesses who bear invincible
testimony of the gospel. Then the text continues:

'And when they shall have finished their testimony
The Beast that ascendeth out of the abyss
Shall make war against them and shall overcome them
    and kill them' (11,7).

This verse, as we have already noted, serves as a prelude
to the next section, which begins with chapter twelve; here
the activities of the Beast are dealt with in greater detail.

Now, when we arrive at Chapter twelve, suddenly a new
personage, called the great red dragon, makes his appearance,
without anything further having so far been said of the Beast
already announced. We are totally unprepared for this new
arrival. In a book as meticulously constructed as this one,
this cannot have happened unintentionally. The author's
intention must have been somewhat as follows.

The revelation of Patmos, we repeat, evolves in accordance
with a series of teachings, the precision of which increases as
their compass is narrowed down. It progresses from generalities to particular. It ends by explaining to the faithful of
the first century the meaning of the persecution which Rome
has launched against them. With the Beast, as we shall
presently see, the ultimate peak of the prophetic explanation
is reached. Now at this point, and in the interests of that
explanation, St John finds it convenient to indulge in a sort
of flash-back. Before showing the Roman pretentions to
divinity in their truly diabolical character, and the persecution
of Christians which results from them, he deems it necessary
to reveal in its supernatural dimensions the mystery of evil
centred in Satan, starting at the very beginning of all creation,
spiritual as well as temporal. Before speaking of the Beast
which is Rome, and in order to view its activities in their
true perspective, we have to be introduced to the Dragon.

'And that great dragon was cast out, that old serpent,
Who is called the devil and Satan,
Who seduceth the whole world' (12, 9).

This is the summit of Christian revelation regarding the

mystery of evil, and St John thought it necessary that all the implications of that mystery should be recognised by anyone hoping to understand the malevolence that dogs temporal history.

So here we have his cumulative comments on the activities of Satan, and the two Beasts through whom he exerts his influence over men and nations.

Leaving on one side, for the moment, the combat between the Dragon and the woman, that is to say, the Church, we get this:

And there was seen another sign in heaven.
And behold, a great red dragon,
Having ten heads and ten horns
And on his heads seven diadems,
And his tail drew the third part of the stars of heaven
And cast them to the earth (. . .)
And there was a great battle in heaven:
Michael and his angels fought with the dragon,
And the dragon fought, and his angels
And they prevailed not:
Neither was their place found any more in heaven.
And that great dragon was cast out,
That old serpent,
Who is called the devil and Satan,
Who seduceth the whole world.
And he was cast unto the earth:
And his angels were thrown down with him.
And I heard a loud voice in heaven saying:
Now is come salvation and strength, and the kingdom of our God
    and the power of his Christ,
Because the accuser of our brethren is cast forth . . .

Therefore rejoice, O heavens, and you that dwell therein.
Woe to the earth and to the sea
Because the devil is come down unto you,
Having great wrath,
Knowing that he hath but a short time. (12, 3 ff.)

Compared with the fantastic demonologies of apocalyptic literature, this passage seems remarkably restrained, which takes nothing from the depth of the revelation it contains.

The two personages who dominate the scene and give it meaning are Michael and Satan, or the Dragon.

Michael, in the angelology of Daniel, is the angel who leads people to God and defends them against his enemies.

(cf. Dan. 10, 13, 21.) We know that the meaning of his name is: 'Who is like unto God.' The role he plays is characterised by these two circumstances, and although this scene takes place in heaven, before the beginning of time, as it were, he already appears in the perspective opened up of the earthly struggle the people of God must pursue with Satan—or, more precisely, the struggle of the Church against the impious nations. His victory already guarantees theirs.

The figure of the dragon also seems to be inspired by Daniel, and it can be traced back to the terrifying visions of the night (Dan. 7, 7). It deals with the same problem, that of the hostility of pagan empires towards the people of God. Like the Beast to whom he suddenly will relegate his power over the earth (13, 2) the Dragon has seven heads and ten horns (12, 3; 13, 1). But while power, symbolised by the horns, enables the Beast to exercise his pseudo-kingship over the earth—a reign of evil, indicated by the diadems—the thoughts in the heads of the Dragon in heaven make the actual pretence to that royalty (12, 3). With his tail, which the previous vision has shown to be the organ used for injecting the poison of error, and which is here shown effectively in action in the sky, he sweeps to earth with him a considerable number of heavenly spirits whom he has been able to snare by his seduction (12, 3-4). He himself is finally thrown out after his defeat in the struggle with Michael. He then appears in his traditional shape, that of the Serpent of Genesis (12, 9; cf. Gen. 3, 1) and thenceforth uses his powers of deception only too effectively among mankind. 'The Serpent deceived me,' Eve pleaded, and St John takes up the same strain with 'Satan, who seduceth the whole world'. All this Satan does because of an incomprehensible jealousy of mankind. The book of Tobias already illustrates the envy of the evil one; and the Apocalypse expresses a similar motive when it describes the devil as 'the accuser of our brethren, who accused them before God day and night' (12, 9-10), and indicates the relentlessness with which he pursues them (12, 9-12).

Obscure as the message is, it is none the less explicit. A great many Christians have practically given up believing in the devil. Maybe as children they were impressed by some picture by Epinal; but the time has passed when Croquemi-taine could inspire fear, and nowadays it is considered rather childish to give the devil a serious place in our outlook on worldly affairs. The gospel did not think so. It opens with our Lord's temptation in the desert, one of the episodes in Jesus's earthly life which is of the very highest importance, and the one which throws the most penetrating light on the mystery of the Incarnation. Throughout his public life our Lord shows himself in pitched battle with the 'Prince of this world', right up to the moment of commencing his Passion, when he declares: 'Now shall the Prince of this world be cast out' (Joh. 12, 31) and from thenceforth 'have not anything in him' (Joh. 14, 30). These words, which the apostle St John reports, must be taken in conjunction with the teachings of the Apocalypse regarding the defeat of Satan.

There is not the slightest doubt that St Paul believed in Satan and the infernal powers. He recognised them at work in the person of the Son of Iniquity (Eph. 2, 2), and in warning the faithful that they would have less trouble in overcoming the flesh and the blood than in dealing with 'principalities and powers, the rulers of this world of dark-ness, the spirits of wickedness in high places' (Eph. 6, 12). When explaining how this diabolical malevolence would operate, like St John he speaks of duplicity and false doctrines (1 Tim. 4, 1-2). This is the picture given of the great mystery of evil actually at work in the world—an activity which will go on and increase towards the end when it is finally vanquished by our Lord Jesus, killing 'with the breath of his mouth' and destroying 'with the brightness of his coming' (2 Thess. 2, 8).

These, then, were the faith and the thoughts on Satan entertained by the early Christians. In the Apocalypse, however, St John makes many points additionally clear. Especially in showing that the great personal struggle between the Prince of Darkness and God, and the Son of God, has its origin in heaven, in the realm of pure spirits which is so mysterious to us.

And there was a great battle in heaven:

Michael and his angels fought with the dragon,
And the dragon fought, and his angels,
And they prevailed not,
Neither was their place found any more in heaven (12, 7-8).

The evil we encounter here below, the instigator of which
our faith teaches us to be the devil, and all the misfortunes in
our world which arise out of that evil, are only the repercussions of this drama, the first scene of which was played
in heaven. There is the mystery of Satan's revolt against God,
and the fight with Michael, champion of God's rights. There
is the mystery of Michael's victory and the defeat of Satan,
whether we look upon this defeat and this victory from their
spiritual aspect, or from their impersonal aspect as the
triumph of good and the arrest of evil in God's creation.
It is difficult to arrive at an exact idea of the real meaning
these statements of faith convey. At least we are assured by
the revelation of Patmos that good triumphs, and will
always triumph, over evil. In heaven, in the realm of spirits,
the battle is already won. Satan has been defeated and
forever expelled from the realm of pure spirit. But on earth,
where the Prince of Darkness remains since his expulsion
from heaven, he will for a time continue his revolt. We are
even warned that he may acquire temporary dominion (the
diadems, 12, 3) and that by his fury (12, 12) and his powers of
deception (12,9) he will not cease to lead the inhabitants of
the earth astray to their ruin.

Now how does this evil operate among us? As Christians
know by the doctrine of temptation, which was already
traditional among the Israelites, it operates in the individual
personal life of each one of us. From the temptation of Adam
and Eve as related in Genesis, to that of our Lord in the
desert, as shown in the synoptic gospels; from teachings like
those of the book of Job and many others, Christians have
learnt to discern the influence of the evil one behind the
weaknesses or attraction of evil with which all are familiar
in their moral life. St John deliberately depicts the devil by
means of traits which characterise him in his traditional role
as tempter. What was new in his inspired message was the
revealing of Satan behind evil factors which are met with

from time to time in all critical stages of human history. He invented the great allegorical figures of the two celebrated Beasts of the Apocalypse in order to drive home this teaching.

So we see Satan, expelled from heaven, incarnated on earth for the short time at his disposal, and waging relentless war upon the woman and her offspring (12, 13, 17). We shall show in the following chapter how the woman, that is to say, the Church, is beyond his power to harm. So he pursues the struggle against her children: he makes war

'. . against the rest of her seed
Who keep the commandments of God
And have the testimony of Jesus Christ' (12, 17).

In accordance with his crafty nature, he keeps himself well in the background, using as his agents the two Beasts, to whom he gives some of his powers. The first rises from the sea—that is to say, taking into account the location of the prophet on Patmos, from the West; the second from the earth, that is to say, from the East. Historians agree that there can be no possible doubt about the identification of the first Beast, hinted at in 11, 7 and clearly described in 13 ff. Passing from particular to general significance, let us say that the symbol is intended to suggest Nero, whose name in Hebraic characters corresponds to 666, the figure of the Beast (12, 18; cf. 13, 3, 12, 14) and at the same time the whole series of persecuting Roman emperors (17, 8-12) and the whole political powers of the Empire (11,7; 13, 1, 2, 3, 4); also, generally speaking, all political powers that, following the example of Rome, shall at any time aspire to divine rights and cause those to be persecuted who will not acquiesce in the idolatry of worshipping them. (13, 12, 15, 17; 14, 9, 11; 16, 2, 10, 13; 17, 8, 11, 12, 17; 19, 19, 20; 20, 4, 10; etc.) It could happen that the persecuting political power might at some time or other be mortally wounded, as happened in the case of the empire at the time of Nero; but it might revive, and by this very resuscitation impose still more easily on the superstitious admiration of mankind.

Now here, according to St John, is the primary power of illusion which Satan exercises, slyly tempting multitudes of human beings and effectively leading them into idolatry, in order to be able subsequently to accuse them before God. Behind every deification of a state, whatever form it may take or by whatever ritual it may be accompanied, St John from the time of Domitian onwards warns Christians to recognise the operations of that evil one whose name is Satan, the very spirit of error and deceit. No longer able to exercise his malice among the celestial beings of heaven, seducing them from God, for whom they have been created, he turns it loose in the world, employing for his particular purpose the political powers that are in a position to enforce idolatry among the masses. And when this plan succeeds, he hypocritically accuses the human multitudes before the throne of justice, whose divine judgements he knows are inevitable. Can one fail to be impressed by the way in which this doctrine of St John, even allowing for the difference in context and literary style, agrees with the account of the temptation in the desert as given in the synoptic gospels? The supreme offer made by the Tempter in order to gain the better of the mysterious Prophet who so much intrigued him and who called himself the Son of God, was universal political domination over all men, if only he would fall down and worship Satan. 'He . . . showed him all the kingdoms of the world and the glory of them, and said to him: All these will I give thee, if falling down thou wilt adore me. Then Jesus saith unto him: Begone, Satan! For it is written: The Lord thy God shalt thou adore, and him only shalt thou serve' (Matt. 4, 8-10 and para. 1, 11). Alas! The Apocalypse shows us that men are not always as clear-sighted and firm of purpose as Jesus in meeting this kind of political pressure from powers that arrogate undue importance to themselves. Despite the manifest blasphemies which they perpetrate against God and against 'those who serve him in heaven' (13, 5-6) too often they receive lip service for a time—but only for a time—from those who 'dwell on the earth' (13, 7). The infernal Dragon lends the Beast all his power, which he is able to use effectively for forty-two months (13, 5; we shall return in our last chapter to the period of time allowed here on earth to the idolatrous Beast). He therefore goes on persecuting the saints, scoring over them occasional temporary and apparent victories, and extending his attentions to 'all tribes and tongues and people and nations'; and they are actually accepted by the 'inhabitants of the earth', but not by those who have their names written in the book of the Lamb, and who refuse him the adoration which is due to God alone (13, 7-8).

We need not go into the detailed characteristics of this central figure in the Apocalypse. In our last chapter we shall refer again to certain features (the wound of the Beast, the number of his horns, his identification with certain emperors, the duration of his power, and so on). Apart from that, it suffices to say that his description on general lines is inspired by Daniel (Cap. 7) and that is another reason that the interpreter is obliged to link him with persecuting empires and blasphemers. The other symbols are quite straight forward. If St John is inclined to multiply them, as in the case of the Beast, he does so by joining up the most concrete effects, that is to say, those most evident in the historic situation he wishes to clarify for the benefit of his correspondents. A little farther on (cap. 17 and ff.) the descriptions of Rome, with its hills, its luxury, its commerce, its universal domination, forsake the allegorical style completely, so clear are the allusions and the developments described. Chapter thirteen is on very similar lines; once in possession of the main keys, everyone can figure out the text for himself, recognising precise historical incidents, and at the same time doctrinal precepts of the highest importance.

The second Beast comes from the earth, that is to say, from Asia and the Orient just as the first one came from the sea, or rather from the West and Rome. Its symbolism, too, is not ambiguous. A little farther on St John gives substance to this explanation by speaking of the false prophet (19, 20). This second Beast, in his power and his method of operating, reminds us of the Lamb. Like the Lamb, the second Beast appeals to religious sentiment, and uses persuasion, instead of compulsion and authority, the means employed by the first Beast. Nevertheless, his mouth, like that of the Dragon, incessantly pours forth blasphemies against God (13, 11). His power is as extensive as that of the other Beast, and thus is wielded over all tribes and tongues and nations and people of 'those who inhabit the earth'. And, moreover, he uses his influence in the interests of the first Beast. He promotes the cult of its adoration, gives it a life it would never have without his aid, among the people who are being led astray. He even multiplies the miracles which are attributed to the first Beast and its cult. Finally he stirs up persecution against those who decline to take part in that adoration and to escape his influence.

All this obviously refers to the religious syncretism and the Gnostic currents of thought we described in the first chapter. Some commentators have read into it a more precise allusion —to Simon the Magician. It is not impossible that something of the kind was intended, especially if it is believed that this same Simon stirred up trouble for St Peter in Italy and in Rome, which is almost certain. Anyway, the symbol extends its orbit beyond any one particular case; it applies to the whole syncretic movement. Derived from the East, these religious currents flourished in Asia Minor, where the addressees of the Apocalypse lived. Here people were favourable to the cult of Caesar and Rome. Having introduced the Caesar-god into their temples, they had by this act given it a kind of soul (13,15), that is to say, they had made this Roman presence alluring. If left to its own purely political and frigid legal demands, it would never have captured the imagination or exercised such powers over a population which remained basically religious. The mysteries and the magic of Gnostic cults or currents (13, 13-14) impressed and effectively won over all those who, not being already united in the worship of the one true God, continued to 'inhabit the earth'. Just as they had previously worshipped the idols in their temples they now adored Caesar and Rome. Thus the second Beast assembled all in servitude to the first, a servitude of thought and of deeds.

And he shall make all
Both little and great,
Rich and poor,

Freemen and bondmen,
To have a character in their right hand or on their foreheads;
And that no man might buy or sell
But he that hath the character,
Or the name of the beast,
Or the number of his name. (13, 16-17.)

This also applies to all time. While the gospel keeps people to the right road, false doctrines, religions and philosophies lead the human masses astray. When they appear, they seem to come from anything but political sources. They all try their best to resemble the Lamb. They claim to have the same rights, and to be just as effective as Christian truth. They seem at first to be very far removed from any desire to favour the worship of political power. Actually, they should be recognised as St Paul recognised Satan, when he described him as being disguised as an Angel of Light (2 Cor. 11, 14). Sooner or later they end by playing the first Beast's game, furnishing him with a mysticism for lack of which he would have no power over the masses. Then they invent a liturgy which is designed to divert to themselves the homage which is due to God alone. Finally they reduce the masses to servitude to their cult. The most ordinary economic necessities are rendered dependent upon the first Beast's whim. People can engage neither in buying nor selling without giving pledges of their servitude to the State idol. From now on, therefore, says St John to the early Christians, you will be able to recognise the spirit of evil at work behind these false doctrines, and realise their power of deception.

For this is the one and only object of the Prince of Darkness; to lead people astray, make them fall into error, and, above all, into the most culpable of all errors, namely, idolatry. This term, 'leading astray', is used seven times in the book, and always to describe the activities of Satan himself or his auxiliaries (2, 20; 12, 9; 13, 14; 19, 20; 20, 3, 8, 10). The second Beast is particularly skilled in this diabolical work. Even as the serpent, in the beginning, led Adam and Eve astray, in the same way he makes the deification of the State, by means of false religious doctrines and philosophies, the most potent means of seducing whole groups of human beings and whole nations from their allegiance to God. For

by these false doctrines, unless they have been immunised
by the gospel and liberated in advance from all servitude,
the nations will be reduced to the adoration of Caesar, which
was the first method of seduction and blasphemy employed
by the infernal Dragon. Indeed, history proves this. Failing
the religious and Gnostic currents of syncretism, the cult of
Caesar and of Rome would have made no headway. From
then on, all other examples have illustrated, or will continue
to illustrate, the doctrine of St John; so there is no need to
spend time in long comment upon it. False mysticisms all
eventually lead to idolatry, by which Satan and evil triumph
among us. The Apocalypse teaches Christians to recognise
the true and diabolical instigator behind all these false
mysticisms and false doctrines, and how they will all end,
unless the gospel steps in to rectify matters.

Thus our book, in its process of composition, once again
justifies itself. With Chapter eight we leave behind us general
considerations, such as the scourges which will overtake
mankind, and especially the wicked; and we come in Chapters
twelve and thirteen to concrete realities of history—the
contemporary history of the author's time, especially as it
affects Domitian and Rome and the Caesar cult, and the
currents of false religions that made these pretensions
possible. But we have now learnt to recognise the personal
intervention of Satan, and the powers of evil at his command.
He and they are the cause of all the sins, and of the moral
torment and misfortunes of the inhabitants of the earth.
From him and from them proceed the scourges with which
the avenging justice demanded by the prayers of the saints
in heaven will finally be fulfilled; and these will be the prelude
to the liberation of the faithful who have the seal of God on
their foreheads. The infernal horsemen, which at the end of
time will increase the torment of those who refuse to be
converted to the true God, also fit into this picture. So much
for Chapters eight and nine.

Chapters twelve and thirteen can then more clearly reveal
the mystery of evil. Here the great adversary of God and the
saints is shown to be the Dragon, the supreme principle of

illusion and blasphemy. Overcome in heaven by Michael, herald and defender of God's transcendence, he tries to involve as many as possible in his fall, out of sheer malice. He is the driving force behind all the blasphemies and deceitful illusions of the Roman Caesar cult, as indeed of all its successors. All the false religious doctrines and philosophies which sooner or later end in servitude to impious political power owe their inspiration to the ceaseless malice of the evil one.

Once this had been demonstrated to them, the Christians persecuted by Domitian had a better grasp of the tragic difficulties by which they were beset. Nor did the consolation the message of Patmos offered end there. We shall see presently that Satan, whom they were now in a position to unmask, already appeared as a vanquished foe. The feverish virulence of his methods could be likened to the last kick of a stricken beast in its death-throes.

Was there anything new in this doctrine? The dominant features deserve to be underlined. The active personal influence of Satan in the temptations every individual has to meet in his personal moral life had always been recognised by Judeo-Christian tradition; this belief can be traced from Genesis to the temptation in the wilderness. St Paul took it a step farther when he discerned, over and above personal temptations, a great mystery of evil, with which our Lord Jesus was in constant combat, and which it had been the purpose of his coming into the world to destroy. And it would be finally and definitely destroyed with his glorious Second Coming—'by the breath of his mouth' (2 Thess. 2, 7). St John, in the Apocalypse defines the methods this spirit of evil utilises in its activity among us. Side-stepping the problem of temptation and sin in the lives of individuals, he concentrates on the diabolical factors of blasphemy and deception in community life as they affect the history of peoples and nations. But by his doctrine of the punishments inherent in the sin of blasphemy, they will inevitably meet with the retribution they deserve. St John shows that all impious tyrants and false prophets are simply the instruments of Satan. His is the driving power behind them and through it he does his best to draw the 'inhabitants of the earth' into his own blasphemies and undoing.

So the mystery of temporal history in which they have their part is gradually unveiled for the benefit of believers. 'Here is Wisdom,' says St John, concluding the passage in which he describes the two Beasts. Wisdom. That is to say, a proper understanding of the divine purpose behind all historic events, no matter how untoward they may appear. And that understanding can only result in serenity—in that self-mastery which is the greatest asset when facing the practical affairs of our daily lives.

Having arrived at this stage in the revelation, the faithful could no longer entertain any doubts as to the ultimate personal victory of the resurrected Christ, and the unfailing triumph of evangelical truth, which he had given to the world. Furthermore they could see the implications of the obstacles that truth was obliged to encounter, and the virulence of the evil which appears from time to time to retard its triumph. This could only put them into better heart for the struggle, confident of ultimate victory over an enemy who habitually fights by underhand methods, and with whom one can deal more effectively once he is unmasked.

The Prince of Evil's main hopes are centred in the offspring of the woman—those who 'keep the commandments of God and have the testimony of Jesus' are the ones he longs to seduce, by approaching them in such disguise that they cannot recognise him. He sows doubts in their minds and shakes their confidence by insidious suggestions of false doctrines and by pressure from political quarters demanding homage for State gods. The revelation of Patmos exposes Satan's game and denounces his diabolical policy so that the faithful can see through it. 'If a stronger than he come upon him and overcome him, he will take away all his armour wherein he trusted and will distribute his spoils' says St Luke (Luke 11, 22) and St John shows the faithful how to disarm the evil one by meeting his lies and deception, forever at work in the course of human history, with the more powerful weapon of evangelical truth.

The message was all the more comforting to the early

Christians because it revealed the enemy already in retreat. To be sure, he would still be in a position to score some apparent victories over the disciples of Jesus. Numerous fellow-servants and brothers would still need to give the supreme testimony before the number of Jesus's martyrs was complete. We shall go into this more fully in the next chapter. But all these apparent victories of Satan would be ephemeral. Ephemeral because all the sufferings the disciples would have to endure in the course of the persecutions would only increase the final victorious testimony of Jesus Christ himself, and, in union with his, hasten the definite defeat of Satan. Apparent, because in spite of temporary successes, Satan is nevertheless already the vanquished enemy. Vanquished in heaven by the archangel Michael and forever expelled from its bliss. Vanquished on earth ever since the Passion and Resurrection of our Lord. He knows himself how little time remains for the continuance of his revolt (12, 12). Not only will he fail in his attempt to ensnare in his temporary triumphs those who have the seal of God on their foreheads—that is to say, believers—but furthermore, as we shall show in our final chapter, he is doomed to pass from defeat to defeat. Of course he will always succeed in drawing 'the inhabitants of the earth' into his own blasphemy and misery; more is the pity. Considered from the point of view of the individual moral life, conditions of human existence will remain unchanged in all essentials until the end of time. Every man may choose either good or evil by his own free will—he may side with the gospel or with error, with Jesus or with Satan, just as he pleases. But the Apocalypse is not primarily concerned with the individual point of view. Collective facts covering the whole span of human history are the main theme of this inspired book. Now in this sphere, it will be noticed, Satan's mastery invariably only lasts as long as the two Beasts get the upper hand in human affairs. And even on this earthly plane he is destined to be overcome eventually by the truth of the gospel and the word of God. This is the real teaching of the Apocalyptical prophecies, as we shall demonstrate in our last chapter.

At the same time, the revelation of Patmos succeeded in solving some of the problems aroused in the minds of early Christians by the apparent contradiction between the old messianic promises of God's universal domination and the apparent triumph of paganism. How accustomed we have become to the repeated revival of blasphemous assumptions on the part of political tyrannies! Let it suffice, at this point, to emphasise the indisputable teaching of our book, namely, that it is by the two Beasts, in other words false doctrines and unjustifiable pretensions of political powers, that Satan exercises whatever authority he can wield over mankind. His instruments are deceit and blasphemy. And for all that, no matter how formidable his weapons may appear, he cannot stand up to the truth of the gospel. Since the Resurrection of their Master, Christians need no longer fear the devil's wiles, for he is already vanquished, and all that now remains is the ultimate regeneration, the coming of the holy Jerusalem to a new earth, to demonstrate the truth of God among men.

CHAPTER VI
THE CHURCH IN HISTORY AND THE HOLY JERUSALEM

We have already said that Christ is the central theme of the Apocalypse. A certain diffidence makes one hesitate to repeat the same assertion as regards the Church, yet, in reality, there is no distinction; the two mysteries are fundamentally identical both in their divine origin and in their implications. The idea of the Church runs right through the book, from the letters at the very beginning, where it figures in such a human, appealing way, taken up with so many local problems, big and little, to its final emergence in the splendour of the holy Jerusalem, on which all the visions irresistibly converge. Between these two extremities we have the major symbols of the Temple, the woman, the two witnesses, and so on, a rapid survey of which will be the object of this chapter.

The Church is a theme on which the Christian commentator cannot embark without a certain awe. How can he express the superabundance of splendour the text suggests, conscious that his impotence springs less from the magnificence of the subject than from his own lack of limpid language with which to describe it? He cannot help being overcome by a kind of religious reserve, I almost said prudishness, before this mystery of the Church as it is presented in the Apocalypse, so completely is it wrapped up in the intimacy and purity of God's own mystery. Let it suffice to say that in this chapter, more than in any other, his chief aim is to persuade the reader to go to the text direct, so that he may read and re-read its sacred message for himself.

In order that the teachings on the Church that came from

137

Patmos may yield their full value, it is essential to approach them in a spirit no different from that of the primitive communities to whom they were first given. For the modern Christian this doubtless involves a certain amount of adjustment. A too individualistic conception of Christianity will certainly prevent a proper appreciation of the balance and the import of St John's doctrine. Let us briefly recall the most elementary facts.

When proceeding from the documents of the Old Testament to the New, as we have said in a previous chapter, one cannot help being struck by the intensely personal character of the latter, in contrast to the primarily collective concern of the Jewish religion. The two messages are poles apart. We have on the one hand the Mosaic code, the institutional charter of a religious and political group; and on the other the Beatitudes—an appeal to every man of good will irrespective of race, nation or class. No other religion exalts human personality as Christianity does, either by the moral stature it demands of the individual, or the responsibilities it places upon him. We have already said this, and we shall return to it.

Nevertheless, it would be unjustifiable to deduce from this an individualistic conception of Christian life, permitting secret, internal communication with God and excluding the intervention of any other element either human or religious. To adopt this attitude would be to overlook the fundamental law of faith, which is brotherly love, as inseparable from Christianity as love of God. Faith, like love, makes the soul, in its innermost intimacy, dependent upon the community as a whole, both visible and invisible; and this community is the Church. From the Church and its apostolic hierarchy Christians receive the truth and the sacraments of the faith, which are the keystones of the structure on which the hierarchy is raised. Failing these, the moral life of Christians cannot receive the grace it needs, nor can their spirit comprehend the objects to which it adheres. Brotherly love is inextricably interwoven with all the souls the Church invisibly embraces, for it has its roots in the mystery of unity, of which Christ is the head and the Holy Ghost the soul.

Christianity, which opens up limitless prospects of intimacy between the soul and the Father in heaven, nevertheless makes nonsense of any sort of 'tête-a-tête' with God. Even if he were to hide himself in the depths of a desert, the Christian's only contact with God would still be through the Church. The more a Christian develops and asserts his personal religious life, the more he realises his radical dependence upon this mystery of the Church.

That at least is what the New Testament teaches. From the Synoptics and their doctrine of the kingdom of God to St John and his theology emphasising the unity founded on the Holy Ghost; through St Paul and his synthesis of the Mystical Body and St Peter looking upon the faithful as 'a chosen race, a holy people of sacerdotal royalty', the teaching never deviates. And that is how the earliest generations of Christians understood it. The idea of an isolated Christian simply had no meaning for them. In their own theoretical and practical conception of life, as well as the impression they made on others, they never sealed themselves off in separate cliques as the community of the faithful is so often inclined to do nowadays. Least of all, from the local community; we need only recall what is said of those in Jersusalem (Acts 2, 42, ff.; 4, 32, ff.); or again, the very detailed descriptions of the Pauline communities—but it applied to the whole of the Church, which was the constant care of each individual community, as the exchanges of letters, the collections for the poor in Jerusalem, the visits of apostolic personages and others inspired by the Holy Ghost, and so on, amply prove. The Christianity of these early Christians, living in the secret intensity of their converted souls, was also a state of great solidarity with one another, united by that charity which was the sign of their membership of the 'ecclesia fratrum', by their submissiveness to the teachings of the apostles and their successors, by their participation in the Holy Eucharist, and by the living faith of the Mystical Body of Christ. This was true at all times, but it came out still more emphatically when any misfortune overtook an individual or a community. When St Peter was thrown into prison, all the brethren in Jerusalem joined in prayer; when

famine reigned in Palestine, all the Churches of the Mediterranean held collections to provide food for the hungry; when
persecution broke out, the links that bound the Churches
to one another were strengthened. The Church came first,
and the fate of each individual could not be separated from
its own.

It was like this during the Domitian persecutions, if we
may judge by the Apocalypse. In the whole of the New
Testament there is scarcely a descriptive book that gives us a
more vivid picture of the times. It sheds a most penetrating
light on Christian life in the first century. The directives sent
to the persecuted Churches stress the responsibility of each
one of them as urgently as possible, at the same time
demonstrating with remarkable clarity the role each Christian
vocation plays in the collective mystery of the holy Jerusalem.
This was its real purpose. The preceding chapters have tried
to analyse the other main teachings of the inspired author,
following him step by step as he developed his undertaking.

The letters at the very beginning bring us face to face with
the visible Church, touching up the picture by means of
concrete realities, so concrete, in fact, that in the absence
of corroborating historical evidence to substantiate them,
the exact meaning of some of the references nowadays
escapes us. What we can follow is sufficient to bring us into
very close contact with the early Christian communities of
Asia Minor, their difficulties, their weaknesses, their
generosity and also their tough tenacity. Here was Christianity of a strongly communal type. We can even detect the
beginnings of the hierarchy's organisation. As to whether
the mention of the angels of the Churches (1, 20) might seem
at first to indicate actual celestial beings, as our Lord
governed each community through the agency of a particular
angel (which indeed would be in conformity with the
general laws of Jewish angelology; cf. 2, 1; 3, 1, etc.),
my own view is that the 'angel' to whom each letter is
addressed (2, 1, 8, 12, etc.) alludes allegorically to its bishop.
In any case it is difficult to deny that this or that characteristic
in the letters applies to the local authority and the way in

which that authority is at the moment being exercised within the community (cf. 2, 14, 20, etc.). The reproach levelled at Ephesus (2,5), above all if we line up this mention of the 'Candlestick' with the interpretation we give of the two candlesticks as representing the two witnesses, leaves little doubt that this refers to the bishop, and the relative pre-eminence which had perhaps already begun to give him the presiding chair over the neighbouring bishoprics. All this remains in doubt because it touches too nearly concrete realities on which history has spared us no information. There is, on the other hand, not the slightest doubt that apostolic personages were the actual founders of this ecclesiastical organisation. This is confirmed even by the description of the holy Jerusalem (21, 14), while the twelve stars which crown the woman of Chapter twelve (12, 1) may also be a further corroboration of it. The Church of Ephesus had greatly distinguished itself by unmasking the false apostles who had tried to usurp divine authority over the faithful (2, 2). We also get an insight into these Christian assemblies, and the readings which took place there (the book which came from Patmos was to be publicly read in this way—see 1, 3), as of the excommunications which were pronounced (2, 6) or which should have been pronounced, if the authorities had been less weak and hesitant (2, 14, 15, 20, etc.). These few instances will suffice to convince the reader that the Church to which St John addressed his message was not a purely spiritual organisation, vague and invisible, but a human association already powerfully organised and provided with its own hierarchy.

All the more striking, therefore, is the responsibility which the message lays on each individual Christian. If the letters are differentiated by the particulars they give us concerning each separate Church, they all agree in addressing the same exhortations to the members, and especially in applying to the faithful the term 'overcomer' (see the ending to each of the letters). 'To him that overcometh I will give . . .' This is repeated seven times, and an eighth reference to it, at the end of the book, shows that St John regarded this as the proper title for a Christian, in the Church, and in history.

With what weapons would the Christian achieve this overcoming, which was also that of his Church? We have already had occasion to point out that they certainly could not be political weapons (13, 9-10). The Church of the Apocalypse, no less than that of St Paul's writings, could not mix itself up in any political cause whatsoever. Its children certainly aspired to regal status in this world; but it was the royalty of priesthood and could not be separated from their sacerdotal office. St Peter already refers to the faithful as having chosen 'a kingly priesthood' (I Pet. 2, 9). St John repeats in the same sense 'that Christ hath made us a kingdom and priests to God and his Father' (1, 6; 5, 10). This royalty and this holiness must be understood as attaching to the reign of the saints on earth, and it is in this religious, and not political, light that the victory, or overcoming, of Christians in this world must be regarded.

The opening of each letter indicates the fervour, or the relaxation of fervour, of the respective communities in grasping their weapons of victory. The most powerful terms in the moral vocabulary of primitive Christians appear in these passages. Faith (2, 13, 19, etc.) and brotherly love (2, 4, 19, etc.) predominate, as they should. But, dependent, we may be sure, on this faith and charity, we also find service (2, 19), unremitting zeal (2, 2, 3, etc.), and above all, strong, confident patience (2, 2, 3, 19; 3, 10, etc.) which must remain constant in the midst of tribulations (2, 9, 10, etc.) of trials (3, 10) and of poverty (2, 9). Each of these terms could be accompanied by a long commentary, in which the perfect resemblance of Christianity as St John taught it, to the Christian life as outlined by St Paul, could be clearly brought out. Briefly, it is only by adhering strictly to this Christian programme, and by a true repentance, if he has fallen short of it, that a Christian may merit the title of overcomer, which shall be his, even as it is that of Christ himself; but he must be prepared to defend that title through trial and persecution, and, if necessary, at the cost of his earthly life.

This overcoming is a personal victory, as personal as was that of our Lord Jesus Christ. The victory of immortality, as typified by the Tree of Life (2, 7; cf. 22, 2, 14, 19; Gen. 2, 9; 3, 22, 24); victory over hell, indicated by the expression of the second death (2, 11; cf. 20, 14; 21, 8); victory of inclusion in the book of Life of the Lamb (3, 5; cf. 13, 8; 17, 8; 20, 12, 15; 21, 27; Ex. 32, 32 ff.; Ps. 69, 29; Dan. 2, 1) victory of the singing of Moses's canticle and that of the Lamb, to the glory of God the Liberator (15, 2 ff.). But above all that victory which will entitle the overcomer to receive the incommunicable name which is known to him alone (2, 7)—which is just as incommunicable as is the word of God (19, 2), as incommunicable as is that even of Jahveh (Wis. 14, 21). The name 'which the mouth of Jahveh shall choose' will be revealed to each individual clearly when the last judgement has established his victory (symbolised by the white stone of 14, 21: of Acts, 26, 10) and from that point onwards hidden manna will sustain him, personally, just as in the desert manna nourished the chosen people (Ps. 78, 24). All these texts, so full of meaning, serve the same purpose of emphasising the Christian's responsibilities, but also the resources at his command, and the ultimate triumph which is the reward of a truly Christian life. No 'spirituality', in the modern sense, is more completely 'personal' than that of the Apocalypse.

But there is still more in it. This does not concern only the salvation and victory of the individual. It concerns the whole edifice of the Church, of the holy Jerusalem. So we can see how the prospect opens out. It takes in triumph over the nations which temporarily persecute, and which they will one day rule with a rod of iron even as the conquering Lamb does (2, 26). It takes in the vision of God's Temple, which will rise with Christian overcomers as its pillars; and of that heavenly Jerusalem whose new name (3, 12) they will share; it takes in finally prospects of the Last Judgement, when, seated on the same throne with God and the Lamb, the saints will judge the world, as St Paul already said they would (3, 21; cf. Matt. 19, 28; I Cor. 6, 2). Actually each individual Christian felt himself involved, by the same exhortations which revealed to him his personal and incommunicable vocation, in a boundless mystery, which was none other than the mystery of the Church. Subsequent visions progressively enlarged the dimensions of that mystery, without in any way lessening the part each personal destiny played in the infinite impersonal aggregate. Finally the divine architecture of the celestial Jerusalem became manifest in all its harmonious proportions, built up out of myriads of precious stones, each separate stone retaining its own inimitable identity and proving indispensable to the glory of the whole.

The Temple is the first of the great Apocalyptic images used to symbolise the Church. Of course St John was not the first to make use of that symbol. It already occurs in St Paul (e.g., I Cor. 3, 16; II Cor. 6, 16; Eph. 2, 21, etc.). The Apocalypse, however, develops it with some important additions. The preliminary sketch which he gives in the letter to the Philadelphians (3, 12) is elaborated with more explicit touches in Chapter eleven, in the section which serves as a prelude, as already shown, to the great visions of the battle between the Church and Satan. This we must now pause to consider.

Notice first of all how the passage is introduced. After the description, in Chapters eight and nine, of the scourges released by the seven trumpets, and in which the infernal powers reveal themselves, the little book suddenly appears. This gives St John his cue to introduce more detailed prophecies. They are the object of the second part of his message, and concern the 'many nations and peoples and tongues and kings' (10, 11). The little book was 'sweet to the mouth' of John (10, 10) because, as in Ezechiel (Ez. 2, 8; 3, 1-3) it is pleasant to know, and to be able to explain, human history. But the same book causes acute discomfort, because it fills the soul with 'bitterness and indignation' (Ez. 3, 14) 'against the nations, people, tongues and kings' (10, 10). Just vengeance will be taken on 'the inhabitants of the earth', after they have been duly segregated from those who are the servants of God. Chapter eleven occupies itself mainly with the details of this segregation. The text is divided up into four parts and offers practically no difficulty.

In order to sum up the first teachings on the mystery of the Church in history, brief comments on these, taking one at a time, will suffice.

1. The Temple and its two parts (11, 1-2).
And there was given me a reed like unto a rod.
And it was said to me:
Arise and measure the temple of God
And the altar,
And them that adore therein.
And the court which is without the temple,
Cast out and measure it not;
Because it is given unto the gentiles.
And the holy city they shall tread underfoot two and forty months.

The general inspiration for this vision was no doubt derived from the prophet Zacharias (2, 5 ff.) when he saw Jerusalem being measured after its final and glorious rebuilding. Zacharias himself depended for this picture on Ezechiel, who also made use of a reed in measuring the ideal temple (Ez. 10, 41 ff.). In Enoch this passage occurs: 'And the angel who walked with me said: These (the angels) carry to the just the measure of the just, so that they may lean upon the Lord of spirits for ages of ages. The elect began to live with the elect, and the measures are those that shall be given to the faith, and those that shall affirm justice'.[1] It was a traditional prophetic scheme to establish 'measures'. According to this scheme, the measure determines who shall be protected against enemy attack or the vengeance of Jahveh. Here, as we have seen, St John, before going on to prophesy the avenging justice of God, had to show the inside and outside of the temple, that is to say, the Church; only the exterior could serve as a stage for the chastisements which the divine wrath inexorably pronounced on the powers of evil. Those inside, where the altar stands, and who worship the true God, are beyond the reach of the infernal powers, and can therefore preserve their tranquillity.

We should note that the reed which serves as the unit of measurement is said to be 'like unto a rod' (11, 1). When John, in the grand finale, sees the holy Jerusalem, the angel who measures it uses a golden rod (21, 5), that is to say, a

[1] 61, 3 ff. Trans. Fr Martin, op. cit. p. 126, 70, 3; pp. 158-159.

perfect and glorified unit of measurement. We are therefore warned that we are at present concerned only with the Church on earth, with the spiritual temple constituted by Christians (cf. St Paul) and which still contains the sacrificial altar of those who worship there (11, 1).

Outside, the earthly temple does not need to be measured, that is to say, to be protected against enemy attack. The courtyard belongs to the temple; in fact, the whole town is sacred (11, 2); but provisionally, for forty-two months all that part is abandoned to the gentiles. They 'crowd' there, says St John precisely, and in this he seems to echo the words of our Lord as reported in St Luke (21, 13 ff.).

'Jerusalem shall be crowded with gentiles
Until the time of the gentiles shall be fulfilled.'

      2. The ministry of the two witnesses (11, 3-6).

And I will give unto my two witnesses:
And they shall prophesy, a thousand two hundred and sixty days,
Clothed in sackcloth.
These are two olive trees
And two candlesticks
That stand before the Lord of the earth;
And if any man will hurt them,
Fire shall come out of their mouths
And shall devour their enemies.
And if any man will hurt them,
In this manner must he be slain.
These have power to shut heaven,
That it rain not in the days of their prophecy;
And they have power over waters,
To turn them into blood
And to strike the world with all plagues
As often as they will.

These two witnesses are also derived from Zacharias (cap. 4) and Zacharias himself borrowed from the first book of Ezra (caps. 5 and 6) which deals with the construction of the Temple after the return of the Israelites from captivity. These two witnesses were Zorobabel, Prince of Juda, and the priest Josue or Jesus, son of Josedec. They therefore represent the religious and political forces of the Israelite State, two quite distinct functions, and each in his own way led the chosen people to victory, 'not by an army, nor by might, but by my spirit, said the Lord of hosts' (Zach. 4, 6).

This particular passage in the prophet's inspired record goes beyond the immediate contingency and bears upon the whole messianic future.[1] St John takes up the same theme but applies it to the Christian Church.

This is very important because, if the prophecy applies to the whole future of the Church the truth already formulated by Zacharias in messianic times, it sanctions for all time this distinction between the two powers, political and religious, in accordance with the truth laid down since the Israelites' return from captivity. The Messiah issues from the people of God, that is to say, the Church, and both powers, without mixing their separate functions, must support one another in giving their testimony on earth before the Lord. There must be a Christian sacerdotal office; but there must also be a body of worshippers, a laity, as we call it. And from both ranks will arise the leaders of the new Israel, and these leaders, whether they be bishops and priests or Christian princes and holders of temporal power, must likewise co-operate in bearing witness to Christ. The whole Church rests on the testimony of both. This passage rules out any theocratic interpretation of the triumphs of the gospel prophesied by the Apocalypse.

Certainly the testimony of the two witnesses for a thousand two hundred and sixty days—the period during which the gentiles enjoy the freedom of the Temple precincts —will stir up the hostility of the 'inhabitants of the earth'. They will render it in contrition, amid trials, as symbolised by the sackcloth and ashes (11, 3). But the testimony will be none the less effective, and will be accompanied, if need be, by signs and wonders comparable with those Elias called forth (I Kings, 17, 1 ff., resumed in James 5, 17-18): 'Thus saith the Lord of hosts: Because you have spoken the word, behold I will make my words in thy mouth as fire and this people as wood; and it shall devour them' (Jer. 5, 14). The same theme is taken up again and again by our book; nothing can deter the ultimate triumph of truth. We will reserve for our last chapter the discussion of when and how this final victory will be accomplished.

[1] Cf. M. J. Lagrange 'Le Judaisme' . . . pp. 281-282.

3. The martyrdom of the two witnesses (11, 7-10).

And when they shall have finished their testimony,
The beast that ascendeth out of the abyss
Shall make war against them and shall overcome them and kill them.
And their bodies shall lie in the streets of the great city
Which is called spiritually Sodom and Egypt:
Where their Lord also was crucified.
And they of the tribes and people and tongues and nations
Shall see their bodies for three days and a half:
And they shall not suffer their bodies to be laid in sepulchres.
And they that dwell upon the earth shall rejoice over them and
make merry:
And shall send gifts one to another,
Because these two prophets tormented them that dwelt upon
the earth.

This text is so admirably clear that it makes any comment
superfluous. 'When they shall have finished their testimony'
—and not before! We have already seen that their invincibility
is not in question. If God permits the Beast to kill a witness of
the gospel, it is because his task has been accomplished. His
very martyrdom is the supreme testimony, and, throughout
all history, makes quite certain that the truth of the gospel
will be passed on. The continuation of the text makes this
quite clear.

For the moment, the Beast and his agents may appear to
triumph. He triumphs in this Sodom of pleasure and
corruption, in this Egypt of servitude, where our Saviour
also was crucified and rendered the supreme and effective
testimony. It is a satanic triumph. Great rejoicing over the
debris of a Church that appears to be destroyed; its destruction seems to be irreparable. The spoils are exhibited in public
places; shrines are converted into museums of anti-religious
art, and the inhabitants of the earth, believing that they have
at last shaken off the mentors whose attentions had so
troubled them, rejoice in their freedom and congratulate one
another. But the triumph is short-lived; three and a half days
after their death, behold, the witnesses rise again, more alive
than ever, and once again take up the cause of evangelical
truth.

4. Resurrection of the two witnesses (11, 11-13).

And after three days and a half,
The spirit of life from God entered into them.

And they stood upon their feet:
And great fear fell upon them that saw them.
And they heard a great voice from heaven,
Saying to them: Come up hither
And they went up to heaven in a cloud:
And their enemies saw them.
And at that hour there was made a great earthquake:
And the tenth part of the city fell.
And there were slain in the earthquake, names of men, seven
thousand;
And the rest were cast into a fear and gave glory to the God
of heaven.

Here we have again, in the form of a vision, the full eschatological prophecy. The triumph of the two witnesses, which is constantly repeated throughout history (11, 11). Then, at last, those who have not been caught up in the punishment reserved for the 'inhabitants of the earth', fall down in homage to the God of heaven (11, 13). This clearly shows that the necessary punishments inherent in God's justice will not overtake those who are converted by the testimony of the two witnesses—testimony which is given generation after generation, as new witnesses appear. Experience in apostolic ministry has often verified this.

And when the witnesses of the gospel arrive at their supreme triumph, the seventh trumpet will sound; then the ultimate kingship of God and his Christ will finally be manifest to the world, for all ages of ages, amid the acclamations of all creation (11, 15-18).

This is the first great Apocalyptic vision of the Church. Its object is to delineate the condition of the Church here on earth for those who are inside it, and to show them clearly that they are inviolable to any attack from the outside. Christians inside the Church can worship God in all security. Whatever disturbances may rage outside, they need have no fear, for no enemy has the power to damage the edifice (cf. Matt. 16, 18). From this impregnable fortress new witnesses of God will incessantly issue, giving their testimony; and even if they may temporarily appear to succumb to the general hostility outside, their strength is in reality irresistible. Sooner or later they will triumph even over the Beast and his persecutions, and succeed in bringing at least some of the 'inhabitants of the earth' to pay homage to the glory of God.

Just as the mention of the seventh seal (8, 1) indicates that the preceding pericopes have summed up the main factors of history, mention of the seventh trumpet, in conjunction with the eschatological pericope that follows, is an indication that the preceding precepts have given an all-over insight into the life of the Church in history. Turning again to the 'little book' introduced in Chapter ten, we realise that Chapter eleven gives a cursory glimpse of its contents. Consequently the chapters which follow, in accordance with the general policy of the book, approach the matter from a new and more analytical angle, and proceed to deal in detail with the whole historical life of the Church.

It is then that the author, rising to fresh heights of invention, introduces a new figure, that of the woman. Not, it should be remarked, without an easy link-up (mention of a Temple which, in contrast to the preceding one, is situated in Heaven: 11, 19), which indicates that he is still occupied with the same subject, that is to say, the Church. After having considered it in a global manner, by its evolution in history till the end of time, he penetrates more deeply into its mystery by showing its heavenly connection. Thus it is necessary first of all to single out the elements of the chapter which concern the woman, just as we did before with the teachings concerning the Dragon.

And a great sign appeared in heaven:
A Woman clothed with the sun,
And the moon under her feet,
And on her head a crown of stars.

And being with child, she cried
Travailing in birth,
And was in pain to be delivered . . .

And the Dragon stood before the Woman
That was ready to be delivered,
That when she might be delivered,
He might devour her son.

And she brought forth a man child,
Who was to rule all nations with a rod of iron,
And her son was taken up to God
And to his throne.

And the Woman fled into the wilderness,
Where she had a place prepared by God;
That there they should feed her
A thousand two hundred and sixty days . . .

And when the Dragon saw
That he was cast on to the earth,
He persecuted the Woman
That had brought forth the man child
And there were given unto the Woman
Two wings of a great eagle,
That she might fly into the desert
Unto her place,
Where she is nourished for a time
And times and half a time
From the face of the serpent.

And the serpent cast out of its mouth,
After the Woman,
Water, as it were a river,
That he might cause her to be carried away by the river.

And the earth helped the Woman,
And the earth opened her mouth and swallowed up the river,
Which the dragon sent out of his mouth,

And the Dragon was angry against the Woman,
And went to make war with the rest of her seed
Who keep the commandments of God
And have the testimony of Jesus Christ (12, 1 ff.).

Hence with consummate skill we are brought back to the most mysterious realities of heaven even at the heart of the Domitian persecutions; for the 'rest of her seed' obviously referred to the victims of that persecution, the Christians who were keeping the commandments of God, and, as John himself did in prison on Patmos (1, 2a) had 'the testimony of Jesus Christ'. Even if we reject the idea that the significance extends to the personal and eternal Word of God, the fact remains that the vision is rooted in the mystery of the Church, and feels its way into the most profound spiritual depths of God's own mystery. Before the prophet of Patmos could contemplate the glorious figure of the woman in heaven, it was necessary that the Ark of God's covenant with man should appear to him, and this Ark itself was in the most secret inner Temple of God in heaven (11, 19). Now we know that, in the heavenly Jerusalem, God himself and his inseparable Lamb are in fact this Temple (21, 22). Dropping all imagery, the Church, as presented here, is of spiritual inception and appears as a thing of light, drawing its inherent illumination from the very depths of God himself (11, 19-21, 1).

The Church is also a pregnant reality (12, 1). Even if we reject the idea of a supernatural conception here, we cannot deny that all the indications force us to see the Church as depicted here in its widest possible ramifications. Its maternity takes in Jesus Christ himself, and the whole multitude of the Elect from the beginning to the end of time. The boundless mystery of creation in the throes and tortures of an endless delivery (12, 2) forecasts the heaven of the Elect and in the very centre of this the Word of God himself has come to take his place. 'For we know that every creature groaneth and travaileth in pain, even till now; and not only it but ourselves also, waiting for the adoption,' says St Paul (Rom. 8, 27 ff.).

In the days of the captivity the prophets already sensed this boundless maternity of the holy Jerusalem:

Before she was in labour she brought forth:
Before her time came to be delivered.
She brought forth a male child—
Who hath ever heard such a thing?
And who hath seen the like of this?
Shall the earth bring forth in one day?
Or shall a nation be brought forth at once
Because Sion hath been in labour and hath
Brought forth her children?
Shall not I that make others to bring forth children
Myself bring forth? Saith the Lord.
Shall I, that give generation to others, be barren? Saith the
  Lord thy God.
Rejoice with Jerusalem and be glad with her,
  All you that love her;
Rejoice for joy with her, all you that mourn for her;
That you may suck and be filled with the breasts of her
  consolations,
That you may milk out and flow with delights
From the abundance of her glory (Isaias 66, 7-11).

Micheas the prophet uses the same imagery and even

emphasises it (Mic. 4, 9-10). The same association of pain and delivery, the same joy of an innumerable progeny, starting with the first, who is a male child (who was to rule the nations with a rod of iron', 12, 5; cf. Is. 66, 7) and the numberless multitude of 'the rest of her seed' (12, 17; cf. Is. 66, 8).

We have no difficulty in identifying the first-born with the Church; if there should be any doubt, St John removes it by his description of the new Ascension and Apotheosis of our Lord in Chapter five.

'And her Son was taken up to God
And to his throne . . . ' (12, 5).

Christians know very well that the whole immense aspiration of creation culminates in this return of the glorious, incarnated Word of God. The boundless motherhood of the Church actually commences with the bringing forth of multitudes of the elect who, by and in Jesus Christ, attain adoption as perfect sons of God.

It is precisely for this reason that the Dragon, in heaven and on earth, is the deadly enemy of the woman, always lying in wait so that he may 'devour the son that she will bring forth' (12, 4). But, like her first-born, she is safely beyond his reach; and this again forces us to recognise her as a completely divine mystery. She is beyond the reach of his power in heaven, whence he has been expelled by the archangel Michael (12, 7-8). She is also beyond his reach on earth. This has already been explained in the vision of the Temple. The precincts of the Temple are given over to the Beast and the auxiliaries of Satan; but they cannot penetrate the inner sanctuary of the Holy Place. Here the same teaching is repeated, but on the threshold of a mighty vision of the Church which is heavenly before belonging to this earth. When the woman has brought forth her child, she escapes to the desert, to the most inaccessible place in the world where God has a place ready prepared for her, and where she will be safe from pursuit by the Dragon (12, 6). The two wings of the great eagle (an Old Testament symbol for Jahveh's aid; see Deuter. 32, 11) are always at her disposal, not only to protect her in this evil world as the shadow of an eagle protects its young in the nest, but also so that she may escape whenever she pleases to that desert of divine preparation where God himself nourishes her during the period of her trial.

And the Dragon knows very well that the Church in its profound mystery will escape him! He becomes infuriated. From his infernal mouth torrents of blasphemy, of lies and deception pour forth. In these, despite all obstacles, he attempts to engulf her; but the earth swallows up the diabolical torrent, and the Church imperturbably continues on her way towards God (12, 15-16).

It is then that he gives up his attempts for the time being to reach the woman or her first-born. Instead, he turns his attention to the rest of her children, that is to say, to faithful Christians who 'keep the commandments of God and have the testimony of Jesus' (12, 17) and who are the children of the Church. These he tries to lead astray, using the two Beasts as his agents (12, 18-13, 1 ff.). In the previous chapter the powers of illusion, blasphemy and misery they symbolise has been shown.

Fundamentally, all this is simple, and tragically true. In studying the history of the last twenty centuries, no historian can fail to have been struck by the contrast between the Church on the one hand, with its roots hidden deep in the divine mystery, from which its perennial fecundity, and also its holiness, are derived, and on the other hand, the frailty of mankind forming 'the rest of her seed', who, alas! are only too easily accessible to the wiles and blasphemies so traitorously suggested to them in the world by Satan and his helpers. A contrast which plainly rests on individual independence, on freedom of will. One might be tempted at times to regret this independence, and to wish, at each epoch and for each individual, that the supertemporal mystery of the Church would more clearly demonstrate the spiritual protection and security of which it is assured. In reality, if one examines it more closely, the problem is one which only concerns those who envisage the Christian life in the individualistic manner denounced at the commencement of this chapter. Truly, the isolated Christian is not invincible in this combat with evil. But it is equally true that the promise, that these evil powers should not prevail, was not made to isolated Christians. The Church alone received this promise, in the person of its head, St Peter (Matt. 16, 18) or in the name of the whole apostolic college (Joh. 16, 23). The message of Patmos, at the time of Domitian, reiterated this promise, and revealed its future realisation. Christians in every period of history will be strong and victorious, and inaccessible to the blandishments of the evil one, but only in so far as they are members of the body, and are willing to listen to the message of the Church. On the other hand, it is only by its members, and only in so far as they consent to act as its delegates and in accordance with the teachings of the Church, that the world can benefit, and the powers of evil suffer defeat. One can go so far as to say that the whole civilising influence of the Church depends entirely on the individual Christian's sense of responsibility, as expressed in his personal life as a member of the Church. The general history of Christianity, no less than the hagiograph itself, bears witness to this sense of responsibility. Those supremely successful Christians who have become saints all showed in their own lives, under varying forms, the utmost solicitude for the Church and for the Christian community. One might even go so far as to demonstrate that there is a direct connection between that solicitude and the victories scored by the Church over the powers of evil at different periods— in other words, between the individual Catholic's conception of Christian life, and the civilising influence of the Church. This close relationship has existed from the earliest community in Jerusalem, right down to the small Catholic villages in outlying missionary stations—taking in the Pauline Churches, the meetings in the catacombs, the age of the great Eastern Councils, the archbishoprics and monasteries of the early middle ages, the great epoch of Mediaeval development and the corporate religious movements which produced successive realisations of monastic ideals. On the other hand, it can be equally proved that religious individualism and the decrease in the sense of unity as incorporated in the Church, after having been tentatively started in the fourteenth and fifteenth centuries, led the way in the sixteenth to the great rift, and were the cause of a profound and incontestable set-back to Christian civilisation in the centuries that followed. It is the Church that has endowed humanity with the healing heritage promised by Jesus Christ. It is to the Church that the promise of victory over the spiritual powers of evil has been given. If Christians withdraw from the Church, if they choose to live, as it were, outside, there is always the wilderness as a place of retreat, a place where the wings of the great eagle are ready to protect her, and where she will be quite secure from the mortal blows which strike down the two faithful witnesses who are loyal enough to testify, and who, in fact, are forever being re-born out of her endless productivity throughout the ages; but she can do nothing for those who, deliberately depriving themselves of the invincibility which she enjoys, are no longer equipped in their own persons to resist the attacks of the Beasts and the Dragon.

From all this we can see that the Christian's first duty is to adhere firmly to the faith and to brotherly love, however hidden his private moral life may be from the eyes of his neighbours. Only by this individual integrity can the community as a whole triumph over the Dragon. Only in this way can the individual Christian emerge victorious, in accordance with the letters to the Churches. The more the spiritual personality of Christians, in desire and in viewpoint, identifies itself with the Church, and by this I mean the whole Church in accordance with the terrestrial and celestial dimensions outlined in the Apocalypse, the more they themselves will share in the enlightenment, the fruitfulness, the invincibility which St John perceived in that mystery. It becomes more and more clear that there is no way except through the Church of Jesus Christ to gain ascendancy over the powers of illusion and blasphemy which Satan exerts over the world, and will continue to exert until his final defeat renders him powerless.

And now the splendour and magnitude of the Church's mystery begins to dawn upon us. It is at once earthly and celestial. Its heavenly origin, so close to God himself, makes it, like Christ, a Mystery of Light, and, like him, invulnerable against the attacks of the enemy. It is earthly by reason of the trials and tribulations it has to undergo, and which are also inherent in the lives of the faithful because of the struggle they must perpetually wage against the snares of the Dragon and the two Beasts—a struggle which they will eventually win through the steadfastness of the two witnesses who, whenever they meet their death, are instantly re-born. The Church is still seen as a collective mystery, as well as a personal one. Personal because it is by each and every believer that it wages its war against the powers of evil, an incessant struggle which must go on, even if it demands the supreme testimony. Collective because it is only within the unity of the Christian community that the individual believer is assured of effective protection against attacks from outside, and because it is this community which, century after century, produces the re-born witnesses through whom evangelical truth scores its victories over Satan. These lessons we have gathered from all that has gone before. Others, no less important, will reward our continued study.

Let us pause here and take a look at the course the book has taken so far. With the seven letters at the beginning we are already aware of the very real and concrete establishment of the Church towards the end of the first century. The vision of the Temple and the two witnesses widens the horizon and tells us something of the general position of the Church in history. But we are still on mundane ground. The vision of the woman 'in heaven' adds a new dimension and reveals the ties that bind the mystery of the Church to a sphere outside, and above, this world. It is only at this point that the author feels the ground is sufficiently prepared for the introduction of the great battle between the Church and the Dragon, which he graphically describes, since it is to become the central theme of the visions that follow.

Now this is the point at which another revelation occurs, which adds further details to those already given concerning the Church and the chosen people who constitute it.

And I beheld:
And lo a Lamb stood upon Mount Sion,
And with him a hundred and forty-four thousand,
Having his name and the name of his Father
Written on their foreheads . . . etc. (14, 1-5).

What is this multitude grouped round the Lamb? To answer this question we must endeavour through the context to visualise the scene. That will not appear to be very difficult. We have just been shown the earthly, historic combat between the Dragon and the Church. The scene which follows it therefore shows the whole world that the hour of God's judgement has at last arrived (14, 1-5). In fact the judgement of Babylon begins immediately; it is the first of a series which carries the historic progression to the end of time. We must therefore conclude that the intermediate vision presents those who will preside at the Dragon's defeat and the victory of the Church, on the one hand, and over the historic unfolding of divine judgements on the other— things, incidentally, which coincide in real life. Now it is precisely in the role of Judge that the Lamb has already appeared (14, 1). There can be no doubt about the significance of 'Mount Sion' if we refer back to the Prophet Joel who inspires the passage, in an eschatological text which forecasts the judgement of the nations (Joel 3, 3 ff.). The Lamb which appears here is definitely the same as the earlier Lamb of the book; but while there, the object was to show his absolute mastery of the facts of history and their unfolding, here he is shown in the exercise of that mastery, to pronounce sentence from which there is no appeal. 'Fear the Lord and give him honour, for the hour of his judgement is come' (14, 6-7).

Now the Lamb is not alone on Mount Sion. He has with him one hundred and forty-four thousand adherents 'having his name and the name of his Father written on their foreheads' (14, 1). Who are they, and where does the scene being enacted here take place? To my mind there is no doubt that this symbolic mount is neither in heaven nor on earth, using these terms in the manner we use when expressing earthly concepts. Just as the resurrected Christ controls human affairs from that mysterious heaven to which he has withdrawn himself from the sight of man since the Ascension, in the same way, and, like him, intervening in these affairs, there are multitudes of martyrs and saints who surround him on Mount Sion. This, it seems to me, is the constant teaching of the book. The saints actively share in the judgements of God. This appears from the breaking of the fifth seal (6, 9-11), from the first act of the vision of the seven trumpets, and from many other texts; subsequently we shall meet it again (for instance in 18, 20, where indeed the Lord appears only to pronounce the judgement of the saints). We are therefore led to accept the one thousand four hundred and forty-four accessories on their obvious description; they are exactly what they seem to be, co-partners with the Judge in the unfolding of divine judgements throughout history. From our point of view, they represent the immense multitude of those who, having kept the commandments of God and the testimony of Christ, have already been redeemed from among men for God and for the Lamb. Wherever he goes, they go also, to assist him in the office of Judge, and, in unity with him, preside over the evolution of human history. If the prophet places their number at one hundred and forty-four thousand, it is not because they are to be identified with the Judeo-Christians already mentioned in the vision of Chapter seven, but because, like the Judeo-Christians of that message, the figure given for them must be taken as merely a token of the numberless multitude of the Elect (14, 4). The limitation—quite relative, as we know—was logical in this vision. Consequently, when it becomes a question of the judgements of Christ and the saints in history, the countless total of the elect can be imagined in the same way. As a matter of fact, when the grand total of them are ultimately assembled, there will be no more history, and no more need for the saints to reign over it. Here then, we get only an inkling of the vast numbers who may assist the Christ-judge in his control of history.

As for the theme of the reign of the saints in general, here on earth, it should be recalled that this agrees in every respect with the eschatological tradition of the Jews. In that tradition it is invariably linked with the reign of the Messiah.

When St John treats history as the gradual unfolding of the judgement of Christ and the triumph of truth, he invariably links with these the judgement of the saints and their effective testimony (cf. 15, 2-4; 16, 5-7; 18, 20; 19, 14; for the Last Judgement, 20, 4). So far as John is concerned, the reign of the saints—like that of Christ—is an invisible reign, while that the prophets imagined and described was entirely mundane, exercised in full view of the living; therein lies the only difference between the old and the new viewpoint.

This theme, although to some extent borrowed from the earlier Jewish tradition, is none the less important as a teaching on the Church laid down for the guidance of the persecuted Christians. According to this teaching, the Church here on earth is a militant Church, and the faithful, in their loyalty and perseverance, are expected to give their testimony as fighters for truth. But they must also be fully aware that, through their testimony, it is the Church which, from generation to generation, scores her victories in the cause of God's truth. If they live in the Lord, their works cannot fail to agree with that blue-print (14, 13); and in their turn, united with the Lord, they are bound to follow him in all his ways, reigning invisibly in the heaven on earth (5, 10). 'Know ye not that the saints shall judge this world?' says St Paul (I Cor. 6, 2). St John enlarges on this teaching inherited from Israel. Describing the whole history of recent events as a judgement in constant progress of realisation, he shows the part the martyrs and the saints, in union with the resurrected Christ, have already played, and will inevitably continue to play in divine judgement through the ages. The values attached to such thoughts have become so strange to us that they may nowadays appear to be of little consequence; but we may well believe that they had a totally different effect upon men of the first century, whose minds were moulded in the school of the prophets. They were more sensitive than we are to reminders of saintly intervention, and the triumph of the saints over the nations was a very real conception stimulated by centuries of profound patriotic hope. Whatever our own reactions may be, an awareness of the religious tradition of the reign of the saints on earth seems indispensable to the proper appreciation of a problem which is perhaps the most debatable the Apocalypse raises —namely, that of the millennium. We shall return to this in the following chapter.

Right through history, therefore, the victory of Christ will be irresistibly extended by the Church—the Church in heaven and the Church on earth. On earth by the power and the steadfastness of its members' testimony, registering victory after victory over the Beasts, in the invisible heaven, however vehemently they may pursue their ceaseless attack. And the Last Judgement will consummate its triumph both in heaven and on earth. Then, 'like a book folded up' (6, 14), 'the first heaven and the first earth' (21, 1), will be gone and 'the new heaven and the new earth' (21, 1) will appear.

And I . . . saw the holy city, the new Jerusalem,
Coming down out of heaven from God,
Prepared as a bride adorned for her husband.
And I heard a great voice from the throne saying:
Behold the tabernacle of God is with men:
And he will dwell with them.
And they shall be his people:
And God himself with them shall be their God.
And God shall wipe away all tears from their eyes
And death shall be no more.
Nor mourning, nor crying, nor sorrow shall be any more:
For the former things are passed away.
And he that sat on the throne said:
'Behold I make all things new'. (21, 2-5.)

Youth and renewal of a universe of light and peace which will never end—a universe more blissfully perfect than the wildest dream of a poet or an imagination roused to religious ecstasy!

Sweet year of the eternal life to come:
Springtime interminable: wings of birds forever spread . . .
Irises . . . and gay parasols . . .
Children's cheerful parasols . . . Thursday laughter, never-ending . . .
Mid-day stillness . . .
A blissful peace that stretches
To the very pastures of heaven . . .

Drained of all evil.   Oh day of a golden day
Having no night within its soul.[1]

For the Christian, this is neither a question of poetic
imagination, nor is it a dream; it is simply an affirmation of
faith. The visible world as we know it will pass away; and
when humanity, which is its crowning expression, has
reached the fullness of the age of Christ, all creation will
also enter a perfect state, a state of complete renewal. It
would be vain to attempt to form any idea of this new state.
We only know that 'death shall be no more' (21, 4; cf. I Cor.,
15, 26) and that 'He who is seated on the throne' makes all
things new in this ultimate creation (21, 5).

In this new creation the perfect alliance between God and
man will come to pass, as Jeremias predicted, and as, indeed,
the coming of Jesus already proved, by bringing to birth
the Church, here on earth. God was made flesh and dwelt
among men; but this time his coming will be in the blazing
light of inseverable co-existence. They will be his people and
he will be their God. They will find themselves so close to
him, so much a part of his own Mystery that he will be, in a
sort of way, no longer alone, but 'God with them' (21, 3;
cf. Jer. 31, 33; Hebr. 8, 8-12). Here we have the promise of
the ineffable bliss this new and eternal alliance with God will
confer on every faithful witness. 'He that shall overcome . . .
I will be his God: and he shall be my son' (21, 7). For every
man who by faith shall have entered into the fellowship of
his Son, Jesus Christ our Lord (I Cor. 1, 9) there shall be
the fullness of adoption, the inexpressible intimacy of the
martyrs with God who 'wipes away all tears from their eyes'
(21, 4; cf. 7, 15-17), the soul-satisfying light which radiates
from God's servants, leaving his imprint on their foreheads
(22, 5)—in short, the triumph of the saints towards which all
history is converging, and which will inaugurate a reign of
divine light, the reign of God and of the Lamb (21, 23; 22, 5)
for all ages of ages. This is the message of Patmos; this is the
future it holds out to Christians as an attainable hope, no
matter what their present sufferings and persecutions may be.

[1]Francis Jammes, Clairieres dans le Ciel ('En Dieu' 1906) Paris 1918.

And in looking at it from a purely personal point of view, as affecting the individual destiny, we have as yet said nothing about the great mystery of the New Jerusalem, in which the mystery of the Church will be consummated—this, which is above all a mystery of linking-up, of synthesis, of unity. In order to give an idea of this great mystery, the prophet made use of many symbols which he scarcely troubled to render coherent. Yet on a doctrinal plane all his teachings are in complete and admirable agreement.

'The new Jerusalem, coming down out of heaven from God,

Prepared as a bride adorned for her husband' (21, 2).

Towering over all else is this mystery of the marriage of the Lamb (19, 9). To approach this delicate subject without symbolism is impossible; but if we may use language a little less dazzling than that which the prophet employs, it suffices to say that all creation is a gift which God wished to give his well-beloved Son. 'Ask of me', as the Psalm says, 'and I will give thee the gentiles for thy inheritance, and the utmost parts of the earth for thy possession' (Ps. 2, 8). The language may vary, but it is always the same gift that God makes to Christ, in text after text. St Paul, in his epistles to the Colossians and the Ephesians, for example, expresses the same central doctrine of Christianity—the absolute primacy of Christ in creation. His from the very principle of his Incarnation, it will be at last fully manifest in all the splendour of its perfection at his Second Coming. The Church itself, in its profound mystery, is nothing but the sum-total of creation offering itself to Christ, and, through Christ, to God, in the perfect alliance. The end of time will be the ultimate total of this offering and in this offering the marriage of the Lamb will be consummated. Then the kingdom of God will become an established fact, and, as Jesus has said, it is like unto 'a king who made a marriage for his son' (Matt. 22, 2 ff.). 'Blessed are they,' says the prophet, 'that are called to the marriage supper of the Lamb.' And this blessing, according to the Sermon on the Mount, can commence here on earth, because of the hope on which it is based, and because in this hope there is no deception.

The Bride which God gives to his Son is 'prepared as a bride adorned for her husband' (21, 2). Another passage makes this more explicit:

Let us be glad and rejoice and give gloɪy to him.
For the marriage of the Lamb is come;
And his wife hath prepared herself.
And it is granted to her
That she should clothe herself with fine linen
Glittering and white,
For the fine linen are the justifications of saints (19, 7-8).

The vestments of the Church, bride of the Lamb, 'are the justifications of saints'. Even Isaias was already aware of these justifications:

I will greatly rejoice in the Lord,
And my soul shall be joyful in my God,
For he hath clothed me with the garments of salvation,
And with the robe of justice he hath covered me
As a bridegroom decked with a crown,
And as a bride adorned with her jewels (Is. 61, 10).

It will be noticed in the Apocalypse that the good deeds of the just are bestowed upon them by God, and they are merely the instruments. Man's saintliness is a gift of God for the glory of his Son. 'For we are his workmen, created in Christ Jesus in good works, which God hath prepared that we should walk in them,' wrote St Paul to the Ephesians (Ep. 2, 10). There is no other purpose for which we are created, except that of adding, by our homage, to the glory of Christ (Eph. Caps. 1 and 2). Can any Christian soul fail to be overwhelmed at the thought that it has actually received from God any holiness it may possess, in order that it may tend to Christ's greater glory? Thus every Christian vocation only makes sense when linked with all other vocations in the unity of the Church, in order that this unity may be offered by God to his Son 'like a bride adorned for her husband'.

When he wishes to give some idea of the splendour of the Church in this state of holiness, St John makes use of the symbol of the holy city, the heavenly Jerusalem. This theme, too, was traditional. It is to be found in Isaias (Is. 54, 11-12; 62, 1-12; 65, 10 ff.) and above all in Ezechiel (Ez. 40 ff.) St Paul also speaks of 'The Jerusalem which is above; which is our mother' (Gal. 4, 26). But no author rises to such heights of doctrinal power as St John in Chapters twenty-one and twenty-two of the Apocalypse. These more than any others call for detailed commentary. We will confine ourselves to a few essential notes.

The dominant impression one gets from these chapters is one of dazzling light and magical colour. From the whole range of an artist's palette the author has drawn with the most sensitive judgement every delicate shade the imagination can conceive. Had he wished to arrange in scintillating harmony the fire of all the precious gems that ever seduced the human eye, he could not have chosen his descriptive matter with more telling effect. Father Allo frequently emphasises the genius of St John in his use of colours. Referring to the gems of which the holy Jerusalem is composed, he writes: 'The harmony of the colours, the nobility with which he blends them, their opulence, their flashing interplay, at once gay and tender, cannot fail to stir emotions of joy, freshness and peace. It is the same inspired artistry that brings to life the throne of God in Chapter four. Violet and blue (amethyst, hyacinth, sapphire); red (sardonyx, sardine); green and golden yellow (jaspar, chalcedony, emerald, beryl, topaz)—altogether a rainbow range of incomparable variety and richness' (Allo, p. 347-348).

In this atmosphere of soft light, seductive, vivid and radiant with the glow of countless precious gems, the Holy City rises on Mount Sion in the new-born cosmos. To an oriental, living in constant dread of nomadic attacks and enemy violence, the perfect town was always one standing on an impregnable mountain which commanded a wide view over the entire countryside (cf. Matt. 5, 14). Such a site was secure against surprise assault, especially when massive walls added to its protection. Thus, upon its luminous mountain the new Jerusalem stands in glorious splendour, fearless and untroubled by any suspicion of rival power. It has 'a wall great and high' (21, 12) of which 'the light is like unto a precious stone, as to a jaspar stone', which, as we know, is the colour associated with divinity; in the great vision of Chapter four it sheds its radiance upon these 'seated on the throne' (4, 3). All this emphasises the idea of its impregnability—it is inaccessible to any cunning enemy, that is to say, to all evil. The city of God is surrounded and protected forever by the most perfect holiness, because it is the holiness of God himself.

Twelve doors open on to the Holy City (21, 12). They must be spiritual entrances, for angels guard them. They open only to the innumerable hordes of God's Israel. These collect from the four corners of the earth, and enter from each point by three linked gates (21, 13)—possibly an allusion to the Trinity. As for the wall of holiness and of truth by which the entire fortress is protected, it rests on twelve foundations which are the twelve apostles of the Lamb (21, 14). Even in heaven, the truth of the gospel, the spreading of which is the sole apostolic mission, remains the indispensable basis of the saints' holiness, the very foundation on which the Holy City is raised.

Twelve is, so to speak, the measurement-unit of the heavenly Jerusalem. It is the unit which John sees in the form of a golden reed (21, 15). The measurement of man, that is to say, of angels, is more precisely defined further on (21, 17) and by this St John seems desirous of indicating that this measurement is perfectly proportioned to a condition arrived at by men when they resemble angels. 'After the resurrection,' Jesus said, 'they shall be as the angels of God in heaven' (Matt. 22, 31). From then on, the prophet is occupied with a description of the actual form of the Holy City. It has all its dimensions equal; and each of them is based on the figure twelve. When he wants to convey an impression of the limitless number of the Elect, he speaks of their being assembled in a space measuring twelve thousand furlongs, that is to say, the perfect measure multiplied by infinity (21, 16). When it is a question of calculating the thickness of the walls, the answer is 144 cubits—the perfect measure multiplied by itself. In this way, by repeating the same figure over and over again, the twelve tribes of Israel and the twelve apostles of the Lamb are recalled and constantly linked with the mystery of the Church in all its splendour.

In this mystery each individual retains and expands his own particular vocation. The precious stones of which the Holy City is built do not merge into one another; all retain their own individual entity, and make their own separate contribution to the harmony of the ensemble. This is probably what the prophet is driving at when he pauses to describe the blaze of splendour (21, 18-21). Thus at the end we are in no doubt about the close inter-relationship between the mystery of each personal destiny and the mystery of the Church's unity, which has been the object of the instruction running right through the book. *Urbs Jerusalem beata*, we sing in the Liturgy, *quae construitur in coelis vivis ex lapidibus*. We are living stones, each equally necessary to the whole, which can only achieve its perfect harmony by the interplay of brilliance from stone to adjacent stone.

St John continues:

And I saw no temple therein.
For the Lord God Almighty is the temple thereof, and the Lamb
And the city hath no need of the sun,
Nor of the moon to shine in it.
For the glory of God hath enlightened it:
And the Lamb is the lamp thereof. (21, 22-23.)

Any comment would be superfluous. We are here at the very source, at the radiating centre of the light with which the holy Jerusalem is ablaze. In the vision of Ezechiel there is a temple (Ez. 40). Here the Christian prophet improves upon his model. In the Beatific Vision the elect are illuminated by the very glory of God. No temple is necessary where they can find his presence within themselves. It is therefore quite remarkable that even at this point St John finds it necessary to emphasise the role of Christ. It is he who is the 'lamp' of the glory of God. We are still, it must be remembered, concerned with the marriage of the Lamb. It is in him and through him that the Elect constantly receive the divine light. Inversely, their ecstasy is the supreme and ultimate triumph of victorious truth.

Indeed, the work culminates in this note of triumph, which is the motif running right through the whole message of Patmos. It is precisely in this description of the holy Jerusalem that John seeks to comfort the faithful and steel them for their struggle against the impious nations. His aim is to show them how these nations may themselves be finally converted by the light of God, and join in paying him that homage which they are for the time being withholding here on earth. No doubt this is yet another trace of the influence the ancient prophecies concerning the triumph of Jerusalem over the nations had upon the whole of the revelation, but it is at the same time the inevitable ending of the theme which the book has adopted, namely, the necessary and inevitable triumph of Jesus, of the gospel truth, of the Church and of the saints over the nations who are at that time persecuting the Church and will continue to do so as long as history continues.

'And the nations shall walk in the light of it:

And the kings of the earth shall bring their glory in to it . . .

And they shall bring the glory and honour of the nations into it' (21, 24, 26).

Thus the victory of truth, which the saints by their testimony have already started to achieve on earth, will be consummated. And thus, in the immortality of God's own mystery, the eternal domination of Christ and of the saints, the ultimate triumph of truth, will be inaugurated in an era of perpetual youth.

'And they shall reign for ever and ever' (22, 5).

In order that this explanation of the Apocalypse may be rounded off, it is necessary to say something about a problem which we almost feel tempted to leave over for the next chapter. I mean the Second Coming of our Lord.

There are two aspects to this problem, and in my opinion they must be carefully distinguished. Spiritual judgement and the soul's aspiration are involved. Judgement is an estimation. It is based on the chronological return of our Lord in glory which may be more or less imminent—a speculation this is not the place to discuss. The aspiration is an emotion of hope and love, both individual and collective —the desire of every Christian soul to enter into possession of its Lord, and the hope of the entire Christian community that it may soon share in the triumph of its king. These two things, the objective estimate, and the religious desire, are quite independent of one another. If, normally, the conviction of our Lord's imminent return must excite desire in the soul, this desire can really only remain strong in the absence of any exact idea of the time when this coming may take place.

Our next chapter will deal with the question of the actual duration, by chronological reckoning, of the 'last days' which precede the glorious Second Coming of our Lord, so we can confine ourselves here to the desire for his return, this being the final characteristic of the Church, and therefore of the Christian in the Apocalypse.

'And the spirit of the bride say: Come!
And he that heareth, let him say: Come!
And he that thirsteth, let him come.
And he that will, let him take the water of life, freely'
(22,17).

In this ineffable dialogue between the Church and her Bridegroom the author touches on the consummation of the marriage of the Lamb. The whole of the Church, which, as we have seen, is the sum-total of all Christians, is the holy bride God gives to his Son. Every single Christian in full consciousness of his responsibility and his own free will belongs to this aggregate animated by the overwhelming desire which St John expresses in the one word, 'Come!' As we have said, there is no Christian messianism, but there is a Christian eschatology or more precisely a Christian hope, an expectation, of a definite reappearance of Christ in the ultimate triumph of truth. This expectation, this hope of Christ's glorious Second Coming, is and must be more powerful than any messianism could ever be, for it is shot through with love, love of the Church and of Christ. In this love and this hope the real aspiration of the Church is summed up; it is the yearning of all creation for the final and definite end in the perfect unity of all things with the Creator, which can only be realised in the glorious Second Coming of the Son. Hence that one word, so charged with emotion: 'Come!' And in this hope is summed up the aspiration of the Holy Spirit itself, which, according to the teachings of St John, is the great agent of the divine unity. Just as St Paul

recognised in each Christian soul the ineffable yearning of
the Spirit for the perfect adoption (cf. Rom. Cap. 8), John
in this passage expresses a similar and definitely divine
aspiration throughout the whole mystery of the Church.
Incidentally, it is clear that both teachings agree in every
respect. The desire of the Church for her divine Bridegroom
is, in fact, hidden deep in the aspiration of each individual
constituting it; and, on the other hand, the voluntary and
conscientious yielding of each individual believer is the
impetus by which the Church increases and grows in her
desire for Christ. This is the secret of her power in the world.

Then, with the Church and in her, the Christian hears
Christ's answer:

'He that giveth testimony of these things saith:
"Surely, I come quickly".' (22, 20).

The more Christians experience this living hope, the more
it is accompanied by the certainty of encountering no
frustration. The more the Church desires the Bridegroom
the nearer he seems. In my opinion we must look for an
explanation to the problem of the early Christians' certainty
of the Second Coming in this idea. Theirs was an intense
religious aspiration. So at least we must conclude from the
texts in the Apocalypse which express that aspiration. The
revelation of Patmos taught Christians not only to believe
in Christ's second coming, but to be convinced that it was
actually at hand; that, indeed, the resurrected Christ was as
much at work in their daily lives, amid all the trials with
which they were surrounded, as if they could actually perceive
his presence in the flesh; and at any moment they would
actually see him in the flesh, glorious and triumphant. Their
very desire to be united with him only served to heighten the
conviction that he was close at hand. It was not a matter of
his being chronologically close; the matter of time scarcely
entered into it. All that really mattered was his spiritual
effectiveness and his manifest mastery. Any Christian who
has perceived even a little of the irresistible victory which
Christ has gained in history since his Resurrection can have
no doubt that his ultimate triumph is approaching. 'I come
quickly' is the reported message (22, 20). This certainty

reinforces the desire, even amid persecution, and the tranquillity that ensues produces the last exquisite sentence: 'Amen. Come, Lord Jesus.' (22, 20).

It is on this note that the revelation of the Church in the Apocalypse ends, a mystery which the Liturgy, following the texts with the most scrupulous care, calls a sweet vision of peace. Whatever may be its future in time—consideration of which will be the object of our next chapter—the Church is assured of its Saviour's triumph. Also, even in times when the increase of that triumph calls for prolongation of the period of trial, it can already enjoy a foretaste of that tranquillity which foreshadows the end, in Christ and with him.

CHAPTER VII

THE EVOLUTION OF HISTORY AND THE END OF TIME

Many people are intrigued with the prophetic nature of the Apocalypse, and look to it for hints as to the end of the world. No greater injustice could be done to its author than to wrap so vital a subject in such obscurity. It puts a quite unwarrantable responsibility on the shoulders of the interpreter, who is expected to clear up that obscurity, and produce evidence that the cataclysms promised for the last days are near at hand, or that they may have already begun their course.

The preceding chapters should have convinced the reader (or at least one would like to hope so) that there is a far deeper purpose to the book than the mere satisfaction of speculative imaginings or vain curiosity. It offers the most profound truths for the spiritual nourishment and the enlightenment of the believer. The Apocalypse certainly does prophetically illuminate the evolution of history till the end of time, but this is not its only purpose. The object of the present work is to marshal these prophecies and to emphasise that their prophetic quality is only of service in so far as it drives home the teachings that must be grasped in connection with them. We must insist upon this, to avoid any misunderstanding. Even when he throws prophetic light on the future, St John's primary object is to instruct. His message is not meant to be applied, with anecdotal superficiality, to this or that particular event, but to enable the Christian to follow and apply the essential affirmations of faith, as they relate to God's providence, to Christ and the establishment of his reign, and to the Church as a living, corporate entity

172

inextricably bound up with men's lives, both as regards their personal destiny and their common fate in communal affairs. Phenomenal events in history do not interest the prophet as such; he touches upon them only in so far as it is necessary to underline religious truths. In the course of the composition, predictions, properly speaking, are only introduced when it is necessary to prove the book's general themes in advance. Consequently, it is not worldly curiosity but deep religious penetration that should be brought to bear upon the Apocalypse, and more so on the prophetic passages than on any others. The reader must be constantly on his guard lest his imagination should run away with him and jump to unjustifiable conclusions—or lest he may miss some apparently negligible point which eventually proves to be of vital importance. Preconceived notions and approaches that the teachings of the prophet do not justify must be most strictly ruled out, always remembering that St John is primarily concerned with communicating religious precepts.

Let us be even more precise and say that, since the book is primarily concerned, as I think I have shown, with the collective facts which form the basis of human history, St John's prophecies must be approached from the religious viewpoint of that history. Political history, military history and what-have-you are not directly concerned. It is legitimate to consult St John only regarding the religious future. We might even enlarge on this and say that *a priori* the book deals with humanity in the mass, and not with any particular nation or group. In its prophetic parts, the book is necessarily catholic. On the one hand we have the people of God, that is to say, the Church; on the other, what the book in its prophetic style calls the nations, the peoples or the tongues, that is to say, the whole human race in whose midst the Church is in course of development and to whom it offers the truth of the gospel. Particular aspects of the religious history of human society are touched upon only in so far as is necessary for the proper understanding of that history.

Having thus disposed of unwarranted expectations and vain curiosity, we must admit that the book still contains a vast amount of prophetic material, the full meaning of which is not immediately apparent at a cursory glance. How, then, shall we separate this essential interpretation from the mysterious literary wrapping in which St John has seen fit to tie up his revelation? Let us briefly formulate three rules. They are elementary in the study of any historical text, but it is particularly useful to remember them in the present case, where interpretation calls for the most delicate perception. The first is that we should approach and read the document in an historical context which is not our own, but that of St John. The prophet of Patmos wrote amid events which were those of the first century, and not of the twentieth, nor of the Hundred Years' War, nor of the barbarian invasions. We must divest ourselves of all notions of any times but his own. But, it may be argued, this is prophecy, and ought not prophecy to embrace the future? Can it be called prophecy if it does not project its vision beyond the author's contemporary experience? This is precisely where we must be cautious, especially when we are concerned with a prophecy belonging to the Judeo-Christian tradition. In this tradition, the prophet, even though he may lift the veil from the future, never does so except from a foundation of contemporary events which he has personally witnessed. He never seems to visualise the more distant future except from his own standpoint at that moment, which embraces nothing but the immediate future. He borrows all the necessary characteristics from facts he knows by personal experience, that is to say, contemporary facts. This applies especially to literary characteristics, symbols and illustrations, with the aid of which he describes future events. He can only express his prophecy by dressing it in the contemporary concrete mode, and we have no authority for thinking that he was able to visualise the concrete mode of a later date. We should be quite wrong in applying his prophetic perspective precisely to events in our own times, because he could not see these events as we see them, clothed in the characteristics which are recognisable to us. If, hypothetically, he knew of their existence, he would still have seen them through the eyes of his own time, that is to say, quite differently from the way in which we see them. He would express them with the aid of characteristics borrowed from contemporary life. In order to understand his prophecy—and this is the necessary first step if we are to test its application by any particular event—we must put ourselves in his place, that is to say, at the cause-end of the prophetic curve, before we can weigh up the effect, because effects can again become causes on their own account. How futile is the attempt to identify tanks with the scorpions of the Apocalypse—or to recognise any modern contemporary in the Beast whose number is 666—or to estimate the length of any war by the figures given in our book! One could, alas! multiply the infantile absurdities that have gained currency even among Christians in this field of speculation. They betray a radical ignorance of the most elementary laws of Judeo-Christian prophecy. To be brief, the Apocalypse, like all the other prophetic sections of the New Testament, must be taken on the basis of contemporary realities of the first century, and only from this point of departure is it legitimate to link them with later events.

This brings us to the next stage in the labour of interpretation. This is concerned not only with ascertaining the exact meaning of the text itself, but comparing the prophetic pronouncements with the actual facts of later history. Here we are faced with another delicate problem. It is essential to be punctiliously careful about the successive processes, in order to avoid passing too quickly, and without adequate consideration, from one step to the other. The vain curiosity against which we have already given warning is sorely tempted to dwell upon the second step. The reader who is anxious for an authentic interpretation must resist this snare and attach greater importance to the first step. Our efforts in this chapter will therefore be essentially directed towards understanding the inspired text, purely and simply on its own account. Only at the end will we attempt to establish some connection between the historic curve prophesied and twentieth century history as the Church knows it in this day and age.

It behoves us in this study of the text to apply a second general rule of historical study; passing from the perfectly clear, through the less clear, to the obscure, in that order.

This will help us to unravel many a mystery. Avoiding chronological progression as we examine the events prophesied, we shall proceed from prophecy to prophecy in accordance with the diminishing certainty as to their meaning. Starting off with events which are properly speaking eschatological, we shall flash back to the starting end of the prophetic curve, to the events of approximately St John's own time, leaving to the last the prophecies which concern the interim period, and which open up the most delicate problems of interpretation.

In doing this we shall reconstruct what we believe to be the prophetic view of humanity expressed by St John at the end of the first century.

Now St John was not the only one at this period of Christian origins to have a doctrine in these matters. There are eschatological pages by other authors in the New Testament. The Christian has advance assurance that there can be no possibility of disagreement between these documents, because the Church vouches for the truth of the divers testimonies, and truth is always the same. Even the ordinary historian knows the fascination of comparing these New Testamental teachings—which are innumerable—and the thrill of discovering that they always agree. We may conclude, then, that the third rule we must formulate in our attempt to explain the prophetic portions of the Apocalypse will have justified itself if these prophecies bear out other eschatological documents in the New Testament, or at least are not in contradiction with them.

Before going into the details of the various problems, we must explain how the general curve of the prophecies works throughout the book.

Prophecies on 'the people, the nations, the tongues and kings' (10, 11) which St John is enabled to make through the consumption of the 'little book', commence with a general view of the Church's future, and more especially the secular struggle between the Beast and the two witnesses (11, 1-14). It seems possible that this may coincide with the second scourge let loose on earth by the fall of Satan (11, 14).

This first general view ends, like each section of the book forming a whole, with an eschatological invocation (11, 15-18).

The same subject of this combat between the Church and the Beast, the central theme of St John's message to the persecuted Churches, is then resumed, in greater detail. The mystery of the Church is no longer represented by the two witnesses, but appears as if literally rooted in the sky, and seems to be directly linked with the personal mystery of Christ. The first Beast, like the second, his assistant (of whom nothing has as yet been said) appears lined up with them, as if incited by the heavenly dragon and working with him here on earth to carry out his work of destruction and blasphemy. (Caps. 12-13.) Thus the forces of good and evil are brought face to face, and the struggle gains momentum. We already know which side has the apparent and ephemeral gains, and which will score the definite, final victory.

And now, on Mount Zion, the awe-inspiring vision of the Lamb appears. The angel introduces it without any mystifying preliminaries: 'Fear the Lord and give him honour, because the hour of Judgement is come' (14, 7). So now the judgements of God will begin to unfold. Another angel at once joins in, and announces the first of the judgements, which is that of Babylon, that is to say, Rome, (14, 8), and a third angel in his turn makes it clear (a new eschatological invocation) that a similar fate awaits all that imitate this city in its idolatry. Its judgement is the symbol and the prelude of theirs (14, 9-11). This first general statement is intended to fortify the saints and give them courage for the supreme testimony. They are assured of the final outcome of their work in the cause for which they will sacrifice their lives (14, 12-15).

Again the author takes up his main theme of God's judgement. As before, he sees the Judge rise up in heaven as if on the threshold of history, surrounded by angels who explain the petitions of the Temple, that is to say, the Church, and who are there to carry out his wishes (14, 14-20). Still in heaven, and under the Judge's command, there appear

'Seven angels having the seven last plagues,
    For in them is filled up the wrath of God' (15, 1).

And at once the heavens ring with acclamations, emphasising the prophetic message of the sections that follow: these describe the judgements of God and confirm, if there is any need for confirmation, the interpretation we have given of the book in general, that it deals with history as a whole.

Great and Wonderful are thy works
O Lord God Almighty;
Just and true are thy ways,
O King of nations!
Who shall not fear thee, O Lord,
And magnify thy name?
For thou only art holy.
For all nations shall come and shall adore in thy sight
Because thy judgements are manifest (15, 3-4).

The following section (15, 5-16) gives the first general notion of the way in which these judgements will be carried out, compelling the nations, by persuasion or by force, to worship their true God. We have come to the vision of the seven vials and the seven plagues. Any who have not been converted on earth shall have no place in the heavenly temple of God, for we have been told that the judgements are only for those who still dwell on earth, the saints, who are inseparably united with the Judge, being already safe inside the temple, which is the Church (see above). Until the judgements of God's wrath have reached fulfilment, the very sky seems to be obscured by the smoke of his anger, giving terrifying evidence of his omnipotence. (15, 5-8.)

Then follows the description of the plagues themselves throughout the course of history (cap. 16). The prophet returns to the traditional themes he has already made use of in Chapter eight (the angels with the trumpets), but he adds many careful details which owe their clarity to the precise particulars that have been given in the intervening chapters. In Chapter eight he contents himself with simply referring to the disasters in history, such as the plagues of Egypt, which were providentially sent to set God's people free from the oppression of impious nations. In Chapter sixteen he becomes more explicit. The people of God are definitely shown to be the martyred saints and prophets (16, 6) that is to say the Church, which the foregoing explanation enables us to recognise. As for the powers that oppress the Church and the saints, these are even more specifically denounced; they include the Beast (12, 2, 10, 13), Babylon (16, 19), the false prophet (16, 13), the Dragon (16,13),all of whom the previous chapters have also alluded to. Again emphasis is laid on the fact that the scourges of God's wrath fall only on those who are obstinate in error, the unconverted 'inhabitants of the earth', who have the mark of the Beast and adore his image. (16, 2.) Insistence on their inconvertibility is stressed here more than in any other chapter (16, 9, 11, 21).

This pericope is itself a complete eschatology; it ends in evocations which are even more emphatic, the sixth vial and the sixth plague (16, 12-14) leading up to the ultimate violent sequence of the Dragon and the two Beasts, to whom more precise reference will be made in the following section, the parenthetical exhortation (16, 15-16) calling attention to the glorious second coming of our Lord, which, quite unforeseen, closely follows the sudden re-emergence of the powers of evil. As for the seventh vial and the seventh scourge, they make their appearance simultaneously with the supreme malevolence of the Devil in the last days. These are the traditional cosmic cataclysms attendant upon the judgement of the Beast, here represented by Babylon (the name which provides a hint of what is to come in the next chapter) and by other towns and nations which, having followed Babylon in her idolatry, will share the same punishments.

The prophetic part of the book, properly speaking, covers Chapters seventeen to twenty, starting with the Judgement of Babylon (persecuting Rome) and passing on to the Last Judgement, which is followed by the description of the Holy City (21 ff.). The prophecies of this section concern the interval between the fall of Rome and the end of the world. We shall return to the analysis in due course.

Because this is simplest, let us start by setting out the items of information that deal with the end of the world.

We have frequently had occasion to remark that in conformity with the style of literature he has adopted for this work, the author brings all his prophecies to a necessary end. This holds good both of the book as a whole and of its varying sections, even if they are only rapid prophetic glances, like that at the very beginning (1, 7).

It is clear that he is not merely concerned with faithfully following a certain literary pattern, but uses this method because he has a definite teaching of the Christian faith to convey; this world is temporal, and will come to an end. However vast the horizon on which the future opens, however unpredictable the extent of that future, as to whether it may be short or long, the Christian may be certain that it is not endless; it has a definite limit, which lies hidden in the will of God. The cosmos we know is moving ceaselessly towards that pre-ordained end. 'In the days of the voice of the seventh angel, when he shall begin to sound the trumpet the mystery of God shall be finished' (10, 7). This is a definite statement, also doubtless in the Judeo-Christian apocalyptic tradition. Just as the world had a beginning, and is not in its origins coeternal with God, it will likewise have an end, at any rate so far as its present state is concerned, the duration of which is still in progress. In the face of this declaration of faith, Christians, to say nothing of others, cannot remain indifferent to St John's predictions of eschatological events. Christian or not, we find it difficult to realise that it will sometime cease to have that stability which seems to us more in keeping with the eternity of God than with our own ephemeral existence— this in spite of what geologists and astronomers tell us about the physical changes that are progressively taking place. Yet for all that we need only read the first chapters of Genesis to learn by the Holy Spirit that the existence of the world, exactly like our own existence, had a beginning, just as, by reading the Apocalypse, we cannot escape the conclusion that the world is moving towards its end just as surely as we are moving towards our death, and that at the time of our own arrival at immortality, it, too, will undergo very definite changes.

In what manner does St John picture the end of the world,

and on what religious values does he base his notion? Here again we must not look for far-fetched tit-bits of imaginary eschatological events. The Church and the faithful need to know the kind of future that demands their testimony. The history of creation is narrated in Genesis within a frame that gives authority to the great precepts of the Law. The Apocalypse likewise instructs Christians in the truths by which they can best meet the immediate crises of this world, and which at the same time shed light on the future of the great religious verity which they are required to witness in thought, word and deed.

The final act of the immense drama of creation is obviously the inauguration of a new heaven and a new earth, which will accompany the manifestation of the holy Jerusalem in all its glory, descending from God himself to a regenerated cosmos and realising for all time the perfect alliance between God and man. It would be even more correct to say that this ultimate phase is already beyond the confines of history; it develops in another dimension, altogether outside our present conception, hemmed in as it is by our human ideas of duration in time—in a dimension 'where time is no more' (10, 6; cf. 15, 7). 'For the first heaven and the first earth was gone' (21, 1). Be that as it may, the book culminates in a description of the bliss which the faithful witnesses of the gospel will experience when earth is no more and the holy Jerusalem is established in its stead. (Caps. 21, 22.) This is the last of the progressive stages which the author began to illustrate by describing the immense multitude of the blessed already on their way towards this very goal. (7, 9-17.) It only remains to point out that in both passages there is definite reference to the nations or other social units whose future forms the general theme of St John's prophecy. (Cf. 7, 9 and 21, 24.) This mention is all the more remarkable in contrast with the absence of any allusion of this kind in the passages dealing with eternal punishment (14, 9-11; cf. 6, 15, 17; 21, 8; above all 20, 11-15). It would almost seem as if the inspired prophet wished to insinuate that human society, at last overcome or saved by the truth of the gospels, were incorporated so to speak in the holy Jerusalem, sharing in its splendour according to its deserts—in an evidently transformed state, leaving nothing of themselves to the power of the Beast. On the other hand, sinners caught up in the punishments of hell, especially those who acquiesced in the worship of the Beast and of his image, appear to be abandoned to complete isolation. In these eternal punishments the Beast has no further power over the human communities that went astray while on earth. The triumph of the Word of God over the nations, prolonged to all eternity, is thus complete.

According to St John, the last general judgement immediately precedes the definite realisation of the new Jerusalem in the regenerated cosmos. The most detailed description of it is given in Chapter twenty (20, 11-15) and it is in perfect accord with certain characteristics furnished by other portions of the book. St John's scenario runs something like this: First of all the Christ-Judge appears in all his majesty on the clouds of heaven (20, 11; cf. 1, 7; 14, 14). According to the description of Chapter twenty, which is the most explicit, we should say that this apparition of Christ would coincide with the last phases of the great cosmic transformation. It is in the midst of the earth's tremors that the Judge appears in the clouds:

'And I saw a great white throne
And one sitting on it
From whose face the earth and heaven fled away,
And there was no place found for them.' (20, 11; cf. 6, 14.)

Before the Judge all the dead have to appear, the mighty and the humble, those of the earth and those of the sea, as well as those who are already in hell (20, 12-13). All therefore are raised in order that they may be judged according to their works, of which an exact account is kept in the book of each individual destiny (Ibid.). Only those whose name is written in the book of life will be saved; this book, as we already know, is also called the book of the Lamb (20, 12-15; cf. 13, 8). In all these illustrations we recognise the doctrine of traditional theology. Those who are damned are condemned by their own works, and none is saved but by the mercy of God exercised through Jesus Christ. The vision of the Last Judgement makes this quite clear. It depicts with equal clarity the doctrine of the end of all things, the eternal bliss of the countless multitudes of the elect (7, 9-11) in the holy Jerusalem (21, 3-4) and the unending torment in hell (20, 10-15) of those who have refused to submit to the Lamb, and more especially the worshippers of the Beast (14, 10-11).

Although the prophetic curve culminates in the end of all things and the resplendence and beatitude of the holy Jerusalem, and although the verdict of the Judge means ineffable bliss in heaven as well as the necessary punishment of hell—the preceding vision shows the Lord reserving for himself the personal recompense of the chosen, whereas the task of administering the divine wrath is left to the Angel of Vengeance—nevertheless, the Day of Judgement leaves the impression of a day devoted to the anger of God and of the Lamb (cf. 6, 16-17, etc.). If the last act is all splendour and intimacy, that which goes before it is stamped with severe and rigorous justice. We should recall, however, that this rigour and this severity only affects sinners, just as secular justice does in our present state. Here on earth the witnesses of Jesus already live in the spiritual radiance of the new Jerusalem towards which they are advancing day by day. Sinners, and especially those who worship the Beast, already have divine judgement hanging over them. Therefore all history from beginning to end is shown as nothing but the continuous working out of God's justice, the recompense and the chastisements being entirely at his discretion. From this point of view it is perfectly clear that the 'last days' commenced with the Resurrection; they have been going on ever since, and are still continuing. We have already seen from the previous chapter that in reality punishment, reward and judgement are interdependent; they all spring from the Word of God, and their out-working continues irresistibly from age to age, carrying with it to the end of time triumphs, salvation and bliss for those who accept the word of God, condemnation and punishment for those who reject it. Nevertheless, it is chiefly from the point of view of God's wrath that the prophet of Patmos has visualised the evolution of history. This is understandable when we recall the tradition in which his thought was moulded, and his uppermost desire to assure God's faithful people that their enemies would certainly not escape divine vengeance. His message left the persecuted Christians in no doubt that God's judgement would descend with irresistible force on the impious powers which were at present persecuting them.

It was also quite in keeping with the pattern to which St John worked that God's judgements should be accompanied by cosmic cataclysms which would usher in the new heaven and the new earth to accommodate the holy Jerusalem. There is no shortage of these great physical upheavals in our book; they occur at the end of practically every prophetic section, in a more or less developed form. Thus, at the opening of the sixth seal (6, 12-17) we have a typical example; there is another immediately following the illustration of the angels holding the four winds of the earth (7, 1-3); then again at the emptying of the seventh vial (16, 17-21); and again at the appearance of the Judge, preceding the Last Judgement (20, 11), etc. We have seen, *a propos* the breaking of the sixth seal, that this was a traditional theme. Every time the old prophets of Israel wanted to convey a terrible and definite impression of God's wrath, they did so to the accompaniment of great earthquakes and othei physical disturbances.

If ever this wrath of God becomes manifest, it can only be because of excess of evil among men. That was how mankind always understood the cataclysms that occurred. The vision which follows the breaking of the sixth seal emphasises this, and shows men running away to hide themselves from God's anger, just as Adam and Eve did in paradise after they had sinned. In Chapter twenty, this recrudescence of evil coincides with the release of Satan after being incarcerated for a thousand years (20, 7-10). The enemies of the Church, having gathered from the four corners of the earth in order to assail her, are devoured by fire which is sent down from heaven, and Satan, who has led them into this final act of aggression, is thrown back into hell (20, 9-10). Since the interpretation of this pericope depends partly on the answer to the question of the millennium, let us leave it for the moment, and return to it when we have explained, to the best of our ability, this mysterious millennium.

To sum up, the eschatological events occur in the following order: The demoniac descent of evil, especially in the form of sudden and violent attacks on the Church—the first cosmic phenomena, terrifying the guilty and at the same time foreshadowing the final transformation of the world; the appearance of the Christ-Judge; the general Resurrection and the Last Judgement; the definite defeat of Satan and those who follow him in his revolt; the inauguration of the new heaven and the new earth, and the appearance of the holy Jerusalem in all its glory 'prepared as a bride adorned for her husband'. All in all the book is not really concerned with future events in a general sense, or with supplying tit-bits of history to come. These eschatological events in St John's work only contribute their traditional and proper note to the prophetic technique. The whole of history, because it must come to an end and because of the events that will accompany that end, here tends only to the triumph of God's Word; its evolution is shown as the working-out of God's punishments and blessings, an evolution now in progress which will end when time itself comes to an end. And this again proves that, so far as St John is concerned, we are already working our way through the 'Last Days', and have been doing so ever since the Resurrection.

We now know the extent of St John's concern with the future; so let us go back to the starting point. We will take up the properly-speaking 'prophetic' part of the book and resume our analysis where we left off. This section is covered by Chapters seventeen to twenty inclusive. Its commencement is quite clear, and the theme there propounded is in perfect agreement with the one we are about to discuss. Both turn on the unfolding of God's judgements, and the concrete historical agents who are the instruments of his justice must be recognised as impious and persecuting political powers. And there came one of the seven angels . . .
Saying: Come, I will show thee
The condemnation of the great harlot

Who sitteth upon many waters:
With whom the kings of the earth have committed fornication
And they who inhabit the earth have been made drunk
With the wine of her prostitution (17, 1-2).

Three different pointers to the future emerge from this message. They are not equally sweeping or precise, but all three are quite definite prophetic declarations and all have the common object of conjuring up more and more grandiose pictures of the Christ-Judge's triumph and that of his saints. The first throws light on the whole history of the Beast (17, 3-5) and clearly foretells the fate of Rome and the ten kings, that is to say the political powers which will succeed the Empire (17, 6-13); it ends with the first general affirmation of the victory of Christ and the saints over the idolatrous Beast (17, 14). The second and third touch on various details which the first general outline does not give. Both centre on the great vision of the horseman who is King of kings and Lord of lords (19, 11-16) and they show his judgements and his mastery in continual progress, the first over the power of Rome (17, 15-19, 9) and the second over successive rulers and the whole future of humanity (19, 17-20, 15). The analysis is a little more detailed in each of the three parts, and the rapid commentary of some of the more important points will, I hope, justify this general division of the text and the interpretation of St John's prophecies as a whole.

Three main symbols obviously dominate the first prophetic vision; they are the Beast, the woman and the ten kings. They symbolise traits which are deliberately mixed and confused. The woman is spoken of at one moment as sitting on the Beast (17,3,7) and at another on Seven Hills (17, 9). The Beast is linked, now with the woman, and now with the ten kings. As for the objects which appear first of all as horns of the Beast (17, 3-7), a little further on they assume a separate identity, and become the ten kings (17, 12). We are accustomed to these incoherencies in the literary works of St John.

Clearly, among all these symbols, the Beast is the one that unifies the whole. He appears in almost every line (17, 3, 7,

8, 11, 12, 13). We know who is meant by this symbol. Let us nevertheless make it quite clear that in this passage he represents, not Rome itself, or the Empire, of which the woman is here the actual symbol, but impious power generally—power of the kind the Dragon calls into being right through history, to make war against the offspring of the other woman in Chapter twelve. This powerful demoniac principle is incarnated successively in Rome and in the ten kings, but it is always the evil one who in reality leads the struggle against truth as we have seen in an earlier chapter. What does this prophetic section tell us of his fate? The same thing that was said of Satan on his expulsion from heaven by the angel Michael—it is the fate of one who is already conquered (cf. 12, 9-12). Doubtless the Beast will have occasional successes and ephemeral triumphs which may make men wonder. This has been mentioned before, and will bear repetition. But, all in all, he is a beaten enemy already on the way to final destruction.

'The beast which thou sawest . . .

Shall go into destruction' (17, 8).

This general affirmation applies right through the prophetic book. All impious and blasphemous political power, revived again and again by Satan as his chief means of leading mankind astray, will one day be overthrown by the Judge who, since the Resurrection, waits on the threshold of the Last Day.

The woman whom St John sees sitting on the Beast— that is to say, supported by him—unquestionably represents Rome and the Roman Empire. Here she is closely linked with the Beast, bearing his names of blasphemy (17, 3), wallowing in his luxury, details of which are forcefully given in the next verse (17, 14), sharing his idolatrous prostitution, his inebriation with the blood of martyrs (17, 6). She is seated like a queen on seven hills, and even the period is clearly established, being indicated by the reigning ruler in a series of emperors. Here St John's prophecies are very precise. Having dealt with generalities and the somewhat impersonal matters that formed the first part, he now inserts a definite fragment of contemporary history, leaving it in

mid-air, as it were, for evolution to provide the continuity.
There are seven kings;
Five have fallen, one is, and the other is not yet come—
And when he is come, he must remain a short time
And the beast which was and is not:
The same also is the eighth,
And is of the seven, and goeth into destruction (17, 9-11).

Can we determine the names of these emperors? There
seems to be no doubt about it. We should notice first of all
that the rulers hinted at here are all represented as auxiliaries
of the Beast. It is therefore not a question of the emperors in
direct succession since Augustus, but only of those who
persecuted Christians, or at least allowed them to be persecuted. We know also that one was in power at the time
the book was written (17, 10); it is Domitian. Five before
him have thus been incarnations of the Beast. If we run
through the series of rulers preceding Domitian, we get
Titus (79-81), Vespasian (69-79) the interregnum with Galba,
Otho and Vitellius (68-69), Nero (54-68) and Claudius (41-54).
This line of succession and the dates are taken from Clement
of Alexandria (Strom. II, XXI; Allo, p.282). Claudius would
thus be the first to have persecuted the Christians, according
to St John at the end of the first century. This should be
borne in mind when the discussion started by historians over
Suetonius's text comes up—over the passage in which this
emperor is said to have expelled the Jews from Rome on
account of the troubles started among them by a certain
Chrestos (Suetonius 'Claudius', 25). This, then, must be
regarded as documentary evidence of the first persecution,
under Claudius, a persecution based on troubles between the
Jews and the Christians. The passage in Suetonius cannot be
taken in any other way, although it does not agree with the
opinion of Eusebius and Tertullian, who looked upon Nero
as the first emperor to persecute the Christians. (Hist.
Eccles. 11, 25.) Nero was the first to persecute the Christians
as such; but this does not exonerate Claudius from being
actually their first persecutor.

As for Nero, we have already seen that he is clearly
distinguished by the figure of the Beast (13,18). He and his
suicide are also definitely recognisable in the mortal wound

in one of the heads of the Beast (13, 3), a wound which would have led to the death of the Empire itself, if it had not been healed, after the interregnum and its disorders, by Vespasian and his reign of conciliation and redressment. All these allusions to the present and the not very distant past must have been crystal clear to the recipients of the letters in the Apocalypse.

Now we come to the prophecy on the future. After Domitian, a series of emperors reigned. St John, speaking of them in the accepted prophetic style, makes use of symbols and especially of numerical symbols, which he uses in accordance with their occult values and symbolic properties. Domitian's successor, a collaborator of the Beast like himself, would thus be both the seventh and the eighth in the series started by Claudius (7, 11). If he were the seventh, that would indicate that the series of emperors had reached its complete number; but since he has to be 'the eighth while also the seventh', that conveys the information that the series will pass beyond the the figure seven, without the inconvenience of tying the author to any definite number, or to any period in time either. St John has not troubled to say how long the reign of the emperors will last. He simply states—and this was all that mattered to his correspondents —that on the one hand the Beast, whose final downfall had already been promised, would continue to be matched by, and to inspire, future persecuting emperors, and on the other hand, these rulers, precisely because their destiny was linked with his, would also shortly be destroyed (17, 10-11). The whole series of persecuting emperors would ultimately end in their definite defeat; that was the burden of St John's prophecy.

After them would come the ten kings, symbolised by the ten horns (17, 12). By this symbol he appears to suggest that it would be waste of time to try and discover those who would follow the fall of Rome as the holders of political power. Let me repeat that, so far as these difficult passages are concerned, I have no intention of mingling with my analysis any research or suggestions regarding their implication when the prophecies they contain have already been proved by the actual events of history. Our task is primarily to concentrate on the text itself, and for its own sake. There will be time presently to point out, in conclusion, how the prophecies of St John seem to agree with the secular history of Christianity. For the time being we are not interested in mixing the pure interpretation of the document with verifications which the prophecies have already received in course of time.

Up to that point of the book at which we have now arrived, the following have been established: the Beast, representing the diabolical power which leads man astray, is definitely doomed to final destruction. Roman power, the incarnation of this beast, will be the first to be destroyed. Other political powers of the same stamp will likewise eventually be destroyed by the Lamb and the saints.

These shall fight with the Lamb and the Lamb shall overcome
  them,
Because he is Lord of lords and King of kings;
And they that are with him are called, and Elect, and faithful
                                          (17, 14; cf. 2, 26; 5, 10; etc.).

Having thus disposed of the general view of the future, the section which follows then proceeds to particulars, taking first those which are nearest in time to the recipients of the letters, and developing them more fully. The fall of the Roman Empire is very vividly portrayed. Like its predecessor, this section opens with a general statement, the profound nature of which can only arouse our admiration. Just as, at the beginning of the previous chapter, the prophet shows the Beast at his diabolical work, using the woman and the ten kings as his instruments, so here, having depicted the fall of Rome with intense realism, he permits his correspondents to foresee that any apparent success the ten kings may score over Rome will only postpone for a time the ultimate victory of the Church and of truth; in other words, the kings' triumph will be a mere illusion. No political power can ever ultimately prevail over the cause of the Church and the truth. The diabolical Beast, even though he may battle against God through these powers, changing his tactics and ever stirring up other enemies to make war upon those who originally carried out his evil work (as in the case of the

ten kings) still has only one design in view—to wean mankind from God and set himself up for worship instead.
He works through new agents as he worked through persecuting Rome. When these new agents turn against the old
persecutors and destroy them, they themselves become
instruments of God's vengeance and the triumph of the
Word. This is the same precept that was conveyed by the
breaking of the second seal and the sounding of the fifth
trumpet. War is a means by which Satan does his evil work;
but it is at the same time a punishment permitted by God
for the sins of man. Here St John admonishes Christians to
guard against the repeated falsehoods of Satan. When he
brings about the fall of a political power which has set itself
up for adoration, it is very often in order that he may raise
another, so innocent-looking that it is not at first suspected,
even though it may turn out to be just as impious as its
predecessor. This diabolical game will go on until the words
of God are fulfilled, by which are meant the words prophesying the final triumph of Christ over the impious
nations (17, 15-17).

This general law having been laid down, the prophet goes
on to state explicitly that his vision refers to Rome and to its
universal empire.

> 'And the woman which thou sawest is the great city,
> which hath kingdom over the kings of the earth.'
>
> (17, 18.)

An awful solemnity surrounds the announcement of the
Roman Babylon's fall—this empire which is the prototype of
all political powers arrogating to themselves divine authority.
(18, 1-3.) Another voice plainly calls upon Christians to
detach themselves from the inevitable doom that hangs over
the condemned city—a message which must have produced
a thrilling effect upon the souls of its recipients just at a time
when Rome, still at the height of her power, persisted in
humiliating them (18, 4-8). There follow, sometimes with
glimpses into the past or peeps at the future, vivid descriptions of the disasters that will overtake Rome. These details
raise no difficulties; we can take the text just as it stands.
Turn by turn reference is made to the kings subjected by the

Empire (18, 9-10) to the merchants who are battening on the
city's love of luxury (18, 11-17) to the great merchant fleets
that sail the oceans in the direction of Rome (18, 18-19).
All are drawn into the disaster which in an hour lays low the
most brilliant capital of the whole world. (18, 10, 16, 19.)
Heaven, on the other hand, proclaims the justice of God
and his powerful judgement, in a form which is worth noting
carefully:

> 'Rejoice over her, thou heaven,
> And ye holy apostles and prophets,
> For God hath judged your judgement on her.' (18, 20.)

This fall of Rome, brought on by the Beast for his own
diabolical ends, but primarily permitted by God who uses
even the Beast as a means of executing his judgements, is
also the triumphant fulfilment of the judgement of the saints,
the apostles and prophets—briefly, of the martyrs of Jesus
whom Rome believed it could persecute with impunity.
God delivers 'their' judgement against the city.

We are nowadays inclined to feel fairly indifferent to this
prophecy about the Roman Empire. It all happened so long
ago. But we can imagine the reaction it must have produced
among the harrassed and anxious Christian communities
at the time when Rome was still bloated with power. Such
explicit assurances! Nowhere is more care lavished on the
minutest details, and although our avid curiosity may not
be entirely satisfied, we cannot help noticing that the description of Rome, with all its craftsmen and musicians (we almost
hear the very sounds!), wiped off the face of the earth as
suddenly and violently as if an angel had cast a mighty
millstone into the sea, is more graphic than any other part
of the book. One can but conclude that this was intended to
answer problems which the persecution had forced the
different churches to face. Even at this distance of time, the
vehemence of St John's emotion comes through quite clearly,
a crescendo rising to the culminating vision of the invincible
horseman who is the very Word of God, King of kings and
Lord of lords. We are borne as if on the wings of an eagle
first to the complete annihilation of the persecuting Roman
Empire (18, 21-24), then to the divine judgements avenging

the blood of the martyrs (19, 1-4) and finally to the evocation of the perfect reign of God, which his judgements have inaugurated, and to the marriage of the Lamb which will be consummated when these judgements are fulfilled (19, 5-9). Then the prophet, as if overcome by the immense prospects opened to his prescient vision, is led to render the highest testimony the spirit of prophecy can conceive (19, 10) and it is the magnificent evocation of the King of kings and Lord of lords, on which we can never sufficiently meditate, and which is truly the summit of the beloved apostle's prediction. It is very remarkable that this evocation, revealing the supernatural name of Christ ('. . . And his name is called The Word of God.' 19, 13) simultaneously with the name by which he is known to history, and which prophetically confirms his dominion over the nations ('King of kings and Lord of lords': 19, 16, cf. 19, 15) should bring to an end the most concrete forecast contained in the message from Patmos—the fate awaiting the Roman Empire. Here the historic and the supernatural planes meet; they meet perfectly, with no rough edges. The Apocalypse is an invitation to the believer never to let them become separated, and never to doubt the victory of the Son of God nor that of the saints, with him (19, 14)—which has already commenced, even though invisibly, in the course of history. It is precisely in history that one can already follow the triumphs of the Word of God.

After the fall of the Roman Empire with its tyranny and its persecutions, the punishments of God and the victories of the King of kings and Lord of lords follow in natural order. They occupy the last of the three parts we singled out for special comment. Like the two preceding, this one opens with a recapitulation of the general theme, which is that of God's judgements (19, 17-18). Here we should note that the passage containing this recapitulation conveys a hint of the prophecy that will shortly be enlarged upon, namely, in showing that God's judgement falls primarily on kings and tribunes. Thus the next, and more explicit, line the prophecy takes is concerned with the royal successors of the Roman Empire. It goes on to include the 'small and the great', so there is no escape, for the heads of nations, for communities or for individuals. All this builds up to the Last Judgement at the end, when men are judged according to their own deeds, good or evil, and it is no longer a question of nations or races.

At the commencement of this new prophetic passage, therefore, St John dwells first on the kings who will successively rule Rome. They appear to him just as they are ranged side by side with the Beast to make war upon the invincible horseman (19, 19). The global nature of this distant perspective of future history evokes the incessant struggle which has been going on through the ages, every period producing new political forces at war with the King of kings and the saints who constitute his army. (19, 19.) The vision is, however, not wholly concerned with this struggle. A moment comes when the Beast is taken, together with the false prophet (who, it will be recalled, is the second Beast—13, 11 ff.) and both are thrown into hell after an irreparable defeat. (19, 20-21.) There has been a great deal of controversy about the exact meaning of this part of the prophecy. Not being able to enter into all the problems raised, and the solutions suggested for them, we will content ourselves with stating our own views, keeping as close as possible to the text and bearing in mind the methods St John habitually uses in expressing himself. If our interpretation agrees with the rest of the book's teachings, and with the whole of the New Testament, we may perhaps assume that we have hit it off correctly.

Of the actualities represented by the false prophet and the Beast there can be no possible doubt. We have already seen that they symbolise on the one hand powers that arrogate to themselves divine rights and consequently tyrannise over the witnesses of the Word of God; and, on the other hand, false religious doctrines and philosophies which, whatever their original aim, invariably end by favouring the undue pretentions of the state. We have seen in a previous chapter that these two powerful agents are the instruments Satan uses to lead men astray. The essential characteristics they embody are emphasised anew in the present prophecy. The long view which unifies this prophecy does, however, give St John his opportunity to show that there will be a point in history when these false religious doctrines and philosophies—I mean those compelling man to worship the Beast, and bow to the pretensions of the idolatrous state—meet with definite defeat at the hand of the King of kings and Lord of lords. How? Not, as will be most readily suggested to our mundane imaginations, by the intervention of political action or authority (the mistake made by material millenniums) but 'by the sword of him who is seated on the horse, which proceedeth out of his mouth' (19, 21) and we know that this represents evangelical truth, founded on the mystery of God's own truth. The victory of the horseman, King of kings and Lord of lords, in Chapter nineteen, is in direct line with that of the white horseman released upon the world by the breaking of the first seal (6, 1). It simply carries the matter a little farther by explaining that human communities will not always be at the mercy of diabolical influences, as they were at the beginning. Sooner or later the truth of the gospel will definitely prevail, and this is the proper way for Christ to overcome.

It is merely a repetition of what has been said all along concerning the outcome of the struggle between the Beast and the Church (cap. 11). The gentiles are at liberty to congregate in, and to befoul, the outer courtyard of the temple only, and for a period of forty-two months (11, 2; 13, 5), and the witnesses will be constrained to deliver their prophecies clothed in sackcloth for one thousand two hundred and sixty days, no more. Their bodies will be exposed to the tribes, and peoples, and tongues, and nations for three and a half days (11, 9-11); the Church here on earth will be forced to seek a hiding place in the desert for a time, and times, and half-a-time (12, 14). All these periods and figures symbolise incomplete and indefinite reckonings, not the whole duration of history. We have seen that the two witnesses, Zorobabel and Jesus, represent the religious and the political authorities of God's people. The Church teaches that Christian leaders having the same roles in human society will also experience times of defeat; but it is expressly said that 'after three days and a half'—and this fractional number also makes it quite clear that their eclipse is temporary—the Spirit of life will re-enter into them, and they will rise firmly to their feet, greatly to the consternation of their enemies (11, 11). This expresses the same idea as the one underlying the section which deals with the unfolding of God's judgements. The time will come, the prophet says when the Beast shall have no more power over the course of events, neither shall the false prophet; the whole substance of human history will then assume a different character. This interpretation, and the one which we shall give of the ensuing section, seem to us the only possible readings, since they agree with what appears to be the central theme of the book from one end to the other, namely, the sovereignty of Christ and the Saints over the Nations—a sovereignty which is perfectly in line with the traditional messianic prophecies, although adjusted in conformity with the spirit of the gospel and the new alliance.

The Beast and the false prophet, whose definite defeat St John foresaw in the course of history, were, you will recall, appointed by the Dragon to lead men astray in their communal life. Their overthrow would not be complete until it was accompanied by the Dragon's defeat. By this, of course, is meant his defeat as a factor in life as a whole; and herein lies the prophetic sequel to the vision. It has nothing to do with the moral life of individuals, nor with the temptations of Satan; such things are quite outside the present orbit of the prophecy. But let us read the text:

And I saw an angel coming down from heaven
Having the key of the bottomless pit;
And a great chain in his hand;
And he laid hold of the dragon,
The old serpent,
Which is the devil and Satan,
And bound him for a thousand years,
And he cast him into the bottomless pit
And shut him up
And set a seal upon him
So that he should no more seduce the nations

Till the thousand years be finished.
And after that he must be loosed a little time. (20, 1-3.)

Thus, by the reference to the bottomless pit, we are led back to the very first vision which had introduced the mystery of Satan, in the explanation of the great universal plagues in human history (8, 10 and 9, 1). The end of this instruction concerning the malevolent power of evil thus links up with the beginning. We have come full circle through human history, and the instruction has not been rendered less effective by bringing actual human society into the struggle against the people of God. The Beast and the false prophet are not to be released from hell. Satan himself, for a thousand years, that is to say for a very long time, will be rendered powerless to go on 'seducing the nations' as he has done in the past. The victory of Christ and the saints, or rather the victory of truth for which they, and he, have given testimony, will at last be established for a long period in history, under this new dispensation. The scandalous struggle between the Church and idolatrous communities will be succeeded by an organisation of society in accordance with the truth of the gospel, in which the two witnesses, that is to say, the political and religious authorities, will stand upright before the Lord, triumphant in their testimony to his truth, as they had stood valiantly in their struggle under the tyrants. (11,3.)

This long period of triumph for the truth of the gospel in human affairs will in reality be the personal reign of Christ and the saints from heaven on this earth. It was prophesied in the very first pages of the book, and everything moves inevitably towards this happy development (1, 6; 2, 26; 17, 14, etc.). The theme is taken up again in an extended form here, just where it can make the prophecy on the future more explicit. Naturally it has a part to play in the picture of the judgement, with which the whole of this section is particularly concerned. The reign of Christ and the saints will be inaugurated by their judgement on the nations. And this reign, the first effect of which will be the shackling of Satan, is to last a thousand years, or a very long time.

It must not be thought that this reign of Christ and his

saints on earth is to be regarded only as their personal triumph in heaven, a triumph which has no connection with the concrete facts of this world. It would be against all the teachings of the book to think so, because St John makes it quite clear that the resurrected and triumphant Christ, invisibly but irresistibly, reigns over human history by virtue of the divine mystery which, through the Incarnation, made him one with us. So far as the saints, and especially the martyrs, are concerned, this is no less true. It goes without saying that they have a personal triumph in heaven. But they also triumph, although invisibly, with their master here on earth. This is expressly stated in the canticle which acclaims the Lamb as master of history:

> 'Thou hast redeemed us to God in thy blood,
> Out of every tribe, and tongue, and people, and nation;
> And hast made us to our God a kingdom and priests.
> And we shall reign on the earth' (5, 9-10).

Clearly it would be useless to try to imagine what the influence of the saints in heaven on our earthly affairs could be, any more than we could imagine that of the resurrected Christ himself. We only know that this influence does merge into that of truth. Beyond that, our almost total ignorance of the condition of souls after death makes it necessary to be very cautious concerning the possible way it works. How a Theresa of Lisieux can intervene from heaven to do good on earth; how a St Martin de Tours, a St Louis or a Jeanne d'Arc can continue to serve their country so that it may become more filled with Christian truth—all this must remain a mystery to us. But the fact remains that, for the believer, the Apocalypse takes up all the threads of the old messianic tradition concerning the reign of the saints with the Messiah, even while adapting them to Christian standards. The saints and martyrs, inseparable from Christ, like him and with him are in control of the progress of evangelical truth on earth and eventually the victory of this truth in the collective life of the human race will inaugurate their invisible reign here below over the nations, in complete conformity with the messianic promises. St John further takes pains to stress that the martyrs and saints, 'living again' thus in history, like

Christ and with him, will go on doing so until the 'thousand years' come to an end. (20, 5-6.) The other dead, that is to say, the old 'inhabitants of the earth', will not return to life until the Last Judgement (20, 13), and will therefore have no evil influence on earth to compare with the blessing extended to it by the saints. It is not surprising, therefore, that good should triumph in the end.

So the continuance of St John's prophecy, in Chapters nineteen to twenty, certainly does seem to suggest a certain millenniarism. But it has obvious limits. It has nothing whatever to do with the Second Coming of Christ, or of Saints materialising in our midst and establishing a theocratic reign; it is by spiritual influence from heaven that they are working for the spread of truth here on earth. Their influence on human institutions is similar to that of the leaven 'hidden in the meal until the whole was leavened' (Matt. 13, 33). We have frequently had occasion to stress that the Apocalypse avoids all suggestions of theocratic action. Of even less weight is the question whether, when the millennium arrives, there will be only Christians on this earth, or whether evil will have disappeared entirely. According to the prophet, the truth of the gospel will end by becoming an integral part of human society and the institutions that compose it. But alas! that certainly does not necessarily mean that all men in those days will be saints, or even Christians. Who can fail to know that even within many excellent institutions, based on directive principles inspired by the highest ideals, there are often men whose moral values vary considerably? Does not the history of the monastic institution itself prove this? The personal moral life of Christians is not conditioned by the collective institutions to which they belong. Till the end of time they will have to struggle against temptation and 'keep the commandments of God' and 'the testimony of Jesus Christ'. Their earthly condition, from the standpoint of their moral life, may be a little easier than that of their forebears in days when the two Beasts were rampant, but certainly it will not differ in essentials; to the very end the moral life of man must remain a constant struggle. And in this struggle it is by no means certain that the shackling of

Satan, as described by St John in his vision, will exclude further activity by the spirit of evil. Once more it must be emphasised that all this does not concern the moral life of individuals; it refers solely to the communal events which constitute the fabric of history. St John's prophecies refer to these alone.

The optimism with which St John's prophecies are too lightly regarded, after twenty centuries of Christianity, prompts us to repeat the caution expressed at the beginning of this chapter. There is always a danger of jumping to conclusions and accepting the more obvious interpretation of texts bearing on the future, thereby often missing their deeper prophetic import. No interpretation should be attempted until the text has been analysed for the statements it contains, and it would be very bad practice to go against these affirmations in order to arrive at a more or less convenient conclusion. Should a possible adversary arise, let us follow him in argument on his own ground. We shall then find that in declining an interpretation because it does not fit in with a conception of history that this interpretation indicated, he will raise a certain number of *a priori* suppositions which are not less debatable. The one, for instance, that twenty centuries represent a sufficiently important factor in the duration of time to form the basis of a general line of thought on the development of Christianity in the history of human society. Or that, among the doctrines which human communities support, Christianity has lost ground, so far as its influence is concerned, even if not in appearance. It seems to me that the very opposite is true and that, as we advance in time, even the enemies of the gospel must in their very crimes, and in the justification they find for them, take as their standard the principles which the Church and the gospel have taught mankind. A conqueror may still, even in our own times, reduce masses of human beings to bondage, but he cannot enforce slavery on principle or include it in his programme, as could a potentate in olden days. It requires sophistry, which moreover could be easily de-masked, to justify the revival of paganism which seems momentarily to have taken possession of the world. This will doubtless be followed by a reaction, as always happens in our civilisation, bringing with it renewed progress for the truth of the gospels. Whatever abuses there may be, on a realistic plane, and these are invariably lapses on the part of individual morality, not of institutional ideas, we must admit that there was more of the gospel influence in the personal fidelity and confidence of feudal times than in the old Roman society, which was essentially a system of slavery; in the free and enthusiastic guild movement of the Middle Ages than in the serfdom which marked feudal times; in the wider horizon of a just liberalism than in the tyrannical government which the ancient corporations ended by imposing. And who can doubt that the gospel is at work, prompting new progress in the aspirations of justice and reasonable equality which is raising the masses of our own time to put down the servitude and oppression of bygone periods? No doubt there will be future crises which, however they may strike the sociologist, will be recognised by the theologian and the Christian as evidence of the gospel leaven at work. In this sense our Lord was also right when he said that he came, not to send peace, but a sword (Matt. 10, 34). The Apocalypse gives us leave to be confident that this militancy of our Lord in history will also end in ultimate triumph.

Therefore nothing in the experience of twenty centuries of Christian history entitles us to reject prospects of unlimited progress, if such progress, as we believe, is foretold in this great prophetic book dealing with the future of Christian history. Their forecasts seem all the more trustworthy if it be true, as the three great stages of St John suggest—the stage of the Roman Empire, the stage of the ten kings, and the millennium of Christ and the saints—that Christianity's course may still have many centuries to run. That is as much as to say—and can any honest observer doubt this?—that the Christian leaven has scarcely yet begun its transforming work in the institutions of human society. A long road probably remains to be covered before Christ and the martyrs surrounding him in heaven achieve the complete victories foretold by the prophet of Patmos.

But, once again, these are speculations far removed from the analysis of the text itself. Now it seems to us that the interpretation we have given is confirmed by the sequel to the vision itself. The description of the millennium is in fact followed, in scrupulous continuity, by the picture of the catastrophies ushering in the last days. These form a prelude to the actual eschatological events.

And when the thousand years shall be finished,
Satan shall be loosed out of prison,
And shall go forth and seduce the nations
Which are over the four quarters of the earth.
Gog and Magog . . . etc. (20, 7-10).

'When the thousand years shall be finished'—the link in the succession is clearly indicated. At the end, therefore, of the long, invisible dominion of Christ and the saints over the world's affairs, Satan will be suddenly set free. He will at once resume his characteristic operations, 'leading the nations astray', which, since his defeat and that of his henchmen, has been beyond his power. Once again he will tempt the nations to rise against the 'encampment of the saints and the well-beloved city' (20, 8); that is to say, he will stir up trouble among the political powers against the Church. Tireless in his tenacity, it never seems to strike him that he is setting himself an impossible target. We know in fact that human communities, no doubt Christianised at least in so far as their principal organisers are concerned, will exist as before during the 'millennium' of Christ and the saints. Nevertheless, no doubt as a result of that general moral decadence which our Lord himself foretold, and St Paul after him, will be open to subversive influences and ready to revolt against Christ and the saints on earth. It will be a violent uprising, open and undisguised. Satan, it will be noticed, leads it in person. Nothing is said of a revival of the Beast and the false prophet. A rapid delineation shows us the attacking army, 'the number of whom is as the sand of the sea,' (20, 8) gathered from the four corners of the earth to fill the length and breadth of the earth (20, 9) and this time the struggle between the forces of evil and the Church and the saints is a war of extermination. The mention of Gog and Magog leaves no room for doubt that we are now really at the end of the world. (Cf. Ezechiel, cap. 38 and 39.) In Ezechiel these symbolic personages represent the enemies who launch the most violent assault on the people of God and the ideal temple. The violence of this assault, on the moral even more than on the material plane (though the possibility of persecution is by no means excluded) deeply impresses anyone who has made a study of parallel eschatological documents in the New Testament. 'Unless these days had been shortened, no flesh should be saved,' says our Lord himself. 'But for the sake of the elect those days shall be shortened' (Matt. 24, 22). The Apocalypse also gives the comforting assurance that the utmost violence of malevolent force will be cut short by heavenly intervention.

And they came upon the breadth of the earth
And encompassed the camp of the saints and the beloved city.
And there came down fire from God out of heaven
And devoured them (20, 8-9).

Then follows the final and utter defeat of Satan, who joins the Beast and the false prophet in hell forever.

'And the devil, who seduced them
Was cast into the pool of fire and brimstone,
Where both the Beast and the false prophet
Shall be tormented for ever and ever' (20, 10).

The scene of the Last Judgement follows immediately. With it we again arrive at the eschatological events which we have already analysed, and with which all the prophetic visions of St John end up, from the persecution of Domitian to the conclusion of history and the apparition of the holy Jerusalem in all its glory.

This then is the evolution of history, as seen by St John in the greatest prophetic vision ever vouchsafed to an inspired author, Jewish or Christian. True to the earlier prophetic tradition, this history, especially as regards the contact of human society with evangelical truth, appears to him as a long series of divine punishments, promulgated by Christ and the saints, a succession each stage of which coincides with a stage in the progress of truth. From the Christians' point of view in their earthly activity, this is a distinctly optimistic concept of history. For even if they are required to give testimony at the cost of their lives, they know that they are making the sacrifice for the future of the world, since in reality they are contributing effectively to the progress of Christian truth.

St John recognises three stages in this unfolding of history. In the first, which is the actual period of the correspondence, the Church squarely faces the idolatrous and persecuting Roman Empire, and scores the first great victory for the resurrected Christ by this valiant stand. The second period, that of the ten kings, will nevertheless witness a continuing of the struggle between the gospel and the political powers which have shared the spoils of the Roman Empire and have also been inspired by the Beast. This period will also end in the victory of Christ and the saints over the idolatrous despots who have so far presided over the organisation of human society. A Christian world is then established, in which the struggle between good and evil, which is inseparable from the condition of man on this earth, will continue under other forms. But the dominion of Christ and his Law will eventually prevail and be established over the nations of the earth. Doubtless men will finally realise that for the salvation of their society there are no other principles than his. This period of Christian civilisation, which brings the invisible reign of Christ and the saints here on earth to pass, will apparently last longer than either the Roman Empire or the period of the ten kings; but it would be futile to speculate as to its duration.

At the end of this period there will be the last release of Satan and a sudden and violent revival of evil among men. This will bring in its wake the decisive intervention of the master of history. After the definite elimination of the Prince of Shadows, the Christ-Judge will appear on the traditional clouds of judgement, followed by the cosmic upheavals expressing for the last time the vehemence of God's wrath. The 'inhabitants of the earth' will reap their deserts; then the dead will rise and present themselves for judgement at the dawn of the new heaven and the new earth. The verdict will be in accordance with each man's works. Then death and all the sufferings in its train will be forever destroyed, and the new Jerusalem will finally appear, 'pre-pared as a bride adorned for her husband', the saints reigning with Christ in the light which is that of God himself, for all ages of ages.

Having thus reconstructed the course of history as seen by St John in his inspired visions and as he in turn revealed it to the persecuted Churches, let us try to discover if there is anything new in this teaching, or whether it simply took up the thread where the earliest Christian revelation had left it. If it should prove to be in direct continuity, it would justify our interpretation—an interpretation which, coming from outside, would not be the less valuable, either from the historian's or the believer's point of view.

On the subject of the last days, St Paul anticipated St John. His writings contain some of the most explicit teachings in this respect. Naturally we must not overlook the great eschatological discourse of our Lord himself (Matt. 24 and parallel). Similar passages occur in the epistles of St Peter and St Jude. It is not necessary here to enter into a detailed discussion on each text. We are, however, entitled to base the following scheme on the different teachings revealed.

Let us take as our starting point the definite conviction shared by all these authors, as well as the witnesses of the first Christian generation, that the reign of Christ com-menced, invisibly but also invincibly, with the Incarnation, or, more particularly, with the Resurrection. (Matt. 28, 18; 24, 24.) St Paul cannot conceive the reign of Christ without seeing it develop until Christ has reduced all his adversaries to submission (1 Cor. 15, 25). Here we have a truth with which the Apocalypse has made us so familiar that we need not emphasise it. Let it suffice to establish the fact that St Paul held the same view.

Nevertheless, simultaneous with the reign of Christ and until the day of its final, all-embracing expansion, there is, according to St Paul, a 'mystery of iniquity '(2 Thess. 2, 6) which also develops and is responsible for all our present misfortunes, which will go on manifesting themselves until the end of time. Our Lord in his own lifetime made no disguise of this aspect of the future, and even warned his disciples to regard it as the 'commencement of sorrows' (Matt. 24, 3-13). Quite suddenly, towards the end of time, we find this iniquity raising its head again, more virulently than ever. For the moment, its malevolence is kept in check by 'that which withholdeth' (2 Thess. 2, 6)—the text suggests it is Christ himself, but the role is interchangeable with that of the angels whom St John sees at the four corners of the earth; they provide a temporary obstacle, that is to say, until the number of the elect shall be complete; then the diabolical malevolence reaches its full force.

Thus, if we are already in the period of the last days, and if the forces of good and evil are already in operation, the latter must be finally overcome by the former (2 Thess. 2, 8; Matt. 24, 30). Nowhere do we find any hint that the consummation is imminent. Both St Peter and St Paul warn their correspondents against the confusion this notion may cause if given free rein in Christian life. From God's standpoint, says St Peter, one day is like a thousand years (2 Pet. 3, 8). As for St Paul, not only does he refuse to teach the imminence of the Second Coming (2 Thess. 2, 2), but he even expresses the view, in other passages of his writings, that two great general facts will ensue before this consummation can take place.

There will be, first of all, what he calls the 'plentitude of nations' (Rom. 11, 25), those entering into the perfect alliance established here on earth by our Lord. This confirms an impression we get when we have finished reading the Apocalypse. St John merely states more explicitly the general affirmation made by St Paul, and thus gives it greater emphasis. The actual historical background at the time of writing gave his prophecies added significance, and he was able to present the 'nations' in a more formal manner than his predecessor, for whom the term meant the gentiles in general without any particular reference to the political institutions symbolised by the Beast in the Apocalypse. Here we can profitably recall the eschatological discourse of our Lord announcing the extension of the gospel to all nations (Matt. 24, 14 and parallel).

Then there will be the 'fulness of the Jews' to enter in their turn (Rom. 11, 12) not without additional spiritual benefits for the nations themselves in the perfect alliance with God, which will inaugurate an age of extraordinary grace (Rom. 11, 12; 11, 15). This stage of the human future will precede the final apostasy. St Paul gives no indication of how long it will last, but we have no reason for imagining that it will be of brief duration. How can we avoid identifying this with the Apocalyptic millennium? Father Allo himself, from whom we differ in the interpretation of millenniarism, admits the affinity between St John's millennium and this period of Christian expansion foreshadowed by the teachings of St Paul.

There is mention of a time, without specifying when it will occur—though logic leads us to locate it in the period spoken of as the 'fulness'—when apostasy and iniquity will make their appearance (2 Thess., 2, 3); when some will turn from their faith (1 Tim., 4, 1; cf. Luke 18, 8); when charity will freeze in the hearts of many men (Matt. 24, 12). Then the man of iniquity, the son of perdition, the enemy of all who call on God (2 Thess. 2, 10) will be at large. It seems legitimate to recognise this personage as the Antichrist of St John (1 Joh. 2, 18), the symbol of a multitude of diabolically inspired agents, in whom we must recognise the false prophets and false saviours predicted by our Lord (Matt. 24, 23-26) and likewise spoken of by St Peter (2 Pet. 3, 3-4) and St John (1 Joh. 2, 18). St Paul frankly states that this increase in human perversity is due to the influence of Satan (2 Thess. 2, 3). All this agrees with what is said in the Apocalypse about the release of Satan at the end of the thousand years. St Paul says the world is plunged into this renewed misery by the seduction of iniquity, operating on those who have no love of God and truth (2 Thess. 2, 10 and ff.). This also agrees with the Apocalyptic teaching of the outbreak of all kinds of vices: egoism, cupidity and so on, making these days difficult, even for the elect. (2 Tim. 3, 1.) St Peter (2 Pet. 3, 3) and St Jude (Jude 18) both warn the faithful in the same sense, and St Peter states explicitly that in giving this warning he is echoing the words of our Lord himself. (Matt. 24, 22.)

The elect nevertheless are completely protected because (Matt. 24, 22) they have been chosen irrevocably by God for the sanctification of the spirit and faith in truth (2 Thess. 2, 12). The Apocalypse has also shown us that inside the Temple, that is to say the Church, the faithful have nothing to fear from the Beast and his helpers.

These days of general iniquity will be of short duration. The Lord will not delay the destruction of Satan and his auxiliaries of all sorts, designated by St Paul under the general title of man of iniquity. He will destroy them by the breath of his mouth and the splendour of his sudden, glorious coming (2 Thess. 2, 8; Matt. 24, 27-28). Of course the day and the hour of this second coming are unknown to us and even to the Son of Man (Matt. 24, 36-37); we can no more foresee them than a man can foretell the exact hour of his own death, even when it is close at hand. In this sense it is true to say, for individuals as for the world as a whole, that our Lord comes like a thief (3, 3; 16, 15 cf. Matt. 24, 27 and ff.; 1 Thess. 5, 2, 4; 2 Pet., 3, 10). It is not less true to say that the final coming of our Saviour will have signs and wonders as its fore-runners (Matt. 24, 32-33). They will consist of those cataclysms and cosmic transformations which the Apocalypse so frequently describes, but which also figure in the eschatological discourse of our Lord (Matt. 24, 27-28), and in St Peter (2 Pet. 3, 7, 10, 12-13).

Then there will be the resurrection of the dead, which our Christian documents refer to primarily as the resurrection of the elect (Matt. 23, 31) or, as St Paul says, 'those of Christ' (1 Cor. 15, 23); the Judgement (Matt. 24, 30; cf. 25, 14-15); and last, the consummation of all things, death and all the powers of evil being destroyed forever, and the Christ established in majesty by the side of the Father. (I Cor., 15, 29.)

From this rapid comparison of the eschatological predictions of St John on the one hand, and of the other inspired Christian authors, especially St Paul, on the other, it seems reasonable to conclude that they agree in all essentials. St John is only more precise, more explicit, and the very nature of his message explains itself. The general line of the future of Christianity, as he depicts it, essentially agrees with all that we can gather from the earlier writings; the struggle between good and evil, or, more precisely, between the Church and the infernal powers, the extension and successive victories of Christ and the perfect alliance which he will inaugurate; the forecast of a period of expansion or 'the fulness of the nations' and 'the fulness of the Jews' of St Paul coincident with the millennium of the Apocalypse; all these, it seems to me, confirm independently the interpretation I have offered of that famous passage. Lastly, to end up this period of Christian expansion, we have a spell of general moral decadence, a recurrence of evil coinciding with the release of the infernal powers, with all their resources of illusion and error; and then the ultimate consummation of the reign of God and the perfect alliance. Step by step all the stages repeat themselves in both series of teachings. The great Apocalypse outstrips its predecessors only from the point of view which is properly its own, namely, that the collective powers, and especially political powers, as represented at that time by the idolatrous Roman Empire, oppose the truth of God's word through the direct inspiration of Satan. All in all, it seems to me that we may well speak of a single teaching concerning the evolution of human history till the end of time, and it runs right through the whole of the New Testament. The Apocalypse is not the only witness, but the most authoritative and the most formal, as it is only right that the last prophetic book of the Judeo-Christian revelation should be.

We must now return to the question which we deliberately left in abeyance at the time we set out to give a straightforward explanation of the book itself; namely: have its prophecies, after twenty centuries, begun to apply, and, if so, at which particular stage of secular evolution do we find ourselves at the present time?

From the Christian standpoint, first of all, the answer to these questions is of altogether minor importance. We cannot, of course, be indifferent to such questions. Our faith assures us that the predictions are inspired, and we must naturally be concerned to know that actual events have not belied the prophecies, but have on the contrary confirmed them. In one particular case this is proved beyond a shadow of doubt. But the believer's faith will not be likely to stumble over such trifling considerations, for the message of the book contains so much of estimable value in other and far more important respects that he will not waste much time over eventual verifications and chronological concordance. It is from the general standpoint of Christian history that the Apocalypse offers him comfort and guidance for his future attitude towards life, just as it was meant to do for the early Christians in their time of trial. From it the Churches and the persecuted communities were able to draw a courageous and hopeful view of the future, just at the moment when the present looked far from rosy. The Christian in every age may turn to it for an impression of the splendour and the supernatural joy towards which his own life is progressing, especially if the testimony he is called upon to give involves superlative sacrifice. Still more, he is assured that even here on earth, in the evolution of events as he sees them, his Christian testimony contributes irresistibly to the ultimate triumph of truth, and that, in Jesus Christ, it will finally prevail. Look at it in any way you like, the combat can only end in victory, and in that victory every faithful witness has his share. The Apocalypse therefore literally compels Christians, in the line of Christian action itself, to take an optimistic view of the future, and is that not more important than to know which particular stage of its progress the Church has arrived at in this, our own day?

But all the same, it is possible and also legitimate to ask this last question, provided the answer is not endowed with an importance it does not deserve, and that it does not bind us to a chronological concordance which may make our position difficult to defend. Here, then, is our opinion. Most commentators agree that the prediction of the fall of the Roman Empire has definitely been fulfilled. Here there is no question about the proof. St John, far from encouraging the Christians under Domitian to expect an early end to their troubles, told them plainly that the malevolence of the Beast against the two witnesses would be re-doubled, and that they would have to go through a period of depression and apparently total defeat. As a matter of history, the obligatory cult of Caesar and the Christian persecutions that resulted from it, only started under Domitian. Father Allo insists again on the manifest proof of St John's prophecy in this respect. One can only imagine that, since the prophet lavished so much care on the minute detail with which he described the fall of Rome (caps. 17 and 18) this was in the highest degree necessary in order to counteract the impression produced on the spirit of his correspondents by the immediate turn of events in the redoubled bitterness of their persecution.

It is equally difficult to deny that the prophecy concerning Christ's victory, and that of his truth, over the Roman Empire has been proved. Which would one say was the culminating moment of that victory? We must remember that this has nothing to do with military or political success, but concerns purely and simply the triumph which Christ pursues throughout history 'by the sword of his mouth', that is to say, the triumph of evangelical truth. Therefore we ought not to be preoccupied with the political collapse of the imperial idea (476, fall of the western part of the Roman Empire; or 1453, fall of the Byzantine Empire; or even the definite disappearance of the title of Roman Emperor with the death of Kaiser Franz-Joseph in 1916); we should think of the moment when the imperial institution inherited from Augustus bowed before Christ, accepting and becoming imbued with his new spirit. So we should think of Constantine in 313, and perhaps still more of Theodosius (379-395), or of Justinian (527-565) whose codes bear witness, within the Roman institutions, of the first indisputable victories of Christian inspiration over the pagan principles of the Augustinian empire. From that time onwards, it was known only as the 'holy' Roman Empire, and even if this holiness remained only relative, there is no doubt that it represented a singular victory of the one whom Pontius Pilate crucified. This same testimony was repeated throughout the centuries, under Charlemagne and under various restorers of the Holy Roman Empire who came after him. It is by these facts, rather than by dates, that one must judge the evolution of history, in accordance with St Peter's statement that for God a thousand years is but as a single day.

These were unquestionable victories over the Roman idea, for Christ and his gospel; yet they were incomplete victories. Would any historian dare to deny that, in the reigns which turn by turn have shared the revival of political power, the Beast has had abundant opportunity to exercise his male-volent power and to sow the seeds of idolatry? Is there any among the collective institutions history has produced since the commencement of the Christian era that has rendered testimony to Christ's victory as resplendently as the Apoca-lypse prophesies? Once again, we are not concerned with princes who from time to time have given Christ's testimony from their thrones. A St Stephen of Hungary, a St Henry of Germany, a St Edward of England, a St Ferdinand of Spain, a St Louis of France—we could easily extend the list. We are concerned with the institutions themselves, and the inspiration which, through them, has influenced human society. Who would dare to maintain that on this plane, and in this order, the Beast was finally defeated by Christ with the downfall of the Roman Empire, to the point of being no longer capable of exercising among men that power of deception which turns the masses from the veneration of the true God? The spirit of Christ did vanquish the Roman Empire, that is incontestable, and, in spite of its many failings, the history of Byzantium confirms this. But it has not yet succeeded in overcoming the ten kings who have succeeded, and who, no less than the Roman Empire itself, have co-operated with the Beast to carry out his evil designs against Christ. The time of expansion of Christian civilisation, the 'fulness' of St Paul, and the 'millennium' of St John, certainly does not yet seem to have arrived. The leaven is far from having done its work in our communal life. Human society has scarcely yet begun to exploit the resources of salvation the gospel affords. So it seems at least to the Christian historian.

If this is correct, we must conclude that we are still in the period of the ten kings prophesied by the Apocalypse. Let us add, with all the necessary reserve this kind of speculation demands, that in view of the geographical vastness of the historical crises that have shaken humanity in our generation, there is a temptation to ask if they might not be caused by that 'last kick' of the two Apocalyptic Beasts, and whether this violent activity may not be the prelude to an important stage in the elimination of pagan idolatry which is invisibly being pursued among us by the master of history.

Pope Pius XI, at the end of his life, spoke with prophetic accents one day, when dealing with the future of the great crisis he saw about to break upon the world during his pontificate. 'We thank God that we are placed in this very moment of time,' he said. 'Truly we cannot look upon youth without a certain envy, especially the very young who still have a long future before them. We have seen many events; but they will see many beautiful things. The immediate preparation may be hard and bitter for them, but there will be no lack of results, even taking into account the short itinerary of a human life . . . How many beautiful things you will see, my dear young people!' (Allocution 29 April, 1938, to the delegates of missionary work to all countries). Quite recently another great Christian witness among us, a witness whose wide experience and lofty views no one thought of denying, gave resolute testimony in the same strain. 'I repeat,' he wrote, 'that the civilising influence of Christianity never had a better chance than it has to-day. I laugh when people speak of the only institution which embraces all eternity as being moribund—an institution which has a future programme certainly more vast and assured than its past, lasting for twenty centuries! For my own part, I think the gospel is only in its earliest stages; that we have not yet begun to know it, so how can we wonder that it has not yet yielded us all its fruits? Christianity, with its long preparation and its profound experience, will prove itself a new force, the only force capable of reviving and directing the resources destined to reorganise the world, by the penetrating power of its spirit, if only men are faithful to it. Christianity alone

is equal to the task of putting an end to the world's enormous
and obscure conflicts.'[1]

Study of the Apocalypse rouses similar thoughts on the
youthful vigour of Christianity, and a parallel optimism as
to the stages yet to be passed through. The victories of Christ,
if we may judge by the prophecies from Patmos, are now,
after two centuries, only just beginning to manifest themselves. They still doubtless have a long evolution before
them. Whether the near future will show further brilliant
progress in Christian civilisation, God alone in his wisdom
knows; but the certainty of Christian hopes is in nowise
lessened. This certainty is of course not limited to any
particular chronological calculation; it rests on the divine
power which will carry the truth of the gospel through
history to its final victory. It is this certainty which in the end
justifies us in accepting the optimistic view of Christianity's
future which these high authorities have submitted to us.
We may hope that these pages have proved the Apocalypse
to be the divinely inspired vehicle of this optimism, for men
of today just as much as for the persecuted Christians of
Domitian's time.

[1]A. D. Sertillanges. 'La Vie Francais', P. Aubier. 1942. pp. 234-235; read also
the following chapter entitled 'Jeunesse de la Civilisation'.

CONCLUSION

For twenty centuries the Church, that irreplaceable foundation on which all Christian civilisation is based, has been ceaselessly offering generation after generation of humanity the grace of redemption, by which the Creator adjusted all human values. The problem of Man's future was solved forever on the Hill of Calvary; but men in their blindness are still stumbling, oblivious to that solution. There have been Empires and other forms of human culture; ages of struggle and ages of prosperity, probable progress and apparent retrogression have succeeded one another. The Church has remained immutably faithful to the dual mission confided to her by the Master: 'Go forth and teach the nations, baptising them . . .' The fluctuations of history have certainly not left her unconcerned; like a mother she has stood by patiently, preparing herself for the meanderings of mankind, while ceaselessly repeating, age after age, the same unchangeable message, and obstinately, if I may use the word, crying out that there is no salvation for mankind, either as individuals or humanity as a whole, except through Jesus Christ and the truth of the gospels.

Centuries have passed and history has been created. Inevitably Christians must ask themselves sometimes whether history has been abandoned by God to the successive incoherent reactions of man, or whether, outside that incoherence, there can possibly be in its temporal evolution some divine purpose—a purpose perhaps only perceptible to the believer, but very much in his interest to know. Precisely in these days of progressive science, when learned specialists are not only discovering new forces but still more are delving into the historical past to arrive at a better understanding of civilisation in its profound continuity. An increasing number of thinkers are approaching this new field of historical

215

research as an avenue, too long unexplored, leading to truth. Philosophies of history are piling up. We may decline to have any part in them on the ground that they are no better than the traditional philosophies and disliking their approach to the past and the future; but we cannot remain indifferent to the fact that, true or false, they have inspired and continue to inspire all the leaders of the masses in our day, without exception. It will suffice to recall the part the philosophies of a Hegel or a Karl Marx have played in recent history, and how these philosophies of history, far from remaining an innocent pastime for thinkers confined to the privacy of their own rooms, have inspired the instigators of the most formidable revolutions of our time. One could multiply the examples and even affirm that there is not one leader of the people to-day who does not base his ideas on some philosophy of history or other, depending upon it to justify his programme of action. Faced with this trend of thought, will Christians, in an isolation lit only by the light of revelation, hold their peace? It is true that, by his faith in the dogma of Providence the Christian knows that God possesses complete mastery over the human events that are the fabric of history, just as he knows that the Apocalypse sheds superior light on human problems. But he must guard against translating this conviction in a manner which overlooks the transcendence of God and relegates his action to the sphere of secondary effects. The dogma of Providence convinces him that nothing can happen that is not in accordance with the will or the sanction of God, or that does not contribute in the end to the glory of the Creator and the blessing of the Elect. But however firmly he may believe in this creative principle as regards historic events and the circumstances of every individual human life, he is still not in a position to say anything about the ties that link it with events in the sphere of historic evolution or with the general sense of that evolution's laws. The doctrine of Providence, if one may say so, applies directly to the mystery of God, affirming his mastery over the successive aspects of created realities; but it throws no direct light on the phenomenal aspect of this succession. Theologians who have studied Providence in the treatise of God, and not in that of the works of creation, know this very well. Starting out from this dogma the historian, no matter how penetrating his faith may be, can never link up without some lack of continuity the concrete facts which science has to handle, in order to discover their historic future. And history, on its part, which is concerned entirely with the order of concrete events and created eventualities, can never by the most penetrating process be related to the omnipotence of Providence and its effect in the world we are conscious of by our human senses. The dogma of Providence therefore can only serve as the basis for a philosophy of its own, or, if you like, of a theology of history, in the sense in which these terms are nowadays employed.

So, once again, can the Christian historian derive any help in his effort to discover, within the confines of strict discipline, whether God, since the incarnation of Christ, has become a personage in history from the standpoint of his faith? When his brother-Christians engaged in Christian action question him on this matter, in order to decide how that action can best serve the evolution of history, is he reduced to his own personal resources, and his own interpretation of the past, in estimating the future, either optimistically or pessimistically? Briefly, does revelation offer any appropriate light for the elaboration which he is bound to make of a philosophy, or, if you like, a theology of history?

It would seem that the Apocalypse, rounding out and synthesising in this respect all the earlier teachings of the New Testament, contains the topical answer to that question. Its author, prompted by the first great historical crisis the Church had to face, presents a veritable theology of history, even though he writes in the fashion of his time and in a literary idiom derived from his place of birth. It is for this reason that the Church has instinctively turned to the Apocalypse for inspiration at any important stage of its progress throughout two thousand years. We can verify this even in our own day, when libraries are flooded with commentaries on St John's message. Thanks to the divinely authenticated visions and prophecies of St John, Christians

need not feel benighted in finding their way through the mazes
of history. They know, from the revelation, 'that which must
be done hereafter' (1, 19).

What, then is this theology of history, and how can it
inspire the believer in his conduct? Let us briefly run over all
the great themes, which are so applicable to our time, and
drink once more from this fountain of living waters.

Since the coming of Jesus of Nazareth the 'Last Days' of
humanity have commenced, and we are now living in them.
The immense aspiration which, from the depths of the
distant past, has lifted the masses of humanity towards God,
has at last come to a head; God is in the possession of man.
Inversely, the unfathomable mystery of love, which made
God give himself to his creation, is accomplished. The perfect
alliance of the human and the divine is now a reality in
history, in the person of the Man-God. Hence our first
certainty: all messianism, being plainly satisfied, has disappeared, as it must. What could man aspire to, that would be
higher and more desirable than God himself given to man?
Certainly the infinite remains to be exploited, and man's
own process of becoming divine is only in its very earliest
stages. But the important thing is that man should realise,
for a start, that in Jesus Christ he *is* divine. He should begin
by making sure to recognise Jesus Christ, and stop giving
his attention to all kinds of messianisms which are unduly
prolonging various powerful aspirations and substituting
them for the homage which is due to God alone. Set-backs
are bound to follow, with all the disappointment they entail.
In these days of ideologies, people are particularly prone to
this kind of blindness, with attendant despair. We have seen
the illusion of liberal messianism, which raised the enthusiasm
of our ancestors in the eighteenth century for created
liberties, and ended in disorder which today is compromising
the most indisputable freedom. We have become acquainted
with Marxist messianism which, turning the masses from
God with the promise that their hunger would be satisfied by
earthly nourishment, has multiplied hatred among men and
in addition produced more hunger and poverty than ever
before—hunger and poverty which are on the increase. It

would be too easy, alas, to add to the list of false messianisms which deny the truth that Christ, the only Messiah, has already come among us; he whose power is alone equal to the despair which follows such manifest set-backs. The Christian has one complete certainty, the first Law of history; much as men may reject the truth that with Christ humanity entered into the perfect alliance with God, it still has nothing more to expect of any Golden Age outside the exploitation of the inexhaustible capital of salvation and expansion which Christ brought with him. Vain messianisms prove only the more malevolent because of the powerful hopes they raise. Their objects are of little importance; they are all *a priori* errors since they do not make the very foundation of their programmes the fact that salvation can only come to mankind through the dominion of Jesus Christ and the triumph of his truth.

For this is the second teaching on which the Apocalypse rests; the cause of Christ and of truth are one and the same. They identify themselves with one another, if one may say so, in the mystery of God himself, where Christ pre-existed for all eternity as the Word, the personal Word of God. They identify themselves in time and in history, where the truth of the gospel prolongs through the centuries the first revelation of Jesus Christ. From that time on no partial truth could save mankind; men could only be saved by surrendering to total truth. The demon knows this well; therefore he sets up false prophets and gives the second Beast a mask which enables him to be mistaken for the Lamb. There are bits of truth in Liberalism, and in all sorts of doctrines that raise false messianic hopes. They are often, as we have said, Christian truths that have gone mad. It is necessary to reintegrate the whole truth of the gospel, otherwise men will be drawn into illusion and misery. Therefore, from the Christian standpoint, moral truth towers over all other truths. One must not of course underrate other orders of truth, like those of science or technique, which are adding so much to the sum-total of human achievement. But the Christian knows very well that all the scientific and technical triumphs in the world, unless they are backed by moral truth, cannot save mankind. However perfect their individual disciplines, their social plans and their politics; however legitimate and idealistic the particular point of view from which such systems spring; however powerful the means they are able to press into their service, the Christian knows in advance that in backing them he is riding towards a fall if they do not measure up to the moral requirements of the truth which commands all others—the truth of the gospel.

And something more. For the Christian, evangelical truth is not just a collection of abstract affirmations, a code of theoretical principles. It is a mysterious link with the Person of Jesus Christ, of whom it is said that he is himself the Truth. Therefore from the Christian standpoint service to truth is the same as service to Jesus Christ, just as in history the two causes are one and the same. The same white horseman, in the Apocalypse, stands turn and turn about for the two aspects of the same idea. In the first instance the impersonal truth of the gospel (Cap. 6) is symbolised; and in the second (Cap. 19) it is he whose personal name is 'Word of God'. The Christian subscribes to the personal cult of Jesus Christ in his devotion to every true cause, and inversely, his love for his Master makes him first and foremost a witness of truth in the world.

The third certainty, which brings us even closer to the evolution of history, is that the dual and single cause of Christ and truth is assured of victory. 'And there was a crown given to him, and he went forth conquering and to conquer' (6, 2). The Christian philosophy of history is absolutely optimistic. We have had so many occasions to point this out in the course of our analysis that there is no need to insist upon it here. The Christian is assured that the truth for which he will give his life if need be cannot possibly fail to triumph in the end over the powers of deception and evil. It will carry the day in each individual destiny, the witnesses of Christ being called to share in his triumphs, and they will judge, by the light that proceeds from their own good works, those others who have obstinately rejected the truth (20, 12-13). But it will also carry the day (and this is of even greater importance to us from our present point of view) in the evolution of human history. It has already demonstrated this in connection with the powerful Roman Empire, in a manner that could not possibly have been imagined by the average person at the time of Domitian. It has triumphed over a number of human institutions so firmly entrenched that their position seemed impregnable. Everything points to our being only at the very beginning of the triumph of evangelical truth in history. The Christian, in serving it, works not only for his own salvation, but also for the salvation of the human race. Thus the doctrine of the Apocalypse formally gives the lie to those who maintain that Christianity keeps men from doing their civic duty. It is true that in seeking the kingdom of heaven he takes on 'these things' as an extra addition. Surely history itself here bears out St John's prophecy. Do not the records of the last twenty centuries prove that progress is intimately linked with the place human beings accord to the truth in their lives —as retrogression is linked with the rejection of it? 'Seek first the kingdom of God' said our Lord, to communities and to individuals, 'and the rest' (which includes all progress and every legitimate human ambition) 'will be added unto you' (Matt. 6, 33).

The progress of truth's victories in history can only be brought about through the co-operation of mankind. Here is perhaps the most profound cleavage between the false messianisms by which the second Beast seeks to lead mankind astray, and the truth by which God saves them. False messianisms mistrust the human personality. They sacrifice whole nations to their shadowy ideologies, and, having led them into this trap, reduce them to a slavery and a spiritual humiliation which are worse than death. We have had many examples of this sort of thing in modern times—messianisms that have demanded the whole lives and the very souls of their dupes, and for what? Christian truth, on the contrary, respects and exalts man, in that it treats him as an in-destructible individual—remember the precious stones in the holy Jerusalem—but still more, it calls for his active co-operation in the work for the redemption of all human values, which is its object throughout history, and for the salvation of mankind. It needs the testimony of the two witnesses who are forever being re-born, and every Christian, whether he be priest or pastor of a community (see the letters to the 'angels' of the Churches of Asia) or whether he have the rank of a chief among laymen, like Zorobabel of old among the people of God, must with his whole life render testimony to the truth and work for the historical development of Christ's ultimate victory. Perhaps no epoch has ever known the need of this testimony as much as our own from every Christian in whatever place it has pleased God to put him. One could even say that the best modern commentary on the teachings which St John expressed by the two witnesses of Zacharias is the encyclical of Pope Pius XI on Catholic Action: 'Participation of the laity in the Apostolate of the Hierarchy'. With the insistence with which we are familiar, this calls upon every Christian, as a duty, to serve the truth of the gospel actively at the post to which he has been appointed by God. If not, the Holy Father affirms, the modern world will not be saved. The reader of the Apocalypse will perfectly appreciate this, for the whole history of modern times is essentially that of Christ's truth confided to the faithful, and spread by them throughout the world till the day of triumph when the consummation will take place.

That is why the Christian has been given the title of 'overcomer'. It applies to him in his supernatural state; but it also expresses a duty on his part. He has earned the hope of attaining it through the very fact of being baptised, in the victorious Resurrection of Christ; and he is as assured of victory as truth itself is, in so far as he remains faithful to it. But it also carries with it the sense of duty, in fact, man's primary duty. In the eyes of the world, the Christian, by the testimony of his whole life, should cut the figure of an over-comer, or conqueror. Like the white horseman leaping across history at the opening of the first seal, a conqueror determined to conquer, *vincens ut vinceret*, he must render his testimony in history. How much one could say on this theme! Too many believers passively lament the evils of our day. They make wickedness responsible for all our ills, without apparently suspecting that wickedness momentarily has the upper hand only because of their weakness. Surely their conscience should be pricked by the generosity and bravery which are at times lavished on the most baleful causes. They have failed to understand the sublime paradox of St John, who insistently saluted the persecuted Christians with the title of overcomers, while, in the sight of men, they were only poor nondescripts born obscurely in Asia Minor. Yet the outcome proved St John right, for even here on earth they were the decisive victors who carried the day before the most powerful of empires and imposed their law upon it, that is to say, the law of the gospel. If Christians today would bring the mentality of overcomers to bear upon contemporary realities in the service of truth, and above all, that of the gospel, the world would once more be compelled to bow to their testimony. It is when witnesses, apparently dead, come back to life, that men give glory to God (11, 13). May our witness be thus revived; may it become strong again, so that the new spirit of life of the gospel (11, 11) may enter into our spirits and into our lives! Then we shall again stand upright on our feet (11, 11) and the enemies of Christ will once more be reduced to silence, false messianisms will lose their attraction and their power of seduction, and that will mark a new stage in the progress of truth through history. All that is needed is that we shall become spiritually strong, behaving like overcomers, so that nothing we do may deserve the terrible denunciation of the Judge, towards the end of the Apocalypse, against the cowardly and the timid (21, 8).

Precisely because it is based on the revelation of Christ's victory and that of his truth throughout history, and because this victory is both dynamic and unique, the spirituality of the Apocalypse is quite the opposite of quietist. It forces one to take part. The Christian who has understood the message of Patmos cannot help being caught up in the great wave of truth that has swept through history since the coming of our Lord Jesus into the world. He cannot help becoming anxious to add his testimony to that of Jesus and the saints. The revelation of the powerful effect the Christian witness has had in the past, and will continue to have in the future, gives the testimony which he must render at the present time solid support, and more than that; it compels him to become aware of the dynamic power of his own soul. This lies at the very root of the testimony and this is the unique victory which, starting with the Resurrection of our Lord, is repeated generation after generation by the victory of the two witnesses. Because the Apocalypse shows how this victory can be recognised by deeds, its impetus is passed on to the one who hears the message, and he can no longer remain inert. And for this reason the theology of history taught by St John prompts and sustains Christian action in history far more than is possible for any mere philosophy of history.

Whereby we see how this action differs from that induced by false messianisms, and in which way the two have a certain resemblance. It resembles the false messianisms in holding that even here on earth the kingdom of God must go on developing to an unlimited extent, which gives rise to the most devoted enthusiasm and inspires optimism regarding the future. It differs in the fact that this devotion and this enthusiasm are not confined to the world, but extend to the whole mystery of truth, which entered into the world and into history with Jesus Christ. The duration of the world, and the ages that succeed one another, are not excluded from the kingdom of God, for the kingdom of God is infinite and when it has reached the preordained extension, the earth itself and its duration in time will mysteriously be transformed in a way adapted to the kingdom of God.

Finally, while we are already involved in this definite expansion, and while the progress of the kingdom will not cease until the end of time, it must be said that it is essential for the action of a Christian to be eschatological. He collaborates actively in what the Apocalypse calls the consummation of the mystery of God (10, 7). This mystery of God is none other than the kingdom of God originally awaited in the messianism of the Jews, and which Christ, Word of God, King of kings and Lord of lords, has inaugurated among us. The Christian, like Christ, helps to realise the kingdom of God, incessantly in process of being inaugurated in these last days. The profound desire which prompts his action, and which expresses itself in the prayer, 'Thy kingdom come' (Matt. 6, 10) has an eschatological import. It cannot become a reality until the mystery of God, which is the kingdom, has arrived at its ultimate expansion. This is not a messianic desire because in Jesus Christ we already possess the essential of that kingdom, and that mystery, which is the object of all messianism. It is an eschatological desire because this kingdom and this mystery, which must expand from the beginning to the end of time throughout the world, have not yet attained their ultimate achievement and their universal extension. That is why the spirit and the bride say: 'Come!' and will go on saying it until the heavenly Jerusalem appears (22, 17).

And we can very well see that this is not any indifferent, ineffective desire. It is a desire that compels action, that is to say, testimony. Every Christian has the mission to participate in the secular witness by which the whole Church, symbolised by the Bride, ardently desires the glorious return of the Lamb and hastens that return by that very desire. 'Yes, I come quickly' answers the Son of Man who reveals these things to John (22, 20).

In this sense the whole apostolate of the Church is also an eschatology. It prepares for the consummation of the mystery of God. It is well illustrated in the report passed on to us of the mission of the Twelve. 'Master, is it now that you will establish your kingdom?' And the Lord, in his reply, while certainly withholding the chronological key to the mystery of the consummation, by its very wording confirms that this eschatological prospect forms the normal context of the apostolic mission. 'It is not for you to know the times or moments which the Father hath put in his own power. But you shall receive the power of the Holy Ghost coming upon you, and you shall be witnesses unto me . . . even to the uttermost ends of the earth.' Then he disappeared mysteriously and an angel, accentuating still more the eschatological note of the scene, announced to the Twelve that the resurrected Saviour would come again in the clouds, as he had gone, on the day of his glorious Ascension (Acts 1, 4-14).

In St Matthew also, the mission of the apostles is mentioned as extending to the consummation of the world (Matt. 28, 20). Attention is fixed on the glorious accomplishment of the 'mystery of God' and the whole energy poured out by the Holy Ghost is directed towards this end, which the witnesses of God must attain here on earth by their testimony. This was done by St Stephen, the first Christian martyr, who already visualised the dominion of Christ over all things, when he died saying: 'Behold, I see the heavens opened and the Son of Man standing on the right hand of God' (Acts 7, 56). All the witnesses of Jesus who come after him do the same and those whom the Apocalypse shows us as being constantly re-born invariably triumph in the end over the infernal powers.

And thus must all Christians to-day face the evils of our time, with indomitable faith in the victory of their Master and in the contribution their testimony will make towards that victory. Then, no matter how many centuries may yet separate us from the final consummation, the faithful will perceive that the last days are actually in progress here and now—that the perfect alliance has already arrived. The Lord will seem very near as they manifest by their faith the irresistible dominion of his word and his truth, and will give their testimony, by this same manifestation, the strength that the revelation of Patmos gave their fathers in faith, at the time of Domitian.

APPENDIX I

GENERAL DIVISION OF TEXT

The numerous literary conventions employed by the inspired writer—septenaries and dove-tailings, antitheses and recapitulation, parallelisms and anticipations, etc., and their various combinations, make it very difficult to establish with certainty any detailed plan of his book. Many systems have been suggested and even the best fail to agree owing to their originators' partiality to their own pet theories. My own leaning is towards the plan arrived at by Fr Allo.

On the whole, the divergencies between the suggested plans are less important than may at first appear. By whatever system one seeks to justify the succession of pericopes, one finds the same line of doctrine running through. It is from the point of view of the doctrinal content, rather than from that of the literary procedure, that the following plan has been compiled. The doctrinal progression here corresponds with that we wished to suggest by the order of chapters in this volume. Inversely these chapters are the justification of the plan, in so far as this is possible with a work of this kind.

1. Title, Address. Doxology. First prophetic evocation (1, 1-8).
2. The messages of the Resurrected Jesus to the churches involved in the persecution (1, 9-3, 22).
3. Jesus Resurrected and the unfolding of History (4, 1-8, 1).
   A. The control of Jesus over the Book of History (4, 1-5, 14).
   B. The components and the end of history (6, 1-7, 17).
4. The evolution of History, from the Resurrection of Christ to the Last Judgement (8, 2-20, 15).
   A. First view of the whole, introducing, after the general condition of the Servants of God and above all the 'inhabitants of the earth', the particular problem of the combat between the Church and the Beast (8, 2-11, 18).
      1) The heavenly agents of the evolution of History (angels of the trumpets and prayers of the saints) (8, 2-5).
      2) General condition of the Servants of God and the inhabitants of the earth (8, 6-9, 21).
         a) The four first trumpets, announcing the liberation of the former and threatening the latter (8, 6-12).

227

b) Warning to the inhabitants of the earth (8, 13).
c) The fifth and sixth trumpets and the first woe; diabolical malevolence directed towards the inhabitants of the earth and an eschatological prospect (9, 1-21).

3) (Dove-tailing) Summing up of the teachings forming the object of the next section (10, 1-11, 18).
a) Introduction of the Little Book and announcement of the consummation which will take place at the end of evolution (10, 1-11).
b) General description of contents of the Little Book: the combat between the Church and the Beast (which forms the second woe) (11, 1-14).
c) The consummation and the heavenly acclamations (eschatological prospect) (11, 15-18).

B. The combat between the Church and Satan (11, 19-20, 10).
1) The heavenly phase of that battle, Defeat of Satan in heaven (11, 19-12, 12).
2) The earthly phase of the battle, up to the Last Judgement.
A. First general view.
1. The opponents:
a) The two Beasts (12, 13-13, 18).
b) Jesus and the Witnesses already united in glory (14, 1-5).
2. General view of the unfolding of the judgements of heaven on the earth (14, 6-11).
a) Solemn announcement of the judgements (14, 6-7).
b) The judgement of Babylon (14, 8).
c) Judgement of all future worshippers of the Beast (14, 9-11).
3. Power of the comfort of these prospects for the Christians (14, 12-13).
4. First description of Judgement, giving the whole its eschatological aspect and dominating the sequel (14, 14-20).
B. Detailed unfolding of the judgement of Christ and the Saints through History (15, 1-20, 15).
1. The instruments of God's wrath.
a) The avenging plagues which will strike down the idolatrous nations but leave the saints unscathed (15, 1-4).
b) The avenging plagues directed against the Beasts and their supporters and

worshippers, described in an eschatological prospect (15, 5-16, 21).

2. The successive unfolding of the Judgement of Christ and the saints, and the defeat of Satan and his supporters (prophetic part) (17, 1-20, 10).

  I. The judgement of Rome (3rd woe) (17, 1-19, 4).
     This first victory of Christ produces heavenly acclamations (19, 5-10) and the brilliant apparition of the King of kings and Lord of lords (19,11-16), whose domination will continue to assert itself in the sequel (19, 17-18).

  II. The judgement of the Kings and the definite defeat of the Beast and the False Prophet (19, 19-21).

  III. The fettering of the Dragon (20, 1-3) and the millennium reign of Christ and the saints (from heaven) over the nations (20, 4-6; cf. 5, 10).

  IV. The last release of Satan and his final defeat (20, 7-10).

C.   The Last and General Judgement (20, 11-15).

5. The heavenly Jerusalem (21, 1-22, 5).

6. Conclusion. Testimony in favour of the prophecy (22, 6-21).

APPENDIX II

THE APOCALYPSE

The following arrangement of the Apocalypse is intended to convey an idea of its rhythm. Characteristic expressions St John borrowed from other books of the Bible, especially the Old Testament, are printed in italics. The notes refer to characteristic expressions or texts of the Bible which St John appears to have used intentionally.

CHAPTER 1.

1. The Revelation of Jesus Christ
   Which God gave unto him,
   To make known to his servants the things which must shortly
     come to pass
   And signified
   Sending by his angel
   To his servant John
2. Who hath given testimony to the word of God
   And the *testimony of Jesus Christ*
   What things soever he hath seen
3. *Blessed* is he that readeth and heareth the words of this
     prophecy:
   And keepeth these things which are written in it.
   For the time is at hand.
4. John to the Seven churches which are in Asia.
   Grace be unto you and peace,
   From *him that is and that was and that is to come*
   And from the *seven spirits* which are before his throne
5. And from Jesus Christ who is the *faithful witness,*
   The first begotten of the dead
   And the *prince of the kings of the earth*
   Who hath loved us
   And *washed us from our sins* in his own blood.
6. And hath made us a *kingdom* and *priests* to God and his father
   To him be glory and empire for ever and ever. Amen.
7. Behold, *he cometh with the clouds,*
   And every eye shall see him: and they also that pierced him.

And *all the tribes of the earth shall bewail themselves because of him*

Even so. Amen.

8. I am *Alpha and Omega,* saith the Lord God,
   Who is and who was and who is to come,
   The *Almighty.*

9. I, John, your brother
   And your partner in tribulation and in the kingdom and patience in Jesus,
   Was in the island which is called Patmos
   For *the word of God and for the testimony of Jesus.*

10. *I was in the spirit* on the Lord's day
    And heard behind me a great voice,
    As a *trumpet,*
    Saying:

11. What thou seest, write in a book,
    And send to the seven churches which are in Asia:
    To Ephesus and to Smyrna and to Pergamos and to Thyatira
    And to Sardis and to Philadelphia and to Laodicea.

12. And I turned to see the voice that spoke with me.
    And being turned I saw *seven golden candlesticks:*

13. And in the midst of the seven golden candlesticks,
    One *like to the Son of Man,*
    Clothed with *a garment down to his feet,*
    And *girt about the paps with a golden girdle.*

14. And *his head and his hairs were white,*
    As white wool and as snow,
    And *his eyes* were as *a flame of fire:*

15. And *his feet like unto fine brass,*
    As in a burning furnace.
    And his voice as the sound of many waters.

16. And he had *in his right hand seven stars.*
    And from his mouth came out *a sharp two-edged sword.*
    And his face was as the *sun* shineth *in his power.*

17. And when I had seen him,
    I *fell* at his feet as dead.
    And he laid his right hand upon me, *saying:*
    Fear not.
    I am the first and the last,

18. And alive, and *was dead.*
    And behold I am living forever and ever
    And have the keys of death and of hell.

19. Write therefore the things which thou hast seen:
    And which are: And *which must be done hereafter.*

20. The mystery of the seven stars, which thou sawest in my right hand,

And the seven golden candlesticks.
The *seven stars* are the angels of the seven churches
And the *seven golden candlesticks* are the seven churches.

NOTES TO CHAPTER 1
v.I: 1, 19; 4, 1; 22, 6; Dan. 2, 28ff., 45.
v.II: 1, 9; 6, 9; 12, 11; 17; 19, 10.
v.III: 14, 13; 16, 15; 19, 9; 20, 6; 22, 7, 14; 22, 10.
v.IV: 1,8;4,8;11,17;16,5;Ex.3,14; 3, 1; 4, 5; 5, 6; Is, 11, 2.
v.V: 3, 14; 19, 11; Ps. 89, 38; 1, 18; 2, 8; Col. 1, 18;
        19, 16; Ps. 89, 28; 5, 9; Is. 40, 2.
v.VI: 5, 10; Ex. 19, 6; Is. 61, 6; 1 Pet. 2, 5, 9.
v.VII: Dan. 7, 13; Zach. 12, 10, 14; Matt. 24, 30.
v.VIII: 21, 6; 22, 13; cf. 1, 4; 4, 8; 11, 17; 15, 3; 16, 7, 14;
        19, 6, 15; 21, 22; Am. 3, 13; 4, 13.
v.IX: cf. 1, 2.
v.X: 4, 2; 17, 3; 21, 10; 10, 4, 8; 4, 1, 8, 2ff.; 9, 14; 10, 7;
        11, 15.
v.XII: 1, 20; 2, 1; Ex. 25, 37.
v.XIII: 14, 14; Dan. 7, 13; Ez. 1, 26; 8, 2; Ez. 9, 2, 11; Dan.
        10, 5.
vv.XIV-XVI: cf. beginning of each letter and 19, 11-16; Dan. 7,
        9ff.; 10, 6ff.
v.XVII: Dan. 8, 18; Is. 44, 2.
v.XVIII: 2, 8; 22, 13; Is. 48, 12; cf. 1, 5.
v.XIX: cf. 1, 1.
v.XX: cf. 1, 16; cf. 1, 12.

CHAPTER 2.
1. Unto the angel of the church of Ephesus write:
   These things saith he who holdeth the *seven stars* in his right
        hand,
   And walketh in the midst of the *seven candlesticks*:
2. I know thy works and thy labour and thy patience
   And how thou canst not bear them that are evil,
   And thou hast tried them that say they are Apostles and
        are not,
   And hast found them liars.
3. And thou hast patience and hast endured
   For my name, and hast not fainted.
4. But I have somewhat against thee, because thou hast left thy
        first charity.
5. Be mindful therefore from whence thou art fallen:
   And do penance and do the first works.
   Or else I come to thee
   And move thy candlestick out of its place,
   Except thou do penance.

6. But this thou hast, that thou hatest the deeds of the *Nicolaites*,
   Which I also hate.
7. He that hath an ear let him hear what the spirit saith to the
   churches:
   To him that overcometh I will give to eat of *the tree of life*
   Which is in the paradise of my God.
8. And to the angel of the church of Smyrna write:
   These things saith the *first and the last*,
   Who was dead and is alive:
9. I know thy tribulation and thy poverty:
   But thou art rich.
   And thou art blasphemed by them that say they are Jews and
      are not,
   But are the synagogue of Satan.
10. Fear none of those things that thou shalt suffer.
    Behold *the devil* will cast some of you into prison,
    That you may be tried:
    And you shall have tribulation *ten days*.
    Be thou faithful unto death:
    And I will give thee the crown of life.
11. He that hath an ear, let him hear
    What the spirit saith to the churches:
    He that shall overcome
    Shall not be hurt by the *second death*.
12. And to the angel of the church of Pergamos write:
    These things saith he that hath the *sharp two-edged sword*:
13. I know where thou dwellest, where the *seat of Satan* is.
    And thou holdest fast my name and
    Thou has not denied my faith.
    Even in those days when Antipas was my faithful witness,
    Who was slain among you, where Satan dwelleth.
14. But I have against thee a few things:
    Because thou hast there them that hold the doctrine of *Balaam*
    Who taught Balac to cast a stumbling block before the
       children of Israel,
    To eat and to commit fornication.
15. So hast thou also them that
    Hold the doctrine of the *Nicolaites*.
16. In like manner do penance.
    If not, I will come to thee quickly
    And will fight against them with the sword of my mouth.
17. He that hath an ear, let him hear
    What the spirit saith to the churches:
    To him that overcometh
    I will give *the hidden manna*,
    And I will give him a white counter:
    And in the counter a *new name* is written,

Which *no man knoweth but him that receiveth it.*

18. And to the angel of the church of Thyatira write:
These things saith the Son of God
Who hath *his eyes like a flame of fire*
And his *feet like to fine brass*:

19. I know thy works and thy faith and thy charity
And thy ministry and thy patience
And thy last works which are more than the former.

20. But I have against thee a few things:
Because thou sufferest the woman Jezabel,
Who calleth herself a prophetess,
To teach and to seduce thy servants,
To commit fornication and to eat
Of *things sacrificed to idols.*

21. And I gave her a time that she might do penance:
And she will not repent of her fornication.

22. Behold, I will cast her into a bed:
And they that commit adultery with her shall be in very
great tribulation,
Except they do penance for their deeds.

23. And I will kill her children with death:
And all the churches shall know that I am he
That *searches the reins and hearts.*
And I will give *to every one of you according to your works.*
But to you I say

24. And to the rest that are at Thyatira:
Whosoever hath not this doctrine and who have not known
The depths of *Satan*, as they say:
I will not put upon you any other burden.

25. Yet that which you have, hold fast till I come.

26. And he that shall overcome,
And keep my works unto the end,
I will give him power *over the nations.*

27. *And he shall rule them with a rod of iron*:
And as the vessels of a potter they shall be broken:

28. As I also have received of my Father.
And I will give him the morning star

29. He that hath an ear, let him hear,
What the spirit saith to the churches.

NOTES TO CHAPTER 2

v.I: cf. 1, 12-16.
v.VI: 2, 15.
v.VII: 22, 2; 14, 19; Gen. 2, 9; 3, 22, 24.
v.VIII: cf. 1, 18; cf. 1, 5.
v.IX: 2, 13, 24; 3, 9; 12, 9; 20, 2, 7.
v.X: 12, 9, 12; 20, 2, 10; Zach. 3, 1; Dan. 1, 12, 14.

v.XI: 20, 6, 14; 21, 8.
v.XII: cf. 1, 16.
v.XIII: cf. 2, 9; 13, 2; 16, 10.
v.XIV: Numbers 31, 16; 25, 1-2.
v.XV: 2, 6.
v.XVII: Ps. 78, 24; 3, 12; Is. 62, 2; 65, 15; 19, 12.
v.XVIII: cf. 1, 14.
v.XX: I K. 16, 31; II K. 9, 22; Numbers 25, 1-2.
v.XXIII: 18, 6; 20, 12, 13; 22, 12; Ps. 7, 10; Jer. 11, 20; 17, 10;
          20, 12; 20, 13; Ps. 62, 13.
v.XXIV: cf. 2, 9.
vv.XXVI-
XXVII: 12, 5; 19, 15; Ps. 2, 8-9.

Chapter 3.

1. And to the angel of the church of Sardis write:
   These things saith he *that hath the seven spirits of God and
   the seven stars.*
   I know thy works,
   That thou hast the name of being alive
   And thou art dead.
2. Be watchful and strengthen the things that remain,
   Which are ready to die.
   For I find not thy works full before my God.
3. Have in mind therefore in what manner thou hast received
   and heard:
   And observe and do penance.
   If then thou shalt not watch, *I will come* to thee *as a thief*:
   And thou shalt not know at what hour I shall come to thee.
4. But thou hast a few names in Sardis
   Which have not defiled their garments:
   And they shall walk with me *in white*,
   Because they are worthy.
5. He that shall overcome shall thus be clothed in white garments;
   And *I will not blot his name out of the book of life*.
   And I will confess his name before my Father and before his
   angels.
6. He that hath an ear, let him hear
   What the spirit saith to the churches.
7. And to the angel of the church of Philadelphia write:
   These things saith the *Holy One and the true One*,
   He that hath *the key of David, he that openeth and no man
   shutteth*,
   Shutteth and no man openeth:
8. I know thy works.
   Behold, I have given thee a door opened,
   Which no man can shut,

Because thou hast a little strength
And hast kept my word and hast denied my name.

9. Behold, I will bring of the synagogue of *Satan*,
Who say they are Jews and are not, but do lie.
Behold *I will make them to come and adore before thy feet.*
And they shall know that I have loved thee.

10. Because thou hast kept the word of my patience,
I will also keep thee from the hour of temptation,
Which shall come upon the whole world
To try *them that dwell upon the earth.*

11. Behold, I come quickly:
Hold fast that which thou hast,
That no man may take thy crown.

12. He that shall overcome, I will make him *a pillar in the temple of my God*:
And he shall go out no more.
And I will write upon him the name of my God
And the *name of the city* of my God, the *New Jerusalem*
Which cometh down out of heaven from my God,
And *my new name.*

13. He that hath an ear, let him hear
What the spirit saith to the churches.

14. And to the angel of the church of Laodicea, write:
These things saith the Amen, the *faithful and true witness,*
Who is the *beginning of the creation of God.*

15. I know thy works,
That thou art neither cold nor hot.
I would thou wert cold or hot.

16. But because thou art lukewarm,
And neither cold nor hot,
I will begin to vomit thee out of my mouth

17. Because thou sayest: *I am rich and made wealthy* and have need of nothing:
And knoweth not that thou art wretched and miserable and poor and blind and naked.

18. I counsel thee to buy of the gold, fine tried,
That thou mayest be rich and mayest be clothed in *white garments*:
And that the shame of thy nakedness may not appear.
And anoint thy eyes with eye-salve,
That thou mayest see.

19. *Such as I love I rebuke and chastise.*
Be zealous, therefore, and do penance.

20. Behold I stand at the gate and knock. If any man
Shall hear my voice and open to me the door,
I will come in to him and sup with him,
And he with me.

21. To him that shall overcome, I will give to sit with me *on my throne*,
    As I also have overcome and am set down with my Father *on his throne*.
22. He that hath an ear, let him hear
    What the Spirit saith to the churches.

NOTES TO CHAPTER 3

v.I: cf. 1, 4.
v.III: 16, 15.
v.IV: 3, 5, 18; 4, 4; 6, 11; 7, 9, 13; 19, 14.
v.V: cf. 3, 4, 20, 15; 13, 8; 17, 8; 20, 12; 21, 27; Ex. 32, 32; Ps. 69, 29; Matt. 10, 32.
v.VII: 6, 10; 19, 11; Is. 22, 22.
v.IX: cf. 2, 9; Is. 60, 14; 43, 4.
v.X: 6, 10; 8, 13; 11, 10; 12, 9; 13, 8, 12, 14; 16, 14; 17, 2, 8.
v.XII: 7, 15; 11, 1, 2, 19; 14, 15, 17; 15, 5, 6, 8; 16, 1, 17; 21, 22, 11, 2; 14, 20; 20, 9; 21, 2, 10, 14, 15, 16, 18, 19, 21, 23; 22, 14, 19; Ez. 48, 35; Is. 62, 2; 65, 15.
v.XIV: cf. 1, 5. Prov. 8, 22.
v.XVII: Os. 12, 9.
v.XVIII: cf. 3, 4.
v.XIX: Prov. 3, 12.
v.XXI: cf. 4, 2 et 22, 3.

CHAPTER 4

1. After these things, I looked
   And behold, a door was opened in heaven.
   And the first *voice* which I heard, as it were of a *trumpet* speaking with me,
   Said: Come up hither and I will show thee
   The *things that must be done hereafter*.
2. And immediately *I was in the spirit*.
   And behold there was a throne set in heaven,
   And *upon the throne one sitting*.
3. And *he that sat* was to the sight
   Like the *jaspar* and the sardine stone.
   And there was a rainbow about the throne,
   In sight like unto an emerald.
4. And round about the throne were four-and-twenty seats:
   And upon the seats four-and-twenty *ancients* sitting,
   Clothed in *white garments*.
   And on their heads were *crowns of gold*.

5. And from the throne proceeded *lightnings*
   And thunders.
   And there were *seven lamps* burning before the throne,
   Which are the *seven spirits of God.*

6. And in the midst of the throne was,
   As it were, a sea of *glass like crystal*:
   And in *the midst of the throne* and *round about the throne,*
   Were *four living creatures, full of eyes before and behind.*

7. And the first *living creature* was like a lion:
   And the second *living creature* was like a calf;
   And the third *living creature,* having the face, as it were,
      of a man
   And the fourth *living creature* was like an eagle flying.

8. And the four *living creatures* had each of them *six wings*
   And round about and within they were *full of eyes.*
   And they rested not by day or by night, saying:
   Holy, Holy, Holy, Lord God Almighty,
   Who was and who is and who is to come.

9. And when those *living creatures* gave glory and honour and
      benediction
   To *him that sitteth on the throne,*
   Who *liveth forever and ever*:

10. The *four and twenty ancients* fell down before *him that sitteth*
      on the throne
   And adored *him that liveth forever and ever,*
   And cast their *crowns* before the throne, saying:

11. Thou art worthy, O Lord, our God,
   To receive glory and honour and power.
   Because thou hast created all things:
   And for thy will they were and have been created.

NOTES TO CHAPTER 4

v.I: cf. 1, 10; cf. 1, 1.
v.II: 1, 10; cf. 3, 21; Ez. 1, 26-28; 10, 1; Is. 6, 1ff.; Ps. 47,
    9; 4, 3, 9, 10; 5, 1, 7, 13; 6, 16; 7, 10, 15; 19, 4;
    20, 11; 21, 5.
v.III: 21, 11, 18, 19.
v.IV: 4, 10; 5, 6, 8, 11, 14; 7, 11, 13; 11, 16; 14, 3; 19, 4;
    Is. 24, 23; cf. 3, 4; 4, 10; 14, 14.
v.V: 8, 5; 11, 19; 16, 18; Ez. 1, 13; Ex. 19, 16; Zach. 4, 2;
    cf. 1, 4.
v.VI: 15, 2; 4, 7, 8, 9; 5, 6, 8, 11, 14; 6, 1, 3, 5, 6, 7; 7, 11;
    14, 3; 15, 7; 19, 4; Ez. 1, 5, 18.
v.VII: 6, 1, 3, 5, 7; cf. 4, 6.
v.VIII: cf. 4, 6; Is. 6, 2; 6, 3; cf. 1, 8; cf. 1, 4; 4, 10.
v.X: 5, 14; 7, 11; 11, 16; 19, 4; cf. 4, 4; cf. 4, 9.

CHAPTER 5.

1. And I saw, in the right hand of *him that sat on the throne*,
   A book, written within and without, sealed with seven seals.

2. And I saw a strong angel, proclaiming with a loud voice:
   Who is worthy to open *the book*,
   And to loose the *seals* thereof?

3. And no man was able,
   Neither in heaven nor on earth nor under the earth,
   To open *the book* nor to look on it.

4. And I wept much,
   Because no man was found worthy to open *the book*,
   Nor to see it.

5. And one of the *ancients* said to me: Weep not:
   Behold, the *lion of the tribe of Juda*, *the root of David*,
   Hath prevailed to open *the book*
   And to loose the *seven seals* thereof.

6. And I saw; and behold, in the midst of *the throne*
   And of the four *living creatures*
   A *Lamb* standing, *as it were slain*,
   Having seven horns and *seven eyes*:
   Which are the seven spirits of God,
   Sent forth into all the earth.

7. And he came and took the book
   Out of the right hand of *him that sat on the throne*.

8. And when he had opened the book
   The four *living creatures* and the four and twenty *ancients*
   Fell down before the Lamb, having every one of them harps
      and golden vials
   Full of odours,
   Which are the *prayers of the saints*.

9. And they sang *a new canticle*, saying:
   Thou art worthy O Lord to take the book
   And to open the *seals* thereof;
   Because thou wast *slain and hast redeemed us to God*,
   In thy blood,
   Out of every tribe and tongue and people and nation;

10. And has made us to our God
    A *kingdom and priests*. And we shall reign on the earth.

11. And I beheld: And I heard the voice of many angels
    Round about the *throne* and the *living creatures* and the
       ancients
    (and *the number of them was thousands of thousands*)

12. Saying with a loud voice:
    The *Lamb that was slain* is worthy
    To receive power and divinity and wisdom and strength
    And honour and glory and benediction.

13. And every creature which is in heaven
    And on earth and under the earth,
    And such as are in the sea, and all that are in them,
    I heard all saying:
    To *him that sitteth on the throne and the Lamb*
    Benediction and honour and glory and power,
    Forever and ever.
14. And the four *living creatures* said: Amen.
    Then the four and twenty *ancients*
    Fell down on their faces and adored
    Him that liveth forever and ever.

NOTES TO CHAPTER 5

v.I: Ez. 2, 9ff.; Is. 29, 11.
v.V: 6, 2; Gen. 49, 8; 22, 16; Is. 11, 1, 10.
v.VI: cf. 4, 6; cf. 4, 4; 5, 8, 12, 13; 6, 1, 16; 7, 9, 10, 14, 17;
      12, 11; 13, 8; 14, 1, 4, 10; 15, 3; 17, 14; 19, 7, 9;
      21, 9, 14, 22, 23, 27; 22, 1, 3; Is. 53, 7; Zach. 4, 10;
      cf. 1, 4.
v.VIII: cf. 4, 6; cf. 4, 4; cf. 5, 6, 8, 3, 4; Ps. 141, 2.
v.IX: 14, 3; 15, 3; cf. 1, 5; 7, 9.
v.X: cf. 1, 6.
v.XI: cf. 4, 4, 6; Dan. 7, 10.
v.XII: cf. 5, 6.
v.XIII: cf. 5, 6.
v.XIV: cf. 4, 4-10.

CHAPTER 6.

1. And I saw
   That the *Lamb* had opened one of the *seven seals*:
   And I heard one of the four *living creatures*
   As it were in a voice of thunder saying:
   Come and see.
2. And I saw:
   And behold a *white horse.*
   And he that sat on him had a bow,
   And there was a crown given unto him.
   And he went forth *conquering, that he might conquer.*
3. And when he had opened the second *seal*
   I heard the second *living creature* saying:
   Come and see.
4. And there went out another *horse that was red.*
   And to him that sat thereon it was given
   That he should take peace from the earth:
   And that they should kill one another.
   And a great sword was given to him.
5. And when he had opened the third seal,
   I heard the third *living creature* saying:

Come and see. And behold, *a black horse*.
And he that sat on him had a pair of scales in his hand.

6. And I heard as it were a voice in the midst of the four *living
   creatures*
   Saying: Two pounds of wheat for a penny,
   And thrice two pounds of barley for a penny;
   And see thou hurt not the wine and the oil.

7. And when he had opened the fourth seal,
   I heard the fourth *living creature* saying:
   Come and see.

8. And behold, a *pale horse*: and he that sat upon him
   His name was death. And hell followed him.
   And power was given to him over the four parts of the earth,
   *To kill with the sword, with famine and with death
   And with the four beasts of the earth.*

9. And when he had opened the fifth seal,
   I saw under the *altar* the souls of them that were slain for the
   word of God
   And for the *testimony* which they held.

10. And they cried with a loud voice, saying:
    How long, O Lord (*holy and true*)
    Dost thou not judge and avenge our blood
    On *them that dwell on the earth*?

11. And white robes were given to every one of them.
    And it was said to them that they should *rest for a little time*
    Till their fellow-servants and their brethren,
    Who are to be slain even as they,
    Should be filled up.

12. And I saw,
    When he had opened the sixth seal:
    And behold there was a great *earthquake*.
    And the *sun became black as sackcloth of hair*:
    And the whole *moon* became as blood.

13. And the *stars* from heaven fell upon the earth,
    As the fig tree casteth its green figs
    When it is shaken by a great wind.

14. And the *heaven departed* as a book folded up.
    And *every mountain and the islands were moved out of their
    places.*

15. And the *kings of the earth* and the princes and *tribunes*
    And the rich and the *strong,*
    And every bondman and every freeman hid themselves in
    the *dens*
    And *in the rocks* of the mountains.

16. And they say to the mountains and to the rocks:
    Fall upon us and hide us
    From the face of *him that sitteth upon the throne*

And from the *wrath of the Lamb.*
17. For the great day of their wrath is come.
And who shall be able to stand?

NOTES TO CHAPTER 6

v.I: cf. 5, 6; cf. 4, 6, 7.
v.II: Zach. 1, 8ff.; cf. 5, 5.
v.III: cf. 4, 6, 7.
v.V: cf. 4, 6, 7.
v.VI: cf. 4, 6.
v.VII: cf. 4, 6, 7.
v.VIII: Ez. 5, 12; 14, 21; 29, 5; 33, 27; Jer. 14, 12; 15, 3.
v.IX: 8, 3, 5; 9, 13; 11, 1; 14, 18; 16, 7; Am. 9, 1; cf. 1, 2.
v.X: cf. 3, 7; cf. 3, 10.
v.XI: 14, 13.
v.XII: 8, 5; 11, 13, 19; 16, 18; 8, 12; Is. 13, 10; 50, 3;
       Ez. 32, 7ff.; Joël 3, 3ff.
v.XIV: 20, 11; 16, 20.
v.XV: 19, 18; Ps. 2, 2; Is. 2, 10ff.
v.XVI: Os. 10, 8; cf. 4, 2 et 5, 6; 6, 17; 11, 18; 14, 10; 16,
       19; 19, 15; Ps. 2, 5, 12.
v.XVII: Joël 2, 11; 3, 4; Soph. 1, 14; Mal. 3, 2.

CHAPTER 7.

1. After these things, I saw four angels
   Standing on the *four corners of the earth,*
   Holding the *four winds of the earth,*
   That they should not blow upon the earth,
   Nor upon the sea nor on any tree.
2. And I saw another angel ascending from the rising of the sun
   Having the *sign of the living God.*
   And he cried with a loud voice to the four angels
   To whom it was given to *hurt* the earth and the sea:
3. Saying: *Hurt not* the earth nor the sea nor the trees
   Till we sign the servants of our God in their foreheads.
4. And I heard the number of them that were *signed.*
   An hundred forty-four thousand were *signed,*
   Of every tribe of the children of Israel.
5. Of the tribe of Juda, twelve thousand *signed;*
   Of the tribe of Ruben, twelve thousand *signed;*
   Of the tribe of Gad, twelve thousand *signed;*
6. Of the tribe of Aser, twelve thousand *signed;*
   Of the tribe of Nepthali, twelve thousand *signed;*
   Of the tribe of Manases, twelve thousand *signed;*
7. Of the tribe of Simeon, twelve thousand *signed;*
   Of the tribe of Levi, twelve thousand *signed;*
   Of the tribe of Issachar, twelve thousand *signed;*

8. Of the tribe of Zabulon, twelve thousand *signed*;
   Of the tribe of Joseph, twelve thousand *signed*;
   Of the tribe of Benjamin, twelve thousand *signed*.
9. After this, I saw a great multitude
   Which no man could number,
   Of *all nations and tribes and peoples and tongues*,
   Standing before the throne and in the sight of the *Lamb*
   Clothed with *white robes*
   And with palms in their hands.
10. And they cried with a loud voice, saying:
    Salvation to our God, *who sitteth upon the throne,*
    And to the *Lamb*.
11. And all the angels stood round about the throne
    And the *ancients* and the four *living creatures.*
    And they fell down before the throne on their faces
    And adored God.
12. Saying Amen.
    Benediction and glory and wisdom and thanksgiving,
    Honour and power and strength to our God
    Forever and ever. Amen.
13. And one of the *ancients* answered and said to me:
    These that are clothed in *white robes*, who are they?
14. And I said to him: My lord, thou knowest.
    And he said to me: These are they who are come out of the
    great *tribulation*
    And have *washed their robes* and made them *white*
    In the blood of the *Lamb*.
15. Therefore, they are before the *throne of God*:
    And they serve him day and night in his temple.
    And he that sitteth on the throne shall dwell over them.
16. They *shall no more hunger or thirst*:
    Neither shall the sun fall on them, or any heat.
17. For the *Lamb*, which is *in the midst of the throne, shall rule
    them,*
    And shall lead them to the *fountains* of the *waters of life*:
    And God shall wipe away all tears from their eyes.

NOTES TO CHAPTER 7

v.I: Ez. 7, 2; 37, 9; Dan. 7, 2.
v.II: 7, 3, 4, 5, 8; 9, 4; Ez. 9, 4, 6; 7, 3; 9, 4, 10, 19; 11,
        5; 22, 11.
v.III: cf. 7, 2; 9, 4; 14, 1; 22, 4.
v.IX: cf. 5, 9; cf. 5, 6; cf. 3, 4.
v.X: cf. 4, 2 et 5, 6.
v.XI: cf. 4, 4; 4, 6; 4, 10.
v.XIII: cf. 4, 4; cf. 3, 4.
v.XIV: Ez. 37, 3; Dan. 12, 1; 22, 14; cf. 3, 4; cf. 5, 6.

v.XV: cf. 3, 12; cf. 4, 2; 12, 12; 13, 6; 15, 5; 21, 3.
v.XVI: Is. 49, 10.
v.XVII: 5, 6; Ez. 34, 23; 21, 6; Jer. 2, 13; Ps. 23, 2; 21, 4;
Is. 25, 8.

CHAPTER 8.

1. And when he had opened the seventh *seal*,
   There was *silence* in heaven,
   As it were for half an hour.
2. And I saw *seven angels* standing in the presence of God
   And there were given to them *seven trumpets*.
3. And another angel came and *stood before the altar*,
   Having a golden *censer*:
   And there was given to him much incense;
   That he should offer
   Of the *prayers of the saints*
   Upon the *golden altar* which is before the *throne of God*.
4. And the smoke of the incense of the *prayers of the saints*
   Ascended up before God from the hand of the angel.
5. And the angel took the *censer*
   And filled it with the *fire of the altar* and cast it upon the
   earth:
   And there were *thunders and voices and lightnings and a great
   earthquake.*
6. And the *seven angels* who had the *seven trumpets*
   Prepared themselves to sound the trumpet.
7. And the first angel sounded the *trumpet*.
   And there followed *hail and fire, mingled with blood*:
   And it was cast on the earth. And the third part of the earth
   was burnt up.
   And all green grass was burnt up.
8. And the second angel sounded the *trumpet*:
   And as it were a great *mountain, burning with fire*, was cast
   into the sea.
   And the third part of the sea became as blood.
9. And the third part of those creatures died which had life
   in the sea:
   And the third part of the ships was destroyed.
10. And the third angel sounded the *trumpet*:
    And a great *star fell from heaven*, burning as it were a torch.
    And it fell on the third part of the rivers
    And upon the fountains of waters.
11. And the name of the *star* is called: Wormwood.
    And the third part of the waters became wormwood,
    And many men died of the waters,
    Because *they were made bitter.*

12. And the fourth angel sounded the *trumpet*:
And the third part of the *sun* was smitten,
And the third part of the moon
And the third part of the stars,
So that the third part of them *was darkened.*
And the day did not shine for the third part of it, and the night likewise.
13. And I beheld:
And heard the voice of an angel flying through the midst of the heaven,
Saying with a loud voice, *Woe, Woe, Woe to the inhabitants of the earth*
By reason of the rest of the voices of the three angels,
Who are yet to sound the *trumpet*!

NOTES TO CHAPTER 8

v.I: Zach. 2, 17; Hab. 2, 20.
v.II: 8, 6, 7, 8, 10, 12, 13; 9, 1, 14; 10, 7; 11, 15.
v.III: cf. 6, 9; 8, 5; cf. 5, 8.
v.IV: cf. 5, 8.
v.V: cf. 6, 9; Ez. 10, 2; cf. 4, 5; 6, 12.
v.VI: cf. 8, 2.
v.VII: 16, 2; Ex. 9, 23-26.
v.VIII: cf. 8, 2; 16, 3; Jer. 21, 25.
v.IX: Ex. 7, 20.
v.X: cf. 8, 2; 16, 4; 8, 11; 9, 1; Is. 14, 12; Lk. 10, 18.
v.XI: Jer. 9, 14.
v.XII: cf. 8, 2; 16, 8; Ex. 10, 21ff.
v.XIII: 9, 12; 11, 14; 12, 12; 18, 10, 16, 19; cf. 3, 10; cf. 8, 2.

CHAPTER 9.

1. And the fifth angel sounded the *trumpet.*
And I saw a *star* fall from heaven upon the earth.
And there was given to him the *key* of the *bottomless pit.*
2. And he opened the *bottomless pit*:
And the *smoke* of the pit arose, as the smoke of a great *furnace.*
And the *sun and the air were darkened* with the *smoke* of the pit.
3. And from the *smoke* of the pit there came out *locusts* upon the earth.
And power was given to them, as the *scorpions* of the earth have power.
4. And it was commanded them that they should not hurt
The grass of the earth nor any tree nor any green thing:
But only the men who have not the *sign of God upon their foreheads,*

5. And it was given unto them that they should not kill them;
   But that they should torment them, five months.
   And their torment was as that of a scorpion when he striketh
   a man.

6. And in those days, man shall *seek death* and shall not find it.
   And they shall desire to die: and death shall fly from them.

7. And the *shapes of the locusts*
   Were *like unto horses* prepared unto *battle*.
   And on their heads were, as it were, crowns like gold;
   And their faces were as the faces of men.

8. And they had hair as the hair of women:
   And *their teeth were as lions*.

9. And they had breastplates as breastplates of iron:
   And the noise of their wings was as the *noise of chariots*
   And many horses *running to battle*.

10. And they had *tails* like to *scorpions*: and there were stings in
    their tails
    And their power was to *hurt* men, five months.
    And they had over them

11. A King, the angel of the *bottomless pit*,
    (Whose name in Hebrew is Abaddon and in the Greek
    Apollyon, in Latin Exterminans)

12. One *woe* is past;
    And behold, there come yet two woes more hereafter.

13. The sixth angel sounded the *trumpet*:
    And I heard a voice from the four horns of the *golden altar*
    Which is before the eyes of God,

14. Saying to the sixth angel who had the *trumpet*:
    Loose the four angels who are bound
    In *the great river Euphrates*.

15. And the four angels were loosed,
    Who were prepared for an hour, and a day, and a month,
    and a year,
    For to kill the third part of men.

16. And the number of the army of horsemen was
    Twenty thousand times ten thousand.
    And I heard the number of them.

17. And thus I saw the horses in the vision.
    And they that sat on them had breastplates of hyacinth and
    of brimstone.
    And the heads of the horses were as the heads of lions;
    And from their mouths proceeded *fire and smoke and
    brimstone*.

18. And by these three plagues was slain the third part of men,
    By the *fire and by the smoke and by the brimstone*
    Which issued from their mouths.

19. For the power of the horses is in their mouths and in their
    tails.
    For their *tails* are like to serpents and have heads;
    And with them they *hurt*.
20. And the rest of the men, who were not slain by these plagues,
    Did not do *penance from the works of their hands*,
    That they should not adore devils and idols of *gold and silver
    and brass*,
    And wood and stone;
    Which *neither can see nor hear nor walk*.
21. Neither did they penance from their murders
    Nor from their sorceries nor from their fornications nor from
    their thefts.

NOTES TO CHAPTER 9

v.I: cf. 8, 2; cf. 8, 10; 9, 2, 11; 20, 1.
v.II: Gen. 19, 28; Ex. 19, 18; Joël 2, 2, 10.
v.III: 9, 7; Ex. 10, 12, 15; Lk. 10, 19.
v.IV: cf. 7, 2; cf. 7, 3.
v.VI: Job 3, 21.
v.VII: cf. 9, 3; Joël 2, 4.
v.VIII: Joël 1, 6.
v.IX: Joël 2, 5.
v.X: 9, 3, 19; cf. 7, 2.
v.XI: cf. 9, 1.
v.XII: cf. 8, 13.
v.XIII: cf. 6, 9.
v.XIV: 16, 12; Gen. 15, 18; Deut. 1, 7; Jos. 1, 4.
vv.XVII-
XVIII: 14, 10; 19, 20; 20, 10; 21, 8; Gen. 19, 24; Ez. 38, 22.
v.XVIII: cf. 9, 9.
v.XIX: cf. 7, 2.
v.XX: 9, 21; 16, 9, 11, 21; Is. 17, 8; 2, 8, 20; Ps. 135, 15-17;
115, 4; Dan. 5, 4, 23; Ex. 20, 13.

CHAPTER 10.

1. And I saw another mighty angel
   Come down from heaven clothed with a cloud.
   And a rainbow was on his head:
   And his face was as the sun, and his feet as pillars of fire.
2. And he had in his hand a *little* book, open.
   And he set his right foot upon the sea,
   And his left foot upon the earth
3. And he cried with a loud voice as when a lion roareth.
   And when he had cried, seven thunders uttered their voices.
4. And when the seven thunders had uttered their voices,
   I was about to write.

And I heard a voice from heaven saying to me:
Seal up the things which the seven thunders have spoken
And write them not.

5. And the angel which I saw standing upon the sea and upon
   the earth
   Lifted up his hand to heaven.

6. And he swore *by him that liveth forever and ever*
   Who created heaven and the things which are therein
   And the earth and the things which are in it
   And the sea and the things which are therein:
   That time shall be no longer.

7. But in the days·of the voice of the seventh angel
   When he shall begin to sound the *trumpet*
   The mystery of God shall be finished,
   As he hath declared by his servants and prophets.

8. And I heard a voice from heaven
   Again speaking to me and saying:
   Go and take *the book* that is open,
   From the hand of the angel who standeth
   Upon the sea and upon the land.

9. And I went to the angel, saying unto him
   That he should give me *the book.*
   And he said to me: take the book and eat it up.
   And it shall make thy belly bitter:
   But *in thy mouth* it shall be sweet as honey.

10. And I took the book from the hand of the angel
    And *ate it up.*
    And it was in my mouth sweet as honey
    And when I had eaten it my belly was bitter.

11. And he said to me:
    Thou must prophesy again to *many nations and peoples and*
    tongues and kings.

NOTES TO CHAPTER 10
v.II: 10, (8), 9, 10; Ez. 2, 8; 3, 1-3.
v.IV: cf. 1, 10; 22, 10; Dan. 8, 26; 12, 4.
vv.V-VI: Dan. 12, 7.
v.VII: cf. 8, 2; 17, 17; 11, 18; Dan. 9, 6, 10; Zach. 1, 6.
v.VIII: 10, 4; 1, 10; cf. 10, 2.
v.IX: Ez. 2, 8; 3, 1-3.
v.XI: Jer. 1, 10.

CHAPTER 11.
And there was given me a *reed* like unto a rod.
And it was said to me:
Arise and *measure the temple* of God
And the *Altar*

And them that adore therein.

2. And the court which is without the *temple*
Cast out and measure it not:
Because it is given unto the gentiles.
And the holy city they shall tread underfoot two and forty
months:

3. And I will give unto my *two witnesses*:
And they shall prophesy a thousand two hundred and sixty
days
Clothed in sackcloth.

4. These are the *two olive trees and the two candlesticks*
That *stand before the Lord of the earth.*

5. And if any man will hurt them,
*Fire shall come out of their mouths and shall devour their
enemies.*
And if any man will hurt them,
In this manner must he be slain.

6. These have power to shut heaven,
That it *rain not in the days of their prophecy*:
And they *have power over waters*,
To *turn them into blood*
And to strike the earth with plagues,
As often as they will.

7. And when they shall have finished their testimony,
The beast that ascendeth out of the abyss
Shall make war against them and shall overcome them and
kill them.

8. And their bodies shall lie in the streets of the *great city*,
Which is called spiritually *Sodom* and Egypt:
Where their Lord also was crucified.

9. And they of the *tribes and peoples and tongues and nations*
Shall see their bodies for three days and a half:
And they shall not suffer their bodies to be laid in sepulchres.

10. And they *that dwell upon the earth*
Shall *rejoice over them and make merry*:
And shall send gifts to one another,
Because these two prophets
Tormented them *that dwelt upon the earth.*

11. And after three days and a half,
The *spirit of life* from God entered into them.
And they stood upon their feet:
And *great fear fell upon them* that saw them.

12. And they heard a great voice from heaven saying:
Come up hither.
And *they went up to heaven* in a cloud: and their enemies
saw them.

13. And at that hour there was made a great earthquake:
And the tenth part of the *city fell.*
And there were slain in the earthquake, names of men, seven thousand:
And the rest were cast into fear and gave glory to *God in heaven.*

14. The second *woe* is past: and behold the third *woe* will come quickly.

15. And the seventh angel sounded the *trumpet*
And there were great voices in heaven,
Saying,
The *kingdom of this world is become our Lord's and Christ's.*
And he shall reign forever and ever.   Amen.

16. And the four and twenty ancients,
Who sit on their seats in the sight of God,
Fell on their faces and adored God, saying:

17. We give thee thanks, O Lord God Almighty,
Who *art and who wast and who art to come*:
Because thou hast taken to the great power,
And thou hast reigned.

18. And *the nations were angry*:
And thy wrath is come.
And the time of the dead, that they should be judged,
And that thou shouldst render reward to *thy servants the prophets,*
And the saints,
And *to them that fear thy name*, little and great;
And shouldst destroy them who have corrupted the earth.

19. And the *temple of God* was opened in heaven
And the ark of his testament was seen in his temple.
And there were *lightnings and voices and an earthquake* and great hail.

NOTES TO CHAPTER 11

v.I: 21, 15; Ez. 40, 3; cf. 3, 12; Zach. 3, 1; cf. 6, 9.
v.II: Zach. 12, 3; Is. 63, 18; Ps. 79, 1; cf. 3, 12; 13, 5; 12, 6, 14.
v.III: cf. 11, 4.
v.IV: Zach. 4, 3, 11-14.
v.V: cf. 7, 2; Jer. 5, 14; II K. 1, 10; II Sam. 22, 9.
v.VI: I K. 17, 1; Ex. 7, 17, 19ff.; I Sam. 4, 8.
v.VII: 13, 1, 2, 3, 4, 12, 14, 15, 17, 18; 14, 9, 11; 15, 2; 16, 2, 10, 13; 17, 3, 7, 8, 11, 12, 13, 16, 17; 19, 19, 20; 20, 4, 10; Dan. 7, 3ff.; 7, 7ff.; 7, 21ff.; 12, 17; 13, 7; 16, 14; 19, 19.
v.VIII: 11, 13; 16, 19; 17, 18; 18, 10, 16, 18, 19, 21; Is. 1, 9ff.

v.X: cf. 3, 10; Ps. 105, 38.

v.XI: Ez. 37, 5, 10; Gen. 15, 12.

v.XII: II K. 2, 11.

v.XIII: cf. 6, 12; cf. 11, 8; Ez. 38, 19ff.; 16, 11; Dan. 2, 19.

v.XIV: cf. 8, 15.

v.XV: cf. 8, 2; Dan. 2, 44; 7, 14, 27; Zach. 14, 9; Abd. 21;
     Ps. 22, 29; 2, 2; 10, 16.

v.XVI: cf. 4, 4.

v.XVII: cf. 4, 10; cf. 1, 8; cf. 1, 4; Ps. 99, 1.

v.XVIII: Ps. 99, 1; cf. 6, 16; cf. 10, 7; Ps. 115, 13.

v.XIX: cf. 3, 12; cf. 4, 5 et 6, 12.

CHAPTER 12.

1. And a great sign appeared in heaven:
   A *woman* clothed with the sun,
   And the moon under her feet,
   And on her head a crown of twelve stars.
2. And being with child, *she cried travailing in birth*:
   And was in pain to be delivered.
3. And there was seen another sign in heaven.
   And behold a great red *dragon*,
   Having seven heads and *ten* horns,
   And on his heads seven diadems.
4. And his tail drew the third part of the *stars of heaven*
   And *cast them to the earth*.
   And the *dragon* stood before the woman
   Who was ready to be delivered:
   That, when she should be delivered,
   He might devour her son.
5. And she *brought forth a man child*
   Who was to *rule all nations with a rod of iron*.
   And her son was taken up to God and to his throne.
6. And the *woman* fled into the wilderness,
   Where she had a place prepared by God,
   That there they should feed her *a thousand two hundred and
   sixty days*.
7. And there was a great battle in heaven:
   Michael and his angels *fought* with the *dragon*,
   And the *dragon* fought, and his angels.
8. And they prevailed not:
   Neither was *their place found any more* in heaven.
9. And that great *dragon* was cast out, that old *serpent*,
   Who is called the *devil* and *Satan*,
   Who *seduceth the whole world*.
   And he was cast on to the earth:
   And his angels were thrown down with him.

10. And I heard a voice in heaven saying:
    Now is come salvation and strength,
    And the Kingdom of our Lord and the power of his Christ :
    Because the *accuser* of our brethren is cast forth,
    Who *accused* them before our God day and night.
11. And they overcame him by the blood of *the Lamb*
    And by *the word of the testimony*:
    And they loved not their lives unto death.
12. Therefore *rejoice*, O heavens, and you that dwell therein.
    Woe to the earth and to the sea,
    Because the *devil is come down unto you*, having great wrath,
    Knowing that he hath but a short time
13. And when the *dragon* saw that he was cast down to the earth
    He persecuted the *woman* who brought forth the *man child.*
14. And there were given to the *woman* two wings of a great *eagle,*
    That she might fly into the desert, unto her place,
    Where she is nourished *for a time and times and half a time,*
    From the face of the serpent.
15. And the serpent cast out of his mouth, after the woman
    Water, as it were a river:
    That he might cause her to be carried away by the river.
16. And the earth helped the woman: and the earth opened her
    mouth
    And swallowed up the river
    Which the *dragon* cast out of his mouth.
17. And the *dragon* was angry against the *woman*:
    And went to *make war with* the rest of her seed,
    Who keep the commandments of God
    And have the *testimony of Jesus Christ.*
18. And he stood upon the sand of the sea.

NOTES TO CHAPTER 12

v.I: 12, 4, 6, 13, 14, 15, 16, 17.
v.II: Is. 66, 7; Mich. 4, 12.
v.III: 12, 4, 7, 9, 13, 16, 17; 13, 2, 4, 11; 16, 13; 20, 2;
    Dan. 7, 7; 13, 1; 13, 3, 7, 12, 16.
v.IV: Dan. 8, 10.
v.V: Is. 66, 7; Jer. 20, 15; cf. 2, 26-27.
v.VII: Dan. 10, 13, 21; 12, 1.
v.VIII: 20, 11; Dan. 2, 35.
v.IX: 20, 2; Gen. 3, 1, 14; cf. 2, 10; cf. 2, 9; cf. 3, 10.
v.X: Job 1, 9-11; 2, 4; Zach. 3, 1.
v.XI: cf. 1, 2.
v.XII: 18, 20; Is. 44, 23; 49, 13; cf. 7, 15; cf. 8, 13; cf. 2, 10.
v.XIV: Is. 40, 31; Dan. 7, 25; 12, 7.
v.XVII: Gen. 3, 15; cf. 11, 7; cf. 1, 2.

CHAPTER 13.

1. And I saw a great beast coming up out of the sea,
Having *seven heads and ten horns*;
And upon his horns ten diadems:
And upon his heads *names of blasphemy*.

2. And the beast which I saw was *like to a leopard*:
And his feet were as the feet of a *bear*,
And his mouth was as the mouth of a *lion*.
And the dragon gave him his own strength
And great power.

3. And I saw one of his heads as it were slain to death:
And his death's wound was healed.
And all the world was in admiration after the *beast*.

4. And they adored the *dragon* which gave power to the *beast*.
And they adored the *beast* saying:
Who is like the *beast*?
And who shall be able to fight with him?

5. And there was given to him *a mouth
Speaking great things and blasphemies*:
And power was given to him to do
Two and forty months.

6. And he opened his mouth unto blasphemies against God,
To blaspheme his name and his *tabernacle
And them that dwell in heaven*.

7. And it was given unto him *to make war with the saints
And to overcome them*.
And power was given him over every tribe and people and
tongue and nation.

8. And all that *dwell upon the earth* adored him,
Whose names are *not written in the book of life* of *the Lamb
Which was slain* from the beginning of the world.

9. If any man have an ear, let him hear.

10. He that shall *lead into captivity* shall *go into captivity*.
He *that shall kill by the sword must be killed by the sword*.
Here is the *patience of the faith and of the saints*.

11. And I saw *another beast* coming up out of the earth:
And he had two horns, like a lamb,
And he spoke as a *dragon*.

12. And he executed all the power of the former *beast* in his sight.
And he *caused the earth and them that dwell therein*
To adore the first beast, whose wound to death was healed.

13. And he did *great signs*,
So then he made also fire to come down from heaven
Unto the earth in the sight of men.

14. And he seduced *them that dwell on the earth*,
For the signs which were given him to do in the sight of the
beast:

Saying to *them that dwell on the earth*
That they should make the image of the beast
Which had the wound by the sword and lived.

15. And it was given him to give life to the image of the *beast*
That the image of the *beast* should speak:
And should cause that whosoever will not adore the image
    of the *beast*
Should be slain.

16. And he shall make all, both little and great, rich and poor,
Freemen and bondmen,
To have a *character* in their right hand or on their foreheads:

17. And that no man might buy or sell, but he hath the *character*,
Or the name of the *beast*, or the number of his name.

18. Here is wisdom. He that hath understanding, let him
Count the number of the *beast*.
For it is the number of a man:
And the number of him is six hundred and sixty-six.

NOTES TO CHAPTER 13

v.I: cf. 11, 7; 17, 3, 9.
v.II: cf. 11, 7; 12, 3; cf. 2, 13.
v.V: Dan. 7, 8, 11, 25; cf. 11, 2.
v.VI: cf. 7, 15.
v.VII: cf. 11, 7.
v.VIII: cf. 3, 10; cf. 3, 5.
v.X: Jer. 15, 2; Matt. 26, 52; 14, 12.
v.XI: 16, 13; 19, 20; 20, 10; Matt. 7, 15; 24, 11, 24; Act.
    13, 6; II Pet. 2, 1; I John 4, 1.
v.XII: cf. 3, 10.
v.XIII: Matt. 24, 24.
v.XIV: cf. 3, 10.
v.XV: Dan. 3, 5ff.
v.XVI: 13, 17; 14, 9, 11; 16, 2; 19, 20; 20, 4.
v.XVIII: 17, 9; 15, 2.

CHAPTER 14.

1. And I beheld:
And lo a *Lamb* stood upon Mount Sion
And with *him one hundred and forty-four thousand,*
Having his name and the name of his Father *written on their
    foreheads.*

2. And I heard a voice from heaven, *as the noise of many waters,*
And as *the voice* of great thunder,
And the voice which I heard was as the voice of harpers
    harping on their harps.

3. And they sang as it were a new canticle,
   Before the *throne* and before the *four living creatures* and the
   ancients:
   And no man could say the canticle
   But those hundred and forty-four thousand
   Who were purchased from the earth.

4. These are they who were not defiled with women:
   For they are virgins.
   These follow the *Lamb* whithersoever he goeth.
   These were purchased from among men,
   The first-fruits to God and to the *Lamb*.

5. And *in their mouth there was found no lie*;
   For they are without spot before the throne of God.

6. And I saw another angel flying through the midst of heaven,
   Having the eternal gospel, to preach unto them that sit upon
   the earth,
   And over every nation and tribe and tongue and people:

7. Saying with a loud voice:
   Fear the Lord and give him honour,
   Because the hour of his judgement is come.
   And adore ye *him that made heaven and earth*,
   The sea and the fountains of waters.

8. And another angel followed, saying:
   That *great Babylon is fallen*, is fallen:
   Which made *all nations to drink*
   Of the *wine* of the wrath of her *fornication*.

9. And the third angel followed them, saying in a loud voice:
   If any man shall adore the *beast* and his image,
   And receive his *character* in his forehead and in his hand,

10. He also shall *drink of the wine of the wrath of God*,
    Which is mingled with pure wine in the *cup of his wrath*:
    And shall be tormented with *fire and brimstone*
    In the sight of the holy angels and in the sight of the *Lamb*.

11. And the smoke of their torments shall *ascend up for ever and
    ever*:
    Neither have they *rest day or night*,
    Who have adored the *beast* and his image,
    And whoever receiveth the *character* of his name.

12. Here is *the patience of the saints*,
    Who keep the commandments of God and *the faith* of Jesus.

13. And I heard a voice from heaven, saying to me:
    Write:
    Blessed are the dead who die in God.
    From henceforth, now, saith the spirit,
    That they may rest from their labours,
    For their works follow them.

14. *And I saw*:
    And behold a white cloud,
    And on the cloud *one sitting like to the Son of Man,*
    Having on his head *a crown of gold,*
    And in his hand a sharp sickle.
15. And another angel came out from *the temple*
    Which is in heaven,
    Crying with a loud voice to him that sat upon the cloud:
    Thrust in *thy sickle* and reap, because *the hour*
    Is come to reap. For the harvest of the earth is ripe.
16. And he that sat on the cloud thrust his sickle into the earth:
    And the earth was reaped.
17. And another angel came out of *the temple* which is in heaven,
    He also having a sickle.
18. And another angel came out from *the altar,*
    Who had power over fire,
    And he cried with a loud voice to him that had the sickle,
        saying:
    Thrust in thy *sharp sickle* and gather the clusters of the
        vineyard of the earth
    Because the grapes thereof are ripe.
19. And the angel thrust in his sharp sickle into the earth
    And gathered the vineyard of the earth
    And cast it into the *great press of the wrath of God.*
20. And the *press was trodden* without the *city*:
    And blood came out of the *press,*
    Up to the horses' bridles,
    For a thousand and six hundred furlongs.

NOTES TO CHAPTER 14

v.I: Ez. 9, 4; cf. 7, 3.
v.II: cf. 1, 15; Ez. 1, 24; 43, 2.
v.III: cf. 5, 9; cf. 4, 4, 6.
v.V: Ps. 32, 2; Soph. 3, 13.
v.VI: cf. 8, 13.
v.VII: 15, 4; cf. 10, 6; Ex. 20, 11.
v.VIII: 16, 19; 17, 5; 18, 2, 10, 21; cf. 11, 8; Is. 21, 9;
    17, 2; 18, 3; Jer. 51, 7, 8.
v.IX: cf. 11, 7 et 13, 16.
v.X: cf. 6, 16; Is. 51, 17; Ps. 75, 9; 14, 19; 15, 1, 7; 16, 1,
    19; 19, 15; cf. 9, 17-18.
v.XI: 19, 3; Is. 34, 9ff.; cf. 11, 7 et 13, 16.
v.XII: cf. 13, 10.
v.XIII: cf. 1, 3; cf. 6, 11.
v.XIV: cf. 1, 13; 4, 4.
v.XV: cf. 3, 12; Joël 4, 13.
v.XVII: cf. 3, 12.

v.XVIII: cf. 6, 9; Joël 4, 13.
v.XIX: 14, 20; 19, 15; cf. 14, 10.
v.XX: cf. 3, 12; Joël 4, 13.

CHAPTER 15.

1. And I saw another sign in the heaven, great and wonderful:
Seven angels having the *seven last plagues*.
For in them is filled up the *wrath of God*.

2. And I saw as it were a *sea of glass* mingled with fire:
And them that had overcome the *beast* and his image
And the *number* of his name,
Standing on the sea of glass,
Having the harps of God:

3. And singing the *canticle of Moses, the servant of God*,
And the *canticle of the Lamb*, saying:
Great and wonderful are thy works, O Lord God Almighty.
Just and true are thy ways, O King of ages.

4. *Who shall not fear thee*, O Lord, *and glorify thy name*?
For thou only art holy.
For all nations shall come and shall adore in thy sight
Because thy judgements are manifest.

5. And after these things, I looked:
And behold the *Temple of the tabernacle of the testimony of heaven*
Was opened.

6. And the seven angels came out of the *temple*, having the *seven plagues*,
Clothed with clean and white linen,
And girt about the breasts with golden girdles.

7. And one of the *four living creatures* gave to the seven angels *golden vials*
Full of the *wrath of God*, who liveth forever and ever.

8. *And the temple was filled* with smoke
From the *majesty* of God and his power.
And *no man was able to enter into the temple*
Till the seven plagues of the seven angels were fulfilled.

NOTES TO CHAPTER 15

v.I: 15, 6, 18; 15, 1.
v.II: cf. 4, 6; cf. 11, 7; cf. 13, 18.
v.III: Ex. 15, 1; cf. 5, 6 et 5, 9; Ps. 111, 2, 4; cf. 1, 8; Ps. 145, 17.
v.IV: Jer. 10, 7; cf. 14, 7; Mal. 1, 11; Ps. 86, 9; Jer. 16, 19.
v.V: cf. 3, 12; 7, 15; Ex. 40, 34.
v.VI: cf. 15, 1; cf. 3, 12.
v.VII: cf. 4, 6; 16, 1, 2, 3, 4, 8, 10, 12, 17; 17, 1; cf. 14, 10.
v.VIII: cf. 3, 12; Ex. 40, 34; I K. 8, 10; Is. 6, 4; Ez. 44, 4; 21, 11, 23; cf. 15, 1.

CHAPTER 16.

1. And I heard a great voice out of the temple saying to the
    seven angels:
    Go and pour out
    The *seven vials of the wrath of God* upon the earth.
2. And the first went and poured out *his vial upon the earth.*
    And there fell *a sore and grievous wound*
    Upon men who had the *character* of the *beast*:
    And upon them that adored the image thereof.
3. And the second angel poured out his *vial upon the sea.*
    And *there came blood* as it were of a dead man:
    And every living soul died in the sea.
4. And the third poured out his vial
    Upon the *rivers and the fountains of waters.*
    And there was made blood.
5. And I heard the angel of the waters saying:
    Thou art just, O Lord,
    Who art and who wast, the holy One,
    Because thou hast judged these things.
6. For they have *shed the blood of saints and prophets*:
    And thou hast given them *blood to drink.*
    For they are worthy.
7. And I heard another, from the *altar*, saying:
    Yea, O Lord *God Almighty,*
    True and just are thy judgements.
8. And the fourth angel poured out his *vial upon the sun.*
    And it was given unto him
    To afflict men with heat and fire.
9. And men were scorched with great heat:
    And they *blasphemed the name of God,*
    Who hath power over these plagues.
    Neither did they penance to give him glory.
10. And the fifth angel poured out *his vial*
    Upon the *seat of the beast.*
    And his kingdom *became dark,*
    And they gnawed their tongues for pain.
11. And they *blasphemed the God of heaven.*
    Because of their pains and wounds:
    And *did not penance* for their works.
12. And the sixth angel poured out *his vial* upon *that great river*
    Euphrates
    And *dried up the water* thereof,
    That a way might be prepared for the kings
    From *the rising of the sun.*
13. And I saw from the mouth of the *dragon*,
    And from the mouth of the *beast* and from the mouth of the
    false prophet,

Three unclean spirits like *frogs*.

14. For they are the spirits of devils, working signs:
And they go forth unto the kings *of the whole earth*
To gather them *to battle against the great day of the Almighty
God.*

15. Behold, *I come as a thief.*
Blessed is he that watcheth and keepeth his garments,
Lest he walk naked, and they see his shame.

16. And he shall gather them together
Into a place which in Hebrew is called *Armagedon.*

17. And the seventh angel poured out his *vial* upon the air.
And there came a great voice out of the temple from the
throne, saying:
It is done.

18. And there were *lightnings and voices and thunders*:
And there was a *great earthquake*,
Such a one as never had been
Since men were upon the earth,
Such an earthquake, so great.

19. And the great city was divided into three parts;
And the cities of the gentiles fell.
And great *Babylon* came in remembrance before God
To give her *the cup*
Of *the wine of the indignation of his wrath.*

20. And *every island fled away*,
And the *mountains were not found.*

21. And the great hall, like a talent,
Came down from heaven upon men;
And men *blasphemed* God, for the *plague of the hail*
Because it was exceeding great.

NOTES TO CHAPTER 16

v.I: cf. 3, 12; Is. 66, 6; cf. 15, 7 et 14, 10; Ps. 69, 25.
v.II: cf. 8, 7; Ex. 9, 10ff.; cf. 11, 7 et 13, 16.
v.III: cf. 8, 8; Ex. 7, 17-21.
v.IV: cf. 8, 10; Ex. 7, 19-24; Ps. 78, 44.
v.V: Ps. 119, 137; cf. 1, 4.
v.VI: Ps. 79, 3; Is. 49, 26.
v.VII: cf. 6, 9; cf. 1, 8; 19, 2.
v.VIII: cf. 8, 12.
v.IX: 16, 11, 21; cf. 9, 20.
v.X: cf. 2, 13 et 11, 7; Ex. 10, 21.
v.XI: cf. 11, 13; cf. 9, 20.
v.XII: cf. 9, 14; Is. 11, 15; 41, 2, 25; 44, 27.
v.XIII: cf. 12, 13; 11, 7; 13, 11; Ex. 8, 3.
v. XIV: cf. 3, 10; cf. 11,7; cf. 1, 8.
v.XV: cf. 3, 3.

v.XVI: Jud. 5, 19; II K. 9, 27; 23, 29; Zach. 12, 11.
v.XVII: cf. 3, 12.
v.XVIII: cf. 4, 5 et 6, 12; Dan. 12, 1.
v.XIX: cf. 11, 8; cf. 14, 8; cf. 14, 10 et 6, 16.
v.XX: cf. 6, 14.
v.XXI: cf. 9, 20 et 16, 9.

CHAPTER 17.

1. And there came one of the seven angels who had the seven *vials*
And spoke with me saying:
Come, I will show thee the condemnation of the *great harlot*,
Who sitteth upon *many waters*:
2. With whom the *kings of the earth have committed fornication*
And *they who inhabit the earth*
Have been made drunk with the *wine of her whoredom*.
3. And he took me away in spirit into the desert.
And I saw a *woman* sitting upon a *scarlet coloured beast*,
Full of the *names of blasphemy*,
Having *seven heads and ten horns*.
4. And the *woman*
Was clothed round about with purple and scarlet,
And gilt with gold and precious stones and pearls,
Having a golden *cup* in her hand,
Full of the abomination and filthiness of her fornication.
5. And on her forehead a name was written:
A mystery:
Babylon the great, the mother of the fornications and abominations of the earth.
6. And I saw the woman drunk with the blood of the saints
And with the blood of the martyrs of Jesus.
And I wondered, when I had seen her, with great admiration.
7. And the angel said to me:
Why dost thou wonder?
I will tell thee the mystery of *the woman*
And the *beast* which carried her,
Which hath the *seven heads and the ten horns*.
8. The *beast* which thou sawest, was, and is not,
And shall come up out of the *bottomless pit*
And go *into destruction*.
And the inhabitants of the earth
(Whose names are not written in the book of life from the foundation of the world)
Shall wonder,
Seeing the beast that was and is not.
9. And here is the understanding that hath the *woman*.

The *seven heads* are seven mountains on which the woman
   sitteth;
And they are *seven kings.*

10. Five are fallen, one is, and the other is not yet come;
    And when he is come, he must remain a short time.

11. And the *beast* which was and is not:
    The same also is the eighth, and is of the seven,
    And *goeth into destruction.*

12. And the *ten horns* which thou sawest are *ten kings*
    Who have not yet received a kingdom:
    But shall receive power as kings,
    One hour after the *beast.*

13. These have one design:
    And their strength and power they shall deliver to the *beast.*

14. These shall fight with the *Lamb*,
    And the *Lamb* shall overcome them,
    Because he is the *Lord of lords and King of kings*:
    And they that are with him
    Are called, and elect, and faithful.

15. And he said to me:
    The *waters* which thou sawest
    Where the harlot sitteth,
    Are peoples and nations and tongues.

16. And the *ten horns* which thou sawest in the *beast*:
    These shall hate the *harlot*,
    And shall make her desolate and naked,
    And shall eat her flesh and shall burn her with fire.

17. For God hath given unto their hearts to do that which
    pleaseth him;
    That they give their kingdom to the *beast*,
    Till the words of God be fulfilled.

18. And the *woman* which thou sawest
    Is the *great city* which hath kingdom over the *kings of the*
    earth.

NOTES TO CHAPTER 17

v.I: cf. 15, 7; 17, 15, 16; 19, 2; cf. 14, 8; 17, 15.
v.II: 18, 3, 9; cf. 14, 8; cf. 3, 10; cf. 14, 8.
v.III: cf. 1, 10; cf. 11,7; cf. 13, 1; cf. 12, 3.
v.IV: Jer. 51, 7.
v.V: cf. 14, 8.
v.VII: cf. 11, 7; cf. 12, 3.
v.VIII: cf. 11, 7; Dan. 7, 3; 17, 11; cf. 3, 10; cf. 3, 5.
v.IX: cf. 13, 18.
v.XI: cf. 17, 8.
v.XII: cf. 12, 3; cf. 11, 7.
v.XIII: cf. 11, 7.

v.XIV: cf. 5, 6; 19, 4; Deut. 10, 17; Dan. 2, 47.
v.XV: cf. 17, 1.
v.XVI: cf. 12, 3; cf. 11, 7; cf. 17, 1.
v.XVII: cf. 11, 7; cf. 10, 7.
v.XVIII: cf. 17, 3 et 11, 18.

CHAPTER 18.

1. And after these things
   I saw another angel come down from heaven,
   Having great power,
   And the earth was enlightened with his glory.
2. And he cried out with a strong voice, saying:
   Babylon the great is fallen, is fallen:
   And is become the habitation of devils
   And the hold of every unclean spirit,
   And the hold of every *unclean and hateful bird*.
3. Because *all nations* have drunk of *the wine of the wrath of her
   fornication*
   And the *kings of the earth* have committed fornication with
   her:
   And the *merchants of the earth* have been made rich for the
   power of her delicacies.
4. And I heard another voice from heaven, saying:
   Go out from her, my people:
   That you be not partakers of her sins
   And that you receive not of her plagues.
5. *For her sins have reached unto heaven*:
   And the Lord hath remembered her iniquities.
6. *Render to her as she also hath* rendered to you:
   And *double unto her double*, according to her works.
7. As much as she hath glorified herself and lived in delicacies,
   So much torment and sorrow give ye to her.
   Because she saith in her heart: *I sit a queen and am no widow*:
   And sorrow I shall not see.
8. Therefore shall her *plagues come in one day*,
   Death and mourning and famine.
   And she shall be burnt with fire,
   Because God is *strong* and will judge her.
9. And the *kings of the earth*, who have *committed fornication*
   And lived in delicacies with her,
   Shall weep and bewail themselves over her,
   When they shall see the smoke of her burning.
10. Standing afar off for fear of her torments,
    Saying: *Alas! Alas! That great city, Babylon*, that mighty city:
    For in one hour is thy judgement come.
11. And the *merchants of the city shall weep and mourn over her*,
    For no man shall buy their merchandise any more.

12. Merchandise of gold and silver and precious stones:
    And of pearls and fine linen and purple and silk and scarlet:
    And all thyine wood: and a manner of vessels of ivory;
    And all manner of vessels of precious stone
    And of brass and iron and of marble

13. And cinnamon and odours and ointment and frankincense
    And wine and oil and fine flour and wheat
    And beasts and sheep and horses and chariots:
    And slaves and *souls of men.*

14. And the fruits of the desire of thy soul are departed from thee:
    And all fat and goodly things are perished from thee:
    And they shall find thee no more at all.

15. *The merchants of these things*, who were made rich,
    Shall stand afar off from her, for fear of her torments,
    Weeping and mourning.

16. And saying, *Alas! Alas! that great city*,
    Which was clothed with fine linen and purple and scarlet
    And was gilt with gold and precious stones and pearls.

17. For in *one hour* are so great riches come to nought.
    And every shipbuilder,
    And all that sail into the lake, *and mariners*,
    And *as many as work in the sea*,
    Stood afar off.

18. And cried, seeing the place of her burning:
    What city is like to this great city?

19. And they cast dust upon their heads and cried,
    Weeping and mourning, saying: *Alas! Alas! that great city*
    Wherein all were made rich, that had ships at sea by reason
       of her prices.
    For in *one hour* she is made desolate.

20. *Rejoice over her*, thou heaven,
    And ye holy apostles and prophets,
    For God hath *judged your judgement* on her.

21. And a mighty angel took up a *stone*,
    As it were a great millstone,
    And cast it into the sea, saying:
    With such violence as this shall *Babylon, the great city*,
    Be thrown down and *shall be found no more at all.*

22. And the voice of the harpers and the musicians,
    And of them that play on the pipe and on the trumpet,
    Shall no more be heard at all in thee;
    And no craftsman of any sort whatsoever shall be found any
       more at all in thee;

23. And the *light of the lamp*
    Shall shine no more at all in thee:
    And the voice of the *bridegroom and bride*
    Shall be heard no more at all in thee.

For thy *merchants were* the *great men of the earth*:
For all nations have been deceived by *thy enchantments*.

24. And in her was found the blood of prophets and of saints
And all that were *slain upon the earth*.

NOTES TO CHAPTER 18

v.II: cf. 14, 8; Is. 13, 21; 34, 11, 14; Jer. 50, 39.
v.III: cf. 14, 8 et 17, 1; 18, 11, 15, 23.
v.IV: Is. 52, 11; Jer. 50, 8; 51, 6, 9, 45.
v.V: Jer. 51, 9; Gen. 18, 20.
v.VI: Ps. 137, 8; Is. 40, 2; cf. 2, 23.
v.VII: Is. 47, 8.
v.VIII: 18, 10, 17; Is. 47, 8; cf. 15, 8; Jer. 50, 34.
v.IX: cf. 17, 1.
v.X: cf. 8, 13 et 14, 8; cf. 18, 8.
v.XI: cf. 18, 3; Ez. 27, 36.
v.XIII: Ez. 27, 13.
v.XV: cf. 18, 3; Ez. 27, 36.
v.XVI: cf. 8, 13 et 11, 8.
v.XVII: cf. 18, 8; Ez. 27, 27-29; Is. 23, 14.
v.XVIII: Ez. 27, 27-29; Is. 23, 14; cf. 11, 8.
v.XIX: Ez. 27, 30-34; cf. 8, 13 et 11, 8; cf. 18, 8; Ez. 26, 19.
v.XX: cf. 12, 12; Deut. 32, 43; Is. 44, 23; Jer. 51, 48.
v.XXI: Jer. 51, 63ff.; cf. 11, 8 et 14, 8.
v.XXII: Ez. 26, 13.
v.XXIII: Jer. 25, 10; 7, 34; 16, 9; cf. 18, 3; Is. 23, 8; 47, 9.
v.XXIV: Jer. 51, 49.

CHAPTER 19.

1. After these things,
I heard as it were the voice of much people in heaven,
Saying:
Alleluia. Salvation and glory and power is to our God.

2. For *true and just are his judgements*, who hath judged the
great *harlot*,
Which corrupted the earth with her fornication,
And hath avenged the blood of his servants, at her hands.

3. And again they said:
Alleluia.
And her *smoke ascendeth for ever and ever*.

4. And the four and twenty *ancients* and the four *living creatures*
Fell down and adored *God that sitteth upon the throne*,
Saying: Amen. Alleluia.

5. And a voice came out from the throne, saying:
Give praise to our *God, all ye his servants*:
And *you that fear him, little and great*.

6. And I heard as it were the voice of a great multitude,
   And as the voice of many waters, and as the voice of great
      thunders,
   Saying:
   Alleluia: for the Lord our God, the Almighty, hath reigned.

7. *Let us be glad and rejoice and give glory to him.*
   For the marriage of the *Lamb* is come:
   And his wife hath prepared herself.

8. And it is granted to her that she should clothe herself with
      fine linen,
   Glittering and white:
   For the *fine linen* are the justification of the saints.

9. And he said to me: Write:
   Blessed are they that are called to the marriage of the *Lamb.*
   And he saith to me:
   These words of God are true.

10. And I fell down before his feet to adore him.
    And he saith to me: See thou do it not.
    I am thy fellow-servant and of thy brethren
    Who have the *testimony of Jesus.*
    Adore God.
    For the testimony of Jesus is the spirit of prophecy.

11. And *I saw heaven opened*: and beheld a *white horse.*
    And he that sat upon him was called *faithful and true;*
    And with justice doth he judge and fight.

12. And his eyes were as a *flame of fire*:
    And on his head were many diadems.
    And he had a *name written,*
    Which *no man knoweth but himself.*

13. And he was clothed with a garment *sprinkled with blood.*
    And his name is called: *The Word of God.*

14. And the armies that are in heaven
    Followed him on *white horses,*
    Clothed in fine linen, white and clean.

15. And *out of his mouth proceedeth*
    A sharp two-edged sword,
    That with it he may strike the nations,
    And he shall rule them with *a rod of iron*:
    And he treadeth the *winepress*
    Of the fierceness of the wrath of God.

16. And he hath on his garment and on his thigh written:
    King of kings and Lord of lords.

17. And I saw an angel standing in the sun:
    And he cried with a loud voice:
    Saying to all the birds that did fly through the midst of heaven:
    Come, gather yourselves together to the great supper of God.

18. That you may eat the flesh of *kings* and the flesh of *tribunes,*
And the flesh of *mighty men,*
And the flesh of *horses* and of them that sit on them:
And the flesh of all freemen and of all bondmen and of little
and great.

19. And I saw the *beast*
And the *kings of the earth* and their armies
Gathered together to make war with him
That sat upon the horse and with his army.

20. And the *beast* was taken
And with him the *false prophet,*
Who wrought signs before him, wherewith he seduced
Those who received the *character of the beast* and adored
his image.
These two were cast alive into the *pool of fire,*
Burning with brimstone.

21. And the rest were slain by the sword of him that sitteth on
the horse,
Which proceedeth out of his mouth;
And all the birds were filled with their flesh.

NOTES TO CHAPTER 19

v.I: 19, 3, 4, 6; Ps. 104, 35.
v.II: cf. 16, 7; cf. 17, 1; Deut. 32, 43.
v.III: cf. 14, 11.
v.IV: cf. 4, 4, 6, 10; cf. 4, 2.
v.V: Ps. 22, 4; 134, 1; 135, 1; 115, 13.
v.VI: Ps. 97, 1; cf. 1, 8.
v.VII: Ps. 118, 24; cf. 5, 6; 19, 9; 21, 2, 9; 22, 17.
v.VIII: 19, 14; 1, 31; cf. 5, 6 et 19, 7.
v.IX: cf. 1, 3; cf. 5, 6 et 19, 7.
v.X: cf. 1, 2.
v.XI: Ez. 1, 1; cf. 6, 2; cf. 3, 7; Is. 11, 4-5.
v.XII: cf. 1, 14; Dan. 10, 6; cf. 2, 17.
v.XIII: Is. 63, 1; Wisd. 18, 15; John 1, 1ff.
v.XIV: cf. 3, 4-5; 19, 8.
v.XV: cf. 1, 16; cf. 2, 26, 27; cf. 14, 19; 14, 10; 6, 16; 1, 8.
v.XVI: cf. 17, 14.
vv.XVII-
XVIII: cf. 6, 15; Ez. 39, 4, 17, 20.
v.XIX: cf. 11, 7.
v.XX: cf. 11, 7; 13, 11; 13, 16; cf. 9, 17-18.
v.XXI: cf. 1, 16; Ez. 39, 17, 20.

CHAPTER 20.

1. And I saw an angel coming down from heaven,

Having the *key of the bottomless pit*
And a great chain in his hand.

2. And he laid hold on the *dragon, the old serpent,*
Which is the devil and Satan,
And bound him for a thousand years.

3. And he cast him into the *bottomless pit* and shut him up
And set a seal upon him,
That he should no more seduce the nations
Till the *thousand years* be finished. And after that,
He must be loosed a little time.

4. And *I saw seats.* And *they that sat upon them*:
And *judgement was given unto them.*
And the souls of them that were beheaded,
For the *testimony of Jesus* and the *Word of God,*
And had not adored the *beast* or his image,
Nor received his *character* on their foreheads or in their hands.
And they lived and *reigned with Christ a thousand years.*

5. The rest of the dead lived not,
Till the thousand years were finished.
This is the *first resurrection.*

6. *Blessed and holy* is he that hath part in the *first resurrection.*
In these the *second death* hath no power.
But they shall be priests of God and of Christ
And *shall reign with him a thousand years.*

7. And when the thousand years shall be finished,
Satan shall be loosed out of his prison
And shall go forth and seduce the nations
Which are over the *four quarters of the earth*
Gog and Magog
Shall gather them together to battle,
The number of them is as the sand of the sea.

8. And they came upon the *breadth of the earth*
And encompassed the camp of the saints and the beloved city.

9. And there came down *fire from God out of heaven*
And *devoured them*; And the *devil, who seduced them,*
Was cast into the *pool of fire and brimstone,*
Where both the *beast*

10. And the *false prophet* shall be tormented
Day and night forever and ever.

11. And I saw a great white throne,
And one sitting upon it,
From *whose face the earth and heaven fled away*:
And *there was no place found for them.*

12. And I saw the dead, great and small,
Standing in the presence of the throne.
And the *books were opened, and another book* was opened,
Which was the book of life.

And the dead were judged by those things which were written
In the books, *according to their works.*

13. And the sea gave up the dead that were in it:
And death and hell gave up the dead that were in them.
And they were judged, everyone *according to his works.*

14. And hell and death were cast into the pool of fire.
This is the *second death.*

15. And *whosoever was not found written in the book of life*
was cast into the pool of fire.

NOTES TO CHAPTER 20

v.I: cf. 9, 1.
v.II: cf. 12, 3, 9; 2, 9, 10; 20, 3, 4, 5, 6, 7.
v.IV: Dan. 7, 9, 22, 27; cf. 1, 2; cf. 11, 7 et 13, **16.**
v.VI: cf. 1, 3; cf. 2, 11; cf. 1, 6.
v.VII: cf. 2, 9.
v.VIII: Ez. 7, 2; 38, 2, 9, 15, 39.
v.IX: Hab. 1, 6; cf. 3, 12; II K. 1, 10, 12.
v.X: cf. 2, 10; cf. 9, 17-18; cf. 11, 7 et 13, 11.
v.XI: cf. 4, 2; cf. 6, 14; Ps. 114, 7, 3; cf. 12, 8.
v.XII: Dan. 7, 10; cf. 2, 23.
v.XIII: cf. 2, 23.
v.XIV: cf. 2, 11.
v.XV: cf. 3, 5.

CHAPTER 21.

1. And I saw a *new heaven and a new earth.*
For the first heaven and the first earth was gone:
And the sea is now no more.

2. And I, John,
Saw the *Holy City, the New Jerusalem,*
Coming down out of heaven from God,
Prepared as a *bride* adorned for her husband.

3. And I heard a great voice from the throne saying:
Behold the *tabernacle* of God with men:
And he will dwell with them,
And they shall be his people;
And God himself with them shall be their God.

4. And God *shall wipe away all tears from their eyes*:
And death shall be no more.
Nor *mourning, nor crying, nor sorrow,*
Shall be any more:
For the former things are passed away.

5. And he *that sat on the throne said*:
Behold, I make all things new.
And he said to me: Write:
For these words are most *faithful and true.*

6. And he said to me:
   It is done.
   I am *Alpha and Omega*:
   The beginning and the end.
   To him that thirstest I will give
   Of the *fountain of the water of life*, freely.
7. He that shall overcome shall possess these things.
   And *I will be his God, and he shall be my son.*
8. But the fearful and unbelieving,
   And the abominable and murders, and whoremongers and
      sorcerers and idolators,
   And all liars,
   They shall have their portion in the poor
   Burning with fire and brimstone, which is the *second death*.
9. And there came one of the seven angels,
   Who had the seven *vials* full of the seven *last plagues*.
   And spoke with me, saying:
   Come,
   And I will show thee the *bride*, the wife of the *Lamb*.
10. And he took me up in spirit
    To a great and high mountain:
    And he showed me the holy city *Jerusalem*,
    Coming down out of heaven from God.
11. Having the *glory of God*.
    And the light thereof was like to a precious stone,
    As to the jaspar stone, even as crystal.
12. And it had a *great wall* and high,
    Having twelve gates; and in the gates *twelve* angels,
    And *names written* thereon,
    Which are the names of the twelve tribes of the children of
       Israel.
13. *On the east, three gates*:
    And on the north, three gates:
    And on the south, three gates:
    And on the west, three gates.
14. And the wall of the *city* had twelve foundations:
    And in them, the names of the twelve apostles of the *Lamb*.
15. And he that spoke with me
    Had a measure of a reed of *gold*.
    To measure the *city* and the *gates* thereof and the *wall*.
16. And the *city* lieth in a *four-square*:
    And the length thereof is as great as the breadth.
    And he measured the *city* with the *golden reed* for twelve
       thousand furlongs
    And the length and height and breadth thereof are equal.
17. And he *measured the wall* thereof, an hundred and forty-four
    cubits,

The measure of a man, which is of an angel.

18. And the building of the *wall* thereof was of *jaspar* stone:
But the city itself pure gold, like to clear glass.

19. And the foundations of the *wall* of the *city*
Were adorned with *all manner of precious stones.*
The first foundation was jaspar;
The second, sapphire;
The third, chalcedony;
The fourth, an emerald;

20. The fifth, sardonyx:
The sixth, sardius;
The seventh, chrysolite;
The eighth, beryl;
The ninth, topaz;
The eleventh, jacinth;
The twelfth, an amethyst.

21. And the *twelve gates* are twelve pearls,
One to each;
And every several gate was of one several pearl.
And the street of the city was pure gold, as it were, transparent glass.

22. And I saw no *temple* therein.
For the Lord God *almighty* is the *temple* thereof, and the *Lamb.*

23. And the *city* hath no need of the *sun,*
Nor the *moon* to shine in it;
For the glory of God hath *enlightened it*:
And the *Lamb* is the lamp thereof.

24. And the *nations shall walk in the light of it*;
And *the kings of the earth shall bring their glory and honour into it.*

25. And the *gates thereof shall not be shut by day*:
For *there shall be no night there.*

26. And they shall bring
The *glory and honour of the nations into it.*

27. And *there shall not enter into it anything defiled,*
Or that worketh abomination or maketh a lie:
But they that are *written in the book of life of the Lamb.*

NOTES TO CHAPTER 21
v.I: Is. 65, 17; 66, 22.
v.II: cf. 3, 12; cf. 19, 7.
v.III: cf. 7, 15; Zach. 2, 14; Ez. 37, 27; Jer. 31, 33.
v.IV: cf. 7, 17; Jer. 31, 16.
v.V: cf. 4, 2; Is. 43, 19; 22, 6; cf. 1, 15.
v.VI: cf. 1, 8; cf. 7, 17; 22, 17; Is. 55, 1.
v.VII: cf. 21, 3; II Sam. 7, 14; Ps. 89, 27ff.; Zach. 8, 8.

v.VIII: cf. 9, 17-18; 2, 11.
    v.IX: cf. 15, 7 et 15, 1; cf. 19, 7.
        v.X: cf. 4, 2; cf. 3, 2.
        v.XI: cf. 15, 8.
vv.XII-
        XIII: Ez. 48, 31-35; Ex. 28, 21; 39, 14.
        v.XIV: cf. 3, 2.
        v.XV: cf. 11, 1.
        v.XVI: Ez. 43, 16.
        v.XVII: Ez. 48, 16.
        v.XVIII: cf. 4, 3.
    vv.XIXff.: Is. 54, 11ff.
        v.XXII: cf. 3, 12; 1, 8; 5, 6.
        v.XXIII: cf. 15, 8; 22, 5; Is. 24, 23; 60, 1, 19; Zach. 14, 7.
vv.XXIV-
        XXVI: cf. 22, 5; Is. 60, 11.
        v.XXVII: Is. 52, 1; cf. 3, 5 et 5, 6.

CHAPTER 22.

1. And he showed me *a river of water of life,*
    Clear as crystal,
    Proceeding from the throne of God and the Lamb.
2. In the midst of the street thereof,
    And on *both sides of the river was the tree of life,*
    Bearing twelve fruits,
    Yielding its *fruits every month*:
    And the *leaves* of the tree were for the *healing of the nations.*
3. And there *shall be no curse any more*:
    But the *throne of God* and the *Lamb* shall be in it.
    And his servants shall serve him.
4. And they shall *see his face*:
    And his name shall be *on their foreheads.*
5. And *night shall be no more.*
    And they shall not need *the light of the lamp*
    Nor the *light of the sun,*
    Because the *Lord God shall enlighten* them.
    And they shall *reign forever and ever.*
6. And he said to me:
    These words are most *faithful and true.*
    And the Lord God of the spirits of the prophets
    Sent his angel to show his servant
    The things which *must be done shortly.*
7. And: *Behold, I come* quickly,
    Blessed is he that keepeth the words of the prophecy of this
        book.
8. And I, John,
    Who have heard and seen these things;

And after I had heard and seen,
I went down to adore before the feet of the angel
Who had showed me these things.

9. And he said to me:
See thou do it not.
For I am thy fellow-servant and of thy brethren the prophets,
And of them that keep the words of the prophecy of this book.
Adore God!

10. And he saith to me:
Seal not the words of the prophecy of this book.
For the time is at hand.

11. He that *hurteth*, let him *hurt still*:
And he that is filthy, let him be filthy still:
And he that is just, let him be justified still;
And he that is holy, let him be sanctified still.

12. *Behold, I come quickly*;
And my *reward is with me*,
To render every man *according to his works*.

13. I am *Alpha and Omega*,
The first and the last,
The beginning and the end.

14. *Blessed* are they that *wash their robes* in the blood of the *Lamb*:
That they may have a right to the *tree of life*
And may enter in by the gates into the *city*.

15. Without are dogs,
And sorcerers and unchaste and murderers and servers of idols,
And everyone that loveth and maketh a lie.

16. I, Jesus, have sent my angel,
To testify to you these things in the churches.
I am the *root and the stock of David*, the bright and *morning star*.

17. And the spirit and the *bride* say:
Come.
And he that heareth, let him say:
Come.
And he *that thirsteth*, let him come.
And he that will, let him take *the water of life*, freely.

18. For I testify to every one
That heareth the words of the prophecy of this book:
If any man shall *add to these things*,
God shall add unto him the *plagues written in this book*,

19. And if any man shall *take away*
From the words of the book of this prophecy,
God shall take away his part out of the *book of life*,
And out of the *holy city*,
And from these things that are written in this book.

20. He that giveth testimony of these things
Saith:
Surely *I come quickly*: Amen. Come, Lord Jesus.
21. And the grace of our Lord Jesus Christ be with you all.
Amen.

NOTES TO CHAPTER 22

vv.I-II: Ez. 47, 1, 7, 12; cf. 2, 7.
v.III: Zach. 14, 11.
v.IV: Ps. 17, 15; 42, 3; cf. 7, 3.
v.V: cf. 21, 23; Is. 60, 19; Ps. 139, 12; Dan. 7, 18, 27.
v.VI: cf. 21, 5; cf. 1, 1.
v.VII: 22, 12, 20; Is. 40, 10; cf. 1, 3.
v.X: cf. 10, 4; cf. 1, 3.
v.XI: cf. 7, 2.
v.XII: cf. 22, 7; Is. 40, 10; cf. 2, 23.
v.XIII: cf. 1, 8.
v.XIV: cf. 1, 13; cf. 7, 14; cf. 2, 7; cf. 3, 12.
v.XVI: cf. 5, 5; Numbers 24, 17.
v.XVII: cf. 19, 7; 22, 20; cf. 21, 6; 7, 17.
vv.XVIII-
XIX: 15, 1, 6; Deut. 4, 2; cf. 2, 7; cf. 3, 12.
v.XX: cf. 22, 7; cf. 22, 17.